Prayer … for t…
Pope Benedict XVI

God of truth and love,
your Son, Jesus Christ, stands as the light
to all who seek you with a sincere heart.

As we strive with your grace
to be faithful in word and deed,
may we reflect the kindly light of Christ
and offer a witness of hope and peace to all.

We pray for Pope Benedict
and look forward with joy
to his forthcoming visit to our countries.
May he be a witness to the unity and hope
which is your will for all people.

We make our prayer through Christ our Lord.
Amen.

Our Lady, Mother of the Church pray for us.
St Andrew pray for us.
St George pray for us.
St David pray for us.

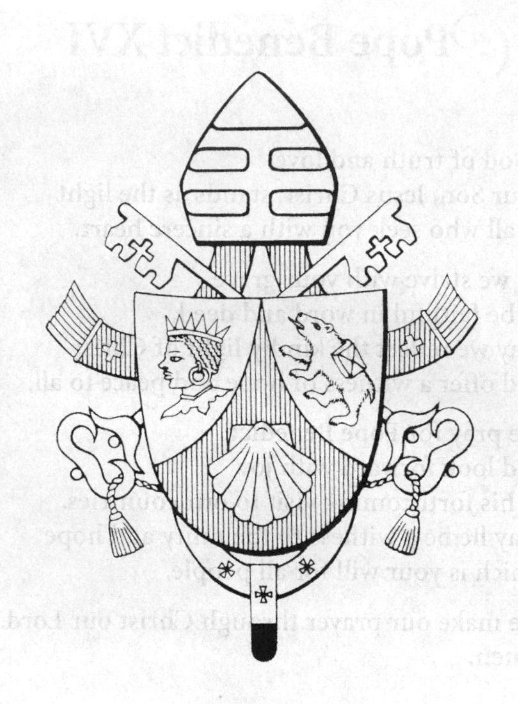

The Papal Visit

Pope Benedict XVI is visiting the United Kingdom from September 16 to 19, 2010. The Holy Father will fly to Scotland and will be received by Her Majesty The Queen. He will also celebrate a public Mass in Glasgow. In England, among other events, His Holiness will make a speech to British civil society at Westminster Hall, meet with the Archbishop of Canterbury, and join with him and other leaders of Christian traditions in Evening prayer at Westminster Abbey, celebrate Mass at Westminster Cathedral and lead a prayer vigil including Exposition of the Blessed Sacrament, and beatify Cardinal John Henry Newman during a Mass in Cofton Park in Birmingham – adjacent, fittingly, to Rednal, where Cardinal Newman was buried.

This booklet contains the texts of the times of public prayer that Pope Benedict will take part in, along with a series of brief articles which help explain something of the context of the prayer and other events of the Papal visit. It also includes texts for the Liturgy of the Church (Morning and Evening prayer, and the Mass) for some days before and after the Papal Visit.

Those attending any of the Papal liturgies are urged to take this booklet with them. It is intended to serve as their participation aid.

After many months of anticipation, it is with great joy that we now welcome the Holy Father Pope Benedict XVI to our shores. In the course of a busy programme involving State occasions and significant public events, we have been looking forward above all to those opportunities when we will gather together at times of prayer with the Successor of St. Peter who was taught to pray by our Blessed Lord himself and who through Pope Benedict continues to "confirm his brethren in the faith".

This missal will help us to pray with the Pope: to follow the prayers of the Mass for the Feast of St. Ninian in Glasgow: Ninian who also came from Rome, to bring the Gospel more than fifteen hundred years ago to the Picts and Britons. We will use this missal to focus our hearts and minds on the celebration of Mass in Westminster Cathedral and during the Mass of Beatification of Cardinal John Henry Newman in Birmingham. The other opportunities for prayer at Twickenham and Hyde Park are also set out for us here.

Whether we are able to be personally present or will be following events on television, radio or over the internet, we all have the opportunity to join our Holy Father the Pope on his pilgrimage to our countries, to accompany him with our prayers and to bear witness with him to the Gospel of Jesus Christ. As he spends these days among us we recall and repeat the prayer he made as he embarked upon his ministry as Pope:

> "Lord, remember your promise. Grant that we may be one shepherd and one flock! Do not allow your net to be torn and help us to be servants of unity!" (24 April 2005).

+Cardinal Keith Patrick O'Brien
Archbishop of St Andrews and Edinburgh

The Beatification of Cardinal John Henry Newman is a great highlight of the Papal Visit. Indeed, in many ways it is a central focus of all our prayer and celebrations, for John Henry Newman represents so many aspects of our mission to proclaim the faith in the United Kingdom today.

This missal will help us all to be united with Pope Benedict throughout his Visit. It enables us to pray with him at every moment of public prayer. It can inspire us to pray with and for him at other moments of these momentous days, too.

The Mass of the Beatification will hold before us, for our inspiration and encouragement, the figure of Cardinal Newman. His life was rich and fruitful in so many ways. I like to think of him as an example and encouragement above all for all priests, especially parish priests.

For thirty years Fr Newman was a parish priest in Birmingham. Indeed, throughout his life his pastoral concern for those in his care was outstanding. As a parish priest he was much loved, precisely because of his regular visiting of the sick and the imprisoned, his care for the poor and the hungry, his support for his parishioners in their work-place, his availability for Confession and counsel. His Beatification highlights yet again the importance of the role and service of the priest in our Catholic life. I hope it inspires many young men to consider the vocation to the priesthood.

At the time of the Mass of Beatification, most of our priests will be at their duties in their parishes. That is right and proper. I invite all who are present at this Mass to remember their priests in a very special way. They will be in the forefront of my prayers!

+Vincent Nichols, Archbishop of Westminster

The Prime Minister and I are delighted that His Holiness Pope Benedict XVI will visit the United Kingdom from the 16th to the 19th of September, following an invitation by Her Majesty The Queen. This is the first official Papal Visit to the UK – Pope John Paul II's visit in 1982 was purely pastoral.

It is a privilege to welcome the Pope, as the head of a Church with so many members in the United Kingdom, and I am very pleased that during his visit the Pope will be celebrating the life of one of the greatest Englishmen of the Nineteenth Century, Cardinal John Henry Newman. This visit will have a special meaning for all Catholics, and I hope that all who wish to do so are able to participate in the visit, directly or through television and internet coverage.

But the visit also has an important official angle. The UK Government are international partners of the Catholic Church world wide, dealing with issues such as poverty, education, health and climate change. This visit will be a chance to take that co-operation further. The Government also sees itself as a partner with all faith groups in the UK including the Catholic Church in building stronger and more resilient communities, and dealing with issues of solidarity and social justice. This visit will help us to make that partnership closer and stronger.

We are determined in Government to do all we can to make the visit a success. I hope it will be a memorable and joyful experience for all those involved.

Lord Patten of Barnes

Twenty eight years ago, Pope John Paul II made his historic visit to Britain, a visit that included an unforgettable act of worship at Canterbury Cathedral in company with my predecessor Archbishop Robert Runcie. It marked a great change in relations between the Roman Catholic Church and the Church of England. Its effects are still making themselves felt.

The warmth of our present friendship, shown in the regular meetings of the bishops of both our communions, and in many local instances, testifies to the continuing work of the Holy Spirit in our ecumenical endeavours. We have learned more and more what it means to share God's mission in Jesus Christ in these islands, recognising that we have the same passion for Jesus Christ to be made known in the lives of faithful and joyful communities gathered around the Lord's Table.

As we now warmly welcome Pope Benedict XVI, we give thanks for his courageous and consistent witness to the abiding and central truths of the faith in a climate so often marked by indifference and ignorance about Christian truth.

Our hope and prayer is that this visit may inspire us to greater energy and imagination in that shared mission. Pope John Paul wrote in his encyclical *Ut unum sint ('May they all be one')* in 1995 of how the papal office could and should be a ministry of unity in the gospel that would serve all Christians. We pray that in this visit, Pope Benedict will draw us closer together in the love of God and the service of Christ, so that the transforming power of the gospel will be proclaimed more effectively to all in our society.

+Rowan Cantuar:
Archbishop of Canterbury

BROADCAST

The Papal Visit will be broadcast live by the BBC, Sky and ITV, and will also be live-streamed on the Papal Visit website: www.thepapalvisit.org.uk.

Full details of these broadcasts will be published in newspapers and magazines nearer the time of the visit. They will also be available from on the Papal Visit website, which in addition will provide a wide range of audio and video files as well as other resources related to the Visit.

WHAT IS MAGNIFICAT?

Launched in France in 1992, then in other European countries and in the United States, MAGNIFICAT has proved a rich resource for laypeople in many countries. With this special issue for the Papal Visit, and beginning on a monthly basis in November, it is available for the first time with readings, texts and calendar appropriate for the British Isles. Beginning on September 12 you can use it to prepare yourself spiritually for the meeting with the Pope, and after the Papal Visit you can continue using MAGNIFICAT right through to the end of the month. We hope that you will find it helpful, and will want to join the growing MAGNIFICAT family around the world by subscribing to the monthly edition.

MAGNIFICAT provides the texts and readings for daily and Sunday Mass, and introduces the reader to the treasures of the Church – her saints, her great spiritual writers, and the prayer-life which we all hold in common. In addition to the daily Missal, you will find for each day a section of Morning and Evening Prayer approved by the Church. This selection from the Psalms, together with readings and canticles, hymns and meditations, offers a simpler alternative to the Divine Office which has been the basis of monastic prayer since the dawn of Christianity. As well as this, articles by our best spiritual writers, and an essay on a beautiful work of Christian art, make MAGNIFICAT an ideal compendium for spiritual reading and reflection in the midst of a busy life. The hard-wearing, pocket-sized format makes it easy to carry around, to be brought out in church or wherever you can find a quiet place to pray – perhaps even in the midst of a crowded commuter train.

PARISH PRAYER IN PREPARATION
for the visit of Pope Benedict

The official prayer of Preparation is presented at the beginning of this booklet. It might be appropriate to have a brief time of silent prayer for the success of the Visit after each Mass, concluding with the prayer of Preparation.

During the nine days immediately prior to the Visit, a parish might offer a novena of prayer, either in the simple form indicated above or in a more extended way, including a reading taken either from the Lectionary and Divine Office provision for The Chair of St Peter (February 22); and Ss Peter and Paul (June 29) or from chapters 14-17 in the Gospel of John.

A more substantial and separate service of preparation might take the form of Evening Prayer as given in the Divine Office of the Church, or of the Worship of the Eucharist outside of Mass (for example Exposition). The Church's ritual books provide guidance on how to prepare and adapt these liturgies for particular occasions.

The form of worship that follows offers a still further alternative, and might be considered more appropriate for an Ecumenical worship service.

OPENING SONG

Choose a song that picks up the focus of the liturgy, and is suitable as an opening song. Choose a song that is familiar to those likely to be present or which can be taught to them before the service begins.

Some suggestions are

We have a gospel to proclaim (778 CHE; 852 LAUD)
Gather us in (253 CHE; 327 LHO&N; 475 LAUD)
Will you come and follow me (812 CHE; 740 LHO&N; 877 LAUD)

We are your people (770 CHE)

We hold a treasure (780 CHE; 717 LHO&N; 915 LAUD)

Some suitable songs have a strong Eucharistic theme, however these may be found to be less suitable for an ecumenical gathering

O thou, who at thy Eucharist… (566 CHE; 559 LHO&N; 833)

We come to share our story (774 CHE; 473 LAUD)

Key: CHE: Celebration Hymnal for Everyone; LHO&N: Liturgical Hymns Old and New; LAUD: Laudate

Greeting

Leader: In the name of the Father, and the Son, and the Holy Spirit.
All: **Amen.**
Leader: The grace and peace of God our Father and the Lord Jesus Christ be with you.
All: **And also with you.**

Welcome and introduction

Opening Prayer

God our Father,
by the promise you made
in the life, death, and resurrection of Christ your Son,
you bring together in your Spirit, from all the nations,
a people to be your own.
Keep the Church faithful to its mission:
may it be a leaven in the world
renewing us in Christ,
and transforming us into your family.
We ask this through our Lord Jesus Christ, your Son,
who lives and reigns with you and the Holy Spirit,
one God, for ever and ever.

All: **Amen.**

• Liturgy of the Word •

Either

A reading from
the letter of St Paul to the Romans **10:9–18**

IF YOUR LIPS confess that Jesus is Lord and if you believe in your heart that God raised him from the dead, then you will be saved. By believing from the heart you are made righteous; by confessing with your lips you are saved. When scripture says: those who believe in me will have no cause for shame, it makes no distinction between Jew and Greek: all belong to the same Lord who is rich enough, however many ask his help, for everyone who calls on the name of the Lord will be saved.

But they will not ask his help unless they believe in him, and they will not believe in him unless they have heard of him, and they will not hear of him unless they get a preacher, and they will never have a preacher unless one is sent, but as scripture says: The footsteps of those who bring good news are a welcome sound. Not everyone, of course, listens to the Good News. As Isaiah says: Lord, how many believed what we proclaimed? So faith comes from what is preached, and what is preached comes from the word of Christ.

Let me put this question: is it possible that they did not hear? Indeed they did; in the words of the psalm, their voice has gone out through all the earth, and the message to the ends of the world.

This is the Word of the Lord.
Thanks be to God.

or

A reading from
the letter of St Paul to the Ephesians 3:2–12

YOU HAVE PROBABLY heard how I have been entrusted by God with the grace he meant for you, and that it was by a revelation that I was given the knowledge of the mystery, as I have just described it very shortly. If you read my words, you will have some idea of the depths that I see in the mystery of Christ. This mystery that has now been revealed through the Spirit to his holy apostles and prophets was unknown to any men in past generations; it means that pagans now share the same inheritance, that they are parts of the same body, and that the same promise has been made to them, in Christ Jesus, through the gospel. I have been made the servant of that gospel by a gift of grace from God who gave it to me by his own power. I, who am less than the least of all the saints, have been entrusted with this special grace, not only of proclaiming to the pagans the infinite treasure of Christ but also of explaining how the mystery is to be dispensed. Through all the ages, this has been kept hidden in God, the creator of everything. Why? So that the Sovereignties and Powers should learn only now, through the Church, how comprehensive God's wisdom really is, exactly according to the plan which he had had from all eternity in Christ Jesus our Lord. This is why we are bold enough to approach God in complete confidence, through our faith in him.

This is the Word of the Lord.
Thanks be to God.

PSALM 97

℟ **The Lord has shown his salvation.**

Sing a new song to the Lord
for he has worked wonders.
His right hand and his holy arm
have brought salvation. ℟

The Lord has made known his salvation:
has shown his justice to the nations.
He has remembered his truth and love
for the house of Israel. ℟

All the ends of the earth have seen
the salvation of our God.
Shout to the Lord all the earth,
ring out your joy. ℟

Sing psalms to the Lord with the harp
with the sound of music.
With trumpets and the sound of the horn
acclaim the King, the Lord. ℟

Gospel Acclamation

Alleluia. You are Peter, and on this rock I will build my church. And the gates of the underworld can never hold out against it. Alleluia.

A reading from
the holy Gospel according to Matthew 16:13–19

WHEN JESUS CAME to the region of Caesarea Philippi he put this question to his disciples, "Who do people say the Son of Man is?" And they said, "Some say he is

John the Baptist, some Elijah, and others Jeremiah or one of the prophets." "But you," he said "who do you say I am?" Then Simon Peter spoke up, "You are the Christ", he said, "the Son of the living God." Jesus replied, "Simon son of Jonah, you are a happy man! Because it was not flesh and blood that revealed this to you but my Father in heaven. So I now say to you: You are Peter and on this rock I will build my Church. And the gates of the underworld can never hold out against it. I will give you the keys of the kingdom of heaven: whatever you bind on earth shall be considered bound in heaven; whatever you loose on earth shall be considered loosed in heaven."

This is the Gospel of the Lord.
Glory to you Lord Jesus Christ.

Homily or reflection

(With a smaller group it might be easier to invite people to share with their neighbour what they hope for from the Papal Visit. There may be particular local initiatives during the visit – don't make this a planning time, but the opportunity might be there for considering how people can best support the initiative.)

General Intercessions

The following simple biddings might be used as they are, with each one being followed by a time of silent prayer for the intention. Alternatively they might be elaborated. It is usual to end the prayer for each bidding with a responsory such as 'Lord in your mercy: hear our prayer.

Let us pray for Pope Benedict

Let us pray for the Church in the United Kingdom

Let us pray for all the peoples and institutions of our nation

Let us pray for our local community

Let us pray for our own needs

Concluding Prayer

Lord, source of eternal life and truth,
give to your shepherd Pope Benedict,
a spirit of courage and right judgement,
a spirit of knowledge and love.
May he, as successor to the apostle Peter and vicar of Christ,
build your Church into a sacrament of unity, love, and peace for all the world.
We ask this through our Lord Jesus Christ, your Son,
who lives and reigns with you and the Holy Spirit,
one God, for ever and ever.

All: **Amen.**

CONCLUDING SONG

If you would follow me (299 CHE; 743 LAUD)

Will you let me be your servant (813 CHE; 924 LAUD)

A new commandment (4 CHE, 133 LHO&N; 920 LAUD)

Make me a channel of your peace (478 CHE, 470 LHO&N; 898 LAUD)

You are salt for the earth (821 CHE; 854 LAUD)

Christ's is the world (198 LHO&N; 882 LAUD)

Key: CHE: Celebration Hymnal for Everyone; LHO&N: Liturgical Hymns Old and New; LAUD: Laudate

MAGNIFICAT has been available in the United States for some years now, and many thousands of readers have found it a wonderful stimulus to daily prayer and a treasury of Christian spirituality. No only does it provide a daily Missal that fits easily in the pocket, but its pages of Morning and Evening Prayer lead the reader gently through the Psalms, and introduce us to the meditations of the Saints, where we encounter the living waters of God's Word, constantly flowing.

In the Mass we can pour ourselves into the mould of the Church, to become freshly-minted Christians once again, able to cooperate creatively with the Spirit of God who lives within us, leading us ever more deeply into prayer and truth.

In the articles and hymns, the lives of the Saints and the meditations of each day, we immerse ourselves in the living culture of faith.

Now for the first time, MAGNIFICAT *is available in an English edition, with the texts and translations appropriate for our own culture and our national calendar. Increasingly it will include appropriate material from Scotland, Wales and Ireland too, as more and more people in these countries come to use* MAGNIFICAT *to pray with the Church each day.*

Magnificat

From September 12th to 15th

Blessings

Blessing of the Fruits of the Eucharist

"The faithful, when worshipping Christ present in the Sacrament of the Altar, should recall that this Presence comes from the Sacrifice of the Eucharist, and tends toward sacramental and spiritual communion."

Rituale Romanum #80

Word of God — John 6: 54, 56

ANYONE WHO does eat my flesh and drink my blood has eternal life, and I shall raise him up on the last day. He who eats my flesh and drinks my blood lives in me, and I live in him.

MEDITATION

Your anguished mind dashes itself against your cage, screaming out blasphemies, but another road leads us to turn our steps toward Jerusalem. You were not deceived in desiring to devour things, poet devoid of the priest's power. *This is*, are words which can instantly serve to unveil Being… Whenever the priest pronounces them, this bread sustains their substance. For us to take in the Word that is the wholly human – fully God and man, we have only to open our mouth… Not only my soul, but also my body can attain contact with this truth! Even during this life the whole man can realise his power to conquer death!

Paul Claudel

LITANY OF THE EFFECTS OF THE EUCHARIST

(based on the Catechism of the Catholic Church)

℟ ***Jesus, be our life!***

"Our way of thinking is attuned to the Eucharist, and the Eucharist in turn confirms our way of thinking." (St Irenaeus, *Adv. haeres.* 4, 18, 5: PG 7/1,1028.) (CCC 1327) ℟

"The Eucharist is the efficacious sign and sublime cause of that communion in the divine life and that unity of the People of God by which the Church is kept in being." (Congregation of Rites, instruction, *Eucharisticum mysterium*, 6) (CCC 1325) ℟

"Those who receive the Eucharist are united more closely to Christ." (CCC 1396) ℟

"By this sacrifice [Christ] pours out the graces of salvation on his Body which is the Church." (CCC 1407) ℟

"Communion renews, strengthens, and deepens... incorporation into the Church." (cf. 1 Cor 12: 13) (CCC 1396) ℟

The Eucharist "is the culmination both of God's action sanctifying the world in Christ and of the worship men offer to Christ." (Congregation of Rites, instruction, *Eucharisticum mysterium*, 6) (CCC 1325) ℟

"The Eucharist commits us to the poor." (CCC 1397) ℟

"Holy Communion separates us from sin." (CCC 1393) ℟

"The Eucharist *preserves us from future mortal sins.*" (CCC 1395) ℟

"The Eucharist strengthens our charity, which tends to be weakened in daily life; and this living charity *wipes away venial sins.*" (cf. Council of Trent (1551): DS 1638) (CCC 1394) ℟

"By giving himself to us Christ revives our love and enables us to break our disordered attachments to creatures and root ourselves in him." (CCC 1394) ℟

"Communion with the flesh of the risen Christ… preserves, increases, and renews the life of grace received at Baptism." (CCC 1392) ℟

Our Father…

Compiled by Father Peter John Cameron, O.P.

Blessings for the Table

GRACE BEFORE THE MEAL:

Blessed are you, almighty Father,
who give us our daily bread.
Blessed is your only begotten Son,
who continually feeds us on the word of life.
Blessed is the Holy Spirit,
who brings us together at this table of love.
Blessed be God now and for ever.

℟ **Amen.**

GRACE AFTER THE MEAL:

Blessed are you, Lord, God of all creation:
you bring forth bread from the earth.
Blessed be God for ever.

℟ **Amen.**

Marian Antiphon

This prayer, first found in a Greek papyrus, c. 300, is the oldest known prayer to the Virgin.

7.
SUB tú-um præsí-di-um confúgimus, * sáncta
Dé- i Génitrix : nóstras depre-ca-ti-ónes ne despíci-as
in ne-ces-si-tá-tibus : sed a per-í-cu-lis cúnctis líbe-ra
nos sem-per, Vírgo glo-ri-ó-sa et be- ne- díc- ta.

**We fly to thy protection, O holy Mother of God.
Despise not our petitions in our necessities,
but deliver us always from all dangers
O glorious and blessed Virgin.**

Hymn of the Month

Virgo virginum praeclara

Hymn for the Memorial of Our Lady of Sorrows, September 15

O noble Virgin of virgins,
be no longer unyielding to me;
allow me to lament with you.

Grant that I may carry the death of Christ,
allow me a share of the passion,
and to contemplate his wounds.

Grant me to be wounded with his wounds,
to be inebriated with this cross
and the blood of your Son.

By you, O Virgin, let me be defended
on the day of judgement,
lest I, set on fire, should be burned in the
flames.

Grant me to be defended by the cross,
protected by the death of Christ,
supported by grace.

When my body shall die,
grant that to my soul may be given
the glory of paradise. Amen.

Translated by James Monti

H.II
VIrgo vírgi-num præclára, mi-hi iam non sis amá-
ra: fac me tecum plángere. 2. Fac ut portem Christi mor-
tem, passi-ó-nis fac me sortem, et plagas recóle-re. 3. Fac
me plagis vulnerá-ri, cruce hac in-ebri-á-ri, et cru-ó-re
Fí-li-i. 4. Flammis urar ne succénsus, per te, Virgo, sim
defénsus in di-e iudí-ci-i. 5. Fac me cruce custodí-ri,
morte Christi præmuní-ri, confovéri grá-ti-a. 6. Quando
corpus mo-ri-é-tur, fac ut á-ni-mæ do-nétur pa-ra-dí-si
gló-ri-a. A-men.

Prayer at Night

Options for September 2010

Prayer at Night is traditionally a short prayer, with fewer variations than the Prayers for Morning and Evening, so that, if desired, it can be memorised. People have most often prayed it alone immediately before retiring for the night. Families or other groups might also want to pray it together.

Two options are suggested for this month.

[Option 1]

O God, come to our aid.
O Lord, make haste to help us.
Glory be to the Father, and to the Son, and to the Holy Spirit, as it was in the beginning, is now, and ever shall be, world without end. Amen. Alleluia.

Examination of Conscience/Penitential Rite (optional)

What have you loved? What have you sought?

If several people are praying together, a penitential rite may be used:

I confess to almighty God,
and to you, my brothers and sisters,
that I have sinned through my own fault
in my thoughts and in my words,
in what I have done, and in what I have failed to do;
and I ask blessed Mary, ever virgin,
all the angels and saints,
and you, my brothers and sisters,
to pray for me to the Lord our God.

May almighty God have mercy on us, forgive us our sins, and bring us to everlasting life. Amen.

HYMN Metre: 55 88 55

This hymn can be sung to the tune used for *Jesus, Lead the Way*

Round me falls the night;
Saviour, be my light:
Through the hours in darkness shrouded
Let me see your face unclouded;
Let your glory shine
In this heart of mine.

PSALM 4

On my bed I remember you./ On you I muse through the night. (Ps 62: 7)

Even in the sleep that prefigures death, we rest in the confident trust that gives true joy because we are safe in the sure promise of the risen Christ.

When I call, answer me, O God of justice;
from anguish you released me, have mercy and hear me!

O men, how long will your hearts be closed,
will you love what is futile and seek what is false?

It is the Lord who grants favours to those whom he loves;
the Lord hears me whenever I call him.

Fear him; do not sin: ponder on your bed and be still.
Make justice your sacrifice and trust in the Lord.

"What can bring us happiness?" many say.
Lift up the light of your face on us, O Lord.

You have put into my heart a greater joy
than they have from abundance of corn and new wine.

I will lie down in peace and sleep comes at once
for you alone, Lord, make me dwell in safety.

Glory be to the Father, and to the Son,
and to the Holy Spirit,
as it was in the beginning, is now,
and ever shall be, world without end. Amen.

Word of God

Isaiah 26: 8-9a

FOLLOWING the path of your judgements, we hoped in you, O LORD, Your name, your memory are all my soul desires. At night my soul longs for you and my spirit in me seeks for you.

Into your hands I commend my spirit.
It is you who will redeem me, LORD.
(Ps 30: 6)

CANTICLE OF SIMEON

Save us, Lord, while we are awake; protect us while we sleep; that we may keep watch with Christ and rest with him in peace.

Now, Lord, you have kept your word:
let your servant go in peace.

With my own eyes I have seen the salvation
which you have prepared in the sight of every people:

a light to reveal you to the nations
and the glory of your people Israel.

Glory be to the Father, and to the Son,
  and to the Holy Spirit,
as it was in the beginning, is now,
  and ever shall be, world without end. Amen.

PRAYER

O God, keep us safe throughout this night that we may rise again with joy for your service, through the same Christ our Lord. Amen.

BLESSING

May the Lord grant a quiet night and a perfect end to us and to all our absent sisters and brothers. Amen.

MARIAN ANTIPHON (Text, page 23)

[Option 2]

O God, come to our aid.
O Lord, make haste to help us.

Glory be to the Father, and to the Son, and to the Holy Spirit, as it was in the beginning, is now, and ever shall be, world without end. Amen. Alleluia.

Examination of Conscience/Penitential Rite (optional)

In what activities have you sought rest? How have they led you to a deeper spirit of prayer, a deeper love of God, a greater patience with your neighbour?

If several people are praying together, a penitential rite may be used:

Lord Jesus, you are peace for our journey.
Lord, have mercy.

All: Lord, have mercy.

Lord Jesus, you are rest on our way.
Christ, have mercy.

All: Christ, have mercy.

Lord Jesus, you are the promise of home at day's end.
Lord, have mercy.

All: Lord, have mercy.

May almighty God have mercy on us, forgive us our sins, and bring us to everlasting life. Amen.

HYMN

Metre: LM
This hymn can be sung to the tune used for *Let All on Earth Their Voices Raise*

We praise you, Father, for your gift
Of dusk and nightfall over earth,

Foreshadowing the mystery
Of death that leads to endless day.

Within your hands we rest secure:
In quiet sleep our strength renew;
Yet give your people hearts that wake
In love to you, unsleeping Lord.

Your glory may we ever seek
In rest, as in activity,
Until its fullness is revealed,
O Source of life, O Trinity.

PSALM 61 2-3, 8-9, 11-13

Full of hope, you will live secure,/ dwelling well and safely guarded. (cf. Jb 11: 18)

As night falls, let us confidently entrust to God the burdens of the day – our hopes and fears, our achievements and failures, our good deeds and our sins – and rest in the stronghold of his unfailing love.

In God alone is my soul at rest;
my help comes from him.
He alone is my rock, my stronghold,
my fortress: I stand firm.

In God is my safety and glory,
the rock of my strength.
Take refuge in God all you people.
Trust him at all times.
Pour out your hearts before him
for God is our refuge.

Do not put your trust in oppression
nor vain hopes on plunder.
Do not set your heart on riches
even when they increase.

For God has said only one thing:
only two do I know:

that to God alone belongs power
and to you, Lord, love;
and that you repay each man
according to his deeds.

Glory be to the Father…

Word of God

Matthew 11: 28-29

COME TO ME, all you who labour and are overburdened, and I will give you rest. Shoulder my yoke and learn from me, for I am gentle and humble in heart, and you will find rest for your souls.

Into your hands I commend my spirit./
It is you who will redeem me, LORD. *(Ps 30: 6)*

CANTICLE OF SIMEON

(Text, page 28)

Save us, Lord, while we are awake; protect us while we sleep; that we may keep watch with Christ and rest with him in peace.

PRAYER

O Lord, support us all the day long of this troublous life, until the shadows lengthen and evening comes, and the busy world is hushed, and the fever of life is over, and our work is done. Then, in your mercy, grant us a safe lodging and a holy rest and peace at the last. Amen.
(Blessed John Henry Newman)

BLESSING

May the Lord grant a quiet night and a perfect end to us and to all our absent sisters and brothers. Amen.

MARIAN ANTIPHON

(Text, page 23)

Rejoice with me,
I have found my sheep that was lost.

Suggested Prayer of the Faithful

(Each local community should compose its own Universal Prayer, but may find inspiration in the texts proposed here.)

The grace of our Lord is abundant, along with the faith and love that are in Christ Jesus. Counting on the Lord's abundance, we turn to the Father and offer him our prayers.

For blessings on Pope Benedict XVI especially as he prepares for his papal visit to the United Kingdom.

For leaders of nations and all civil authorities: that they will govern in such a way as to promote the tranquillity and dignity of all people.

That our parish community may grow in faith, hope, and love.

For firemen, police officers, and emergency medical technicians: that the Lord will watch over them and reward them for their service.

For the needy and the disadvantaged: that the Lord will lift up the poor, and that we will be generous in aiding and comforting the unfortunate.

For the grace this week to live in obedience to God the Father.

Loving Father, the grace of your Son has been abundant in our lives. Keep us true to all that Christ has done for us and grateful for his favour. We ask this through Christ our Lord. Amen.

SUNDAY, SEPTEMBER 12

Twenty-Fourth Sunday in Ordinary Time

Prayer for the Morning

Our God is the seeker of the lost. Let us praise him!

Glory be to the Father, and to the Son, and to the Holy Spirit, as it was in the beginning, is now, and ever shall be, world without end. Amen. Alleluia!

HYMN Metre: 77 77

This hymn can be sung to the tune used for *Saviour of the Nations, Come*

Drained the wine and sung the songs,
Scattered friends like leaves on wind,
Dead the fire and cold the hearth –
Dust and ashes: we have sinned.

Hunger prowls this hollow house;
Thirst laps up the drying lees
Left in cups none cared to drink
Once the feast had ceased to please.

Dry the rustling of the husks,
Fragile walls for emptiness;
Dry the whispering heart within,
Shell for dreams grown meaningless.

Others eat the bread we left,
Careless as we cast aside
Love that held the door and wept
Tears unnoticed by our pride.

Still the table stands prepared,
Lonely till we cease to roam.
Fools! Why do we linger here?
Let us go: love waits at home.

PSALM 50 12-21

In the waste lands he adopts him,/ in the howling desert of the wilderness./ He protects him, rears him, guards him/ as the pupil of his eye. (Dt 32: 10)

No matter how far we stray and how lost we feel, God the Father is always right there waiting for us with open arms. We may feel sinful and unworthy of his love, but all we need to do is make a move toward him and he will run to meet us as his beloved sons and daughters. Let us run to receive his love!

A pure heart create for me, O God,
put a steadfast spirit within me.
Do not cast me away from your presence,
nor deprive me of your holy spirit.

Give me again the joy of your help;
with a spirit of fervour sustain me,
that I may teach transgressors your ways
and sinners may return to you.

O rescue me, God, my helper,
and my tongue shall ring out your goodness.
O Lord, open my lips
and my mouth shall declare your praise.

For in sacrifice you take no delight,
burnt offering from me you would refuse,
my sacrifice, a contrite spirit.
A humbled, contrite heart you will not spurn.

In your goodness, show favor to Sion:
rebuild the walls of Jerusalem.
Then you will be pleased with lawful sacrifice,
burnt offerings wholly consumed.

Glory be to the Father…

Word of God — Genesis 37: 23-28

SO, WHEN JOSEPH REACHED his brothers, they pulled off his coat, the coat with long sleeves that he was wearing, and catching hold of him they threw him into the well, an empty well with no water in it.

They then sat down to eat. Looking up they saw a group of Ishmaelites who were coming from Gilead, their camels laden with gum, tragacanth, balsam and resin, which they were taking down into Egypt. Then Judah said to his brothers: "What do we gain by killing our brother and covering up his blood? Come, let us sell him to the Ishmaelites, but let us not do any harm to him. After all, he is our brother, and our own flesh." His brothers agreed. They sold Joseph to the Ishmaelites for twenty silver pieces.

I am your brother Joseph whom you sold into Egypt. *(Gn 45: 4)*

CANTICLE OF ZECHARIAH (Text, back cover B)
The man who fears the LORD bears repentance in his heart. (Sr 21: 6)

INTERCESSIONS

We have all sinned and are in need of God's forgiveness, so we pray:

℟ Run to us in your mercy.

When we have departed far from you: ℟

When we seek to return to your house: ℟

When we have squandered the gifts you have given us: ℟

Personal intentions

Our Father…

God, our Father, you are great and merciful. Pursue us when we are far from you, that we may return to your loving arms. We ask this through Christ our Lord. Amen.

MASS

Twenty-Fourth Sunday in Ordinary Time

The Pharisees and scribes complain about Jesus, "This man welcomes sinners and eats with them." Yet, if they had the decency to be the least bit mindful of their own history, they would have recalled how their ancestors at the base of Mount Sinai had "become depraved" and had turned aside from the way that God pointed out to them. God uses the experience of our being lost like the sheep, the coin, and the son to demonstrate compellingly that "Christ Jesus came into the world to save sinners." Christ welcomes sinners and eats with them because only that closeness with Christ's human presence changes sinners into saints. To this Saint Paul attests: "I was once a blasphemer and a persecutor and arrogant, but I have been mercifully treated… The grace of our Lord has been abundant, along with faith and love."

ENTRANCE ANTIPHON

O Lord, give peace to those who wait for you and your prophets will proclaim you as you deserve. Hear the prayers of your servant and of your people Israel. (See Sr 36: 18)

GLORIA ——————————————— **page 450**

OPENING PRAYER

Almighty God,
our creator and guide,
may we serve you with all our heart
and know your forgiveness in our lives.
We ask this through our Lord Jesus Christ, your Son,
who lives and reigns with you and the Holy Spirit,
one God, for ever and ever.

ALTERNATIVE OPENING PRAYER

Father in heaven, Creator of all,
look down upon your people in their moments of need,

for you alone are the source of our peace.
Bring us to the dignity which distinguishes the
poor in spirit
and show us how great is the call to serve,
that we may share in the peace of Christ
who offered his life in the service of all.
We ask this through Christ our Lord.

● *The Lord relented and did not bring on his people the disaster he had threatened.* ●

A reading from the Book of Exodus 32: 7-11, 13-14

THE LORD SPOKE TO Moses, "Go down now, because your people whom you brought out of Egypt have apostasised. They have been quick to leave the way I marked out for them; they have made themselves a calf of molten metal and have worshipped it and offered it sacrifice. 'Here is your God, Israel,' they have cried, 'who brought you up from the land of Egypt!'" The LORD said to Moses, "I can see how headstrong these people are! Let me, now, my wrath shall blaze out against them and devour them; of you, however, I will make a great nation."

But Moses pleaded with the LORD, his God. "LORD," he said, "why should your wrath blaze out against this people of yours whom you brought out of the land of Egypt with arm outstretched and mighty hand? Remember Abraham, Isaac, and Jacob, your servants to whom by your own self you swore and made this promise: 'I will make your offspring as many as the stars of heaven, and all this land which I promised I will give to your descendants, and it shall be their heritage for ever.'" So the LORD relented and did not bring on his people the disaster he had threatened.
This is the word of the Lord.

• PSALM 50 •

℟ (Lk 15: 18) I will leave this place and go to my father.

Have mercy on me, God, in your kindness;
in your compassion blot out my offence.
O wash me more and more from my guilt
and cleanse me from my sin. ℟

A pure heart create for me, O God,
put a steadfast spirit within me.
Do not cast me away from your presence,
nor deprive me of your holy spirit. ℟

O Lord, open my lips
and my mouth shall declare your praise.
My sacrifice is a contrite spirit;
a humbled, contrite heart you will not spurn. ℟

• *Christ Jesus came into the world to save sinners.* •

A reading from
the first Letter of Saint Paul to Timothy 1: 12-17

I THANK Christ Jesus our Lord, who has given me strength, and who judged me faithful enough to call me into his service even though I used to be a blasphemer and did all I could to injure and discredit the faith. Mercy, however, was shown me, because until I became a believer I had been acting in ignorance; and the grace of our Lord filled me with faith and with the love that is in Christ Jesus. Here is a saying that you can rely on and nobody should doubt: that Christ Jesus came into the world to save sinners. I myself am the greatest of them; and if mercy has been shown to me, it is because Jesus Christ

meant to make me the greatest evidence of his inexhaustible patience for all the other people who would later have to trust in him to come to eternal life. To the eternal King, the undying, invisible and only God, be honour and glory for ever and ever. Amen.
This is the word of the Lord.

Alleluia, alleluia! May the Father of our Lord Jesus Christ enlighten the eyes of our mind, so that we can see what hope his call holds for us. Alleluia!

Longer Form

● *There will be rejoicing in heaven over one repentant sinner.* ●

A reading from
the holy Gospel according to Luke **15: 1-32**

THE TAX COLLECTORS and the sinners were all seeking the company of Jesus to hear what he had to say, and the Pharisees and the scribes complained. "This man," they said, "welcomes sinners and eats with them." So he spoke this parable to them: "What man among you with a hundred sheep, losing one, would not leave the ninety-nine in the wilderness and go after the missing one till he found it? And when he found it, would he not joyfully take it on his shoulders and then, when he got home, call together his friends and neighbours? 'Rejoice with me,' he would say, 'I have found my sheep that was lost.' In the same way, I tell you, there will be more rejoicing in heaven over one repentant sinner than over ninety-nine virtuous men who have no need of repentance.

"Or again, what woman with ten drachmas would not, if she lost one, light a lamp and sweep out the house and search thoroughly till she found it? And then, when she had found it, call together her friends and neighbours? "Rejoice with me," she would say "I have found the drachma I lost." In the same way, I tell you, there is rejoicing among the angels of God over one repentant sinner."

He also said, "A man had two sons. The younger said to his father, 'Father, let me have the share of the estate that would come to me.' So the father divided the property between them. A few days later, the younger son got together everything he had and left for a distant country where he squandered his money on a life of debauchery. When he had spent it all, that country experienced a severe famine, and now he began to feel the pinch, so he hired himself out to one of the local inhabitants who put him on his farm to feed the pigs. And he would willingly have filled his belly with the husks the pigs were eating but no one offered him anything. Then he came to his senses and said, 'How many of my father's paid servants have more food than they want, and here am I dying of hunger! I will leave this place and go to my father and say: Father, I have sinned against heaven and against you; I no longer deserve to be called your son; treat me as one of your paid servants.' So he left the place and went back to his father. While he was still a long way off, his father saw him and was moved with pity. He ran to the boy, clasped him in his arms and kissed him tenderly. Then his son said, 'Father, I have sinned against heaven and against you. I no longer deserve to be called your son.' But the father said to his servants, 'Quick! Bring out the best robe and put it on him; put a ring on his finger and sandals on his feet. Bring the calf we have been fattening, and kill it; we

are going to have a feast, a celebration, because this son of mine was dead and has come back to life; he was lost and is found.' And they began to celebrate. Now the elder son was out in the fields, and on his way back, as he drew near the house, he could hear music and dancing. Calling one of the servants he asked what it was all about. 'Your brother has come,' replied the servant, 'and your father has killed the calf we had fattened because he has got him back safe and sound.' He was angry then and refused to go in, and his father came out to plead with him; but he answered his father, 'Look, all these years I have slaved for you and never once disobeyed your orders, yet you never offered me so much as a kid for me to celebrate with my friends. But, for this son of yours, when he comes back after swallowing up your property – he and his women – you kill the calf we had been fattening.' The father said, 'My son, you are with me always and all I have is yours. But it was only right we should celebrate and rejoice, because your brother here was dead and has come to life; he was lost and is found.'"
This is the Gospel of the Lord.

Or Shorter Form

● *There will be rejoicing in heaven over one repentant sinner.* ●

A reading from
the holy Gospel according to Luke **15: 1-10**

THE TAX COLLECTORS and the sinners were all seeking the company of Jesus to hear what he had to say, and the Pharisees and the scribes complained. "This man," they said, "welcomes sinners and eats with them." So he spoke this parable to them: "What man among you with a hundred sheep, losing one, would not leave the ninety-nine in the wilderness and go after the missing one till he found it? And when he found it, would he not joyfully take it on his shoulders and then, when he got home, call together his friends and neighbours? 'Rejoice with me,' he would say, 'I have found my sheep that was lost.' In the same way, I tell you, there will be more rejoicing in heaven over one repentant sinner than over ninety-nine virtuous men who have no need of repentance.

"Or again, what woman with ten drachmas would not, if she lost one, light a lamp and sweep out the house and search thoroughly till she found it? And then, when she had found it, call together her friends and neighbours? 'Rejoice with me,' she would say, 'I have found the drachma I lost.' In the same way, I tell you, there is rejoicing among the angels of God over one repentant sinner."

This is the Gospel of the Lord.

CREDO ——— page 452

PRAYER OVER THE GIFTS

Lord,
hear the prayers of your people
and receive our gifts.
May the worship of each one here
bring salvation to all.
Grant this through Christ our Lord.

PREFACE OF SUNDAYS IN ORDINARY TIME ——— page 455

COMMUNION ANTIPHON

O God, how much we value your mercy! All mankind can gather under your protection. (Ps 36: 8)

Or:

The cup that we bless is a communion with the blood of Christ; and the bread that we break is a communion with the body of the Lord. (See 1 Co 10: 16)

PRAYER AFTER COMMUNION

Lord,
may the Eucharist you have given us
influence our thoughts and actions.
May your Spirit guide and direct us in your way.
We ask this in the name of Jesus the Lord.

DAY BY DAY

The Prodigal Son

We read that our Lord God is so anxious for our love that he acted in the same way when the sinner arrived from a distant land, treating him as if he were his own servant, or more. It is said that God went out to welcome the one who arrived whereas the mother usually does not move except to stretch out her arms to the child. But God, moved by pity, as Saint Luke writes, went out to welcome the one who came, and, clasping him in friendship, kissed his face in peace, and, what is more, ordered a cloak with new adornments brought, placed a ring on his finger to seal the friendship; nor did he neglect to give him shoes. Then God had a fatted calf slaughtered, invited guests, and celebrated the day with songs of joy. If all of this is an image for the way God spiritually treats the hardened sinner, and his own Son assures us it is, think how he will welcome the just person who diligently and continuously searches for him. I know without a doubt that just persons enjoy paradise in this life as well as the next, as sinners, if you think on it, suffer their hell not only later but now. If you let the world give you what you look for and feed your vanity on pleasure, do you think that God will merely sleep or turn a deaf ear? In your wickedness you will think ill of God and pervert the concern of servants who seek him and renounce vanity into laziness and negligence, and you will believe that nothing more exists now than what will perish and is common to everyone. You should know, as Saint Augustine tells us, that God does not deceive, and if he did not intend to sustain us, he would not urge us over and over again to come to him. Ordinary things are in the Church for ordinary people, but God has other things for special people, and even the ordinary contains something special, which those who love more deeply can understand.

FRANCISCO DE OSUNA

Francisco de Osuna († c. 1540), known as Fray Francisco, was a Franciscan friar and ascetic writer from the Seville region of Spain.

Prayer for the Evening

Our God is the lover of our souls. Let us adore him!

Glory be to the Father, and to the Son, and to the Holy Spirit, as it was in the beginning, is now, and ever shall be, world without end. Amen. Alleluia!

HYMN Metre: CM 86 86

Amazing grace! How sweet the sound
That saved a wretch like me!
I once was lost, but now am found,
Was blind but now I see.

'Twas grace that taught my heart to fear,
And grace my fears relieved;
How precious did that grace appear
The hour I first believed.

The Lord has promised good to me,
His word my hope secures;
He will my shield and portion be
As long as life endures.

PSALM 65 1-3a, 8-9, 16-17, 20

There is nothing I cannot master with the help of the One who gives me strength. (Phil 4: 13)

God loves each one of us very much and has a special vocation for us. He gives us the strength to fulfil our unique mission in life. We merely need to remain humble before him and be responsive to his gifts. In this way we will be given everything that is necessary.

Cry out with joy to God, all the earth,
O sing to the glory of his name.
O render him glorious praise.
Say to God: "How tremendous your deeds!"

O peoples, bless our God,
let the voice of his praise resound,
of the God who gave life to our souls
and kept our feet from stumbling.

Come and hear, all who fear God.
I will tell what he did for my soul:
to him I cried aloud,
with high praise ready on my tongue.

Blessed be God who did not reject my prayer
nor withhold his love from me.

Glory be to the Father…

Word of God 2 Timothy 1: 6-10

THAT IS WHY I AM reminding you now to fan into a flame the gift that God gave you when I laid my hands on you. God's gift was not a spirit of timidity, but the Spirit of power, and love, and self-control. So you are never to be ashamed of witnessing to the Lord, or ashamed of me for being his prisoner for his sake; but with me, bear the hardships for the sake of the Good News, relying on the power of God who has saved us and called us to be holy – not because of anything we ourselves have done but for his own purpose and by his own grace.

This grace had already been granted to us, in Christ Jesus, before the beginning of time, but it has only been revealed by the Appearing of our saviour Christ Jesus.

Here is a saying you can rely on:/ If we have died with him,/ then we shall live with him. (2 Tm 2: 11)

CANTICLE OF MARY (Text, back cover A)
God, from our mothers' wombs, has called us through his grace. (cf. Ga 1: 15)

INTERCESSIONS

We seek to share in Christ's redemption and so we say:

℟ Lord, uphold us in your salvation.

When we feel that our sins are too much to be forgiven:
– give us the confidence to repent. ℟

When our situation looks hopeless:
– comfort us in your love. ℟

When we fear for those who have abandoned their faith:
– give them the insight to return to you. ℟

Personal intentions

Our Father…

May God keep us firm to the end, irreproachable on the day of our Lord Jesus Christ. Amen. (cf. 1 Co 1: 8)

MARIAN ANTIPHON (Text, page 23)

[MONDAY, SEPTEMBER 13
Saint John Chrysostom]

Prayer for the Morning

Let us proclaim the greatness of our God!

Glory be to the Father, and to the Son, and to the Holy Spirit, as it was in the beginning, is now, and ever shall be, world without end. Amen. Alleluia!

HYMN **Metre: 8 6 8 6 88**

How shall they hear the word of God
Unless the truth is told?
How shall the sinful be set free,
The sorrowful consoled?
To all who speak the truth today
Impart your Spirit, Lord, we pray.

How shall the gospel be proclaimed
If heralds are not sent?
How shall the world find peace at last
If we are negligent?
So send us, Lord, for we rejoice
To speak of Christ with life and voice.

CANTICLE **Deuteronomy 32: 1-4**

As for God, his ways are perfect;/ the word of the LORD, purest gold. (Ps 17: 31)

"Chrysostom" means "Golden Mouth". Saint John is remembered for his eloquence in preaching God's word to small and great alike.

Listen, O heavens, while I speak;
earth, hear the words that I am saying
May my teaching fall like the rain,
may my word drop down like the dew,

like showers on fresh grass,
and light rain on the turf.

For I proclaim the name of the LORD.
Oh, tell the greatness of our God!
He is the Rock, his work is perfect,
for all his ways are Equity.
A God faithful, without unfairness,
Uprightness itself and Justice.

Glory be to the Father…

Word of God

Isaiah 50: 4

THE LORD GOD has given me/ a disciple's tongue./ So that I may know how to reply to the wearied/ he provides me with speech./ Each morning he wakes me to hear,/ to listen like a disciple.

Only say the word and your servant will be healed.
(cf. Mt 8: 8)

CANTICLE OF ZECHARIAH (Text, back cover B)
You have the words of eternal life. (Jn 6: 68)

INTERCESSIONS

The preacher's is the voice, but the word of life is Christ. Let us pray through the intercession of Saint John Chrysostom for the grace to hear Christ in his word and to live by what we hear:

℟ Open our ears that we may hear and live!

By your word, you carved creation out of chaos:
– create in us a Gospel order of life. ℟

By your word, you brought light from darkness and stilled the storm:
– enlighten and quiet us to hear your voice in the midst of daily life. ℟

By your word, you healed the sick and raised the dead to life:
– give new life to all who live in the shadow of death. ℟

Personal intentions

Our Father…

O God, you speak the word of life through the eloquence of the faithful servants whom you call to proclaim the good news of salvation. By the example and intercession of Saint John Chrysostom, raise up courageous and convincing preachers in our day to stir faith to life, to heal the broken-hearted, and to offer new life, through Jesus Christ our Lord. Amen.

Mass

Monday of the Twenty-Fourth Week in Ordinary Time

Saint John Chrysostom *Memorial*

● *Saint John Chrysostom was born in Antioch about the year 349. After an extensive education he embraced a life of asceticism. He was ordained a priest and distinguished himself by his preaching which achieved great spiritual results among his hearers. He was elected bishop of Constantinople in 397 and proved himself a capable pastor, committed to reforming the life of the clergy and the faithful. Twice he was forced into exile by the hatred of the imperial court and the envy of his enemies. After he had completed his difficult labours, he died at Comana in Pontus on*

September 14, 407. His preaching and writing explained Catholic doctrine and presented the ideal Christian life. For this reason he is called Chrysostom, or Golden Mouth. ●

ENTRANCE ANTIPHON

I will look after my sheep, says the Lord, and I will raise up one shepherd who will pasture them. I, the Lord, will be their God. (Ezk 34: 11, 23-24)

OPENING PRAYER

Father, the strength of all who trust in you,
you made John Chrysostom
renowned for his eloquence
and heroic in his sufferings.
May we learn from his teaching
and gain courage from his patient endurance.
We ask this through our Lord Jesus Christ, your Son,
who lives and reigns with you and the Holy Spirit,
one God, for ever and ever.

● *If there are separate factions among you, it is not the Lord's Supper that you are eating.* ●

A reading from the first Letter of Saint Paul to the Corinthians 11: 17-26, 33

ON THE SUBJECT of instructions, I cannot say that you have done well in holding meetings that do you more harm than good. In the first place, I hear that when you all come together as a community, there are separate factions among you, and I half believe it – since there must no doubt be separate groups among you, to distinguish those who are to be trusted. The point is, when you hold these meetings, it is not the Lord's Supper that you are eating, since when the time comes to eat, everyone is in such a hurry to start his own supper that one person goes hungry while another is getting drunk.

Surely you have homes for eating and drinking in? Surely you have enough respect for the community of God not to make poor people embarrassed? What am I to say to you? Congratulate you? I cannot congratulate you on this.

For this is what I received from the Lord, and in turn passed on to you: that on the same night that he was betrayed, the Lord Jesus took some bread, and thanked God for it and broke it, and he said, "This is my body, which is for you; do this as a memorial of me." In the same way he took the cup after supper, and said, "This cup is the new covenant in my blood. Whenever you drink it, do this as a memorial of me." Until the Lord comes, therefore, every time you eat this bread and drink this cup, you are proclaiming his death. So to sum up, my dear brothers, when you meet for the Meal, wait for one another.
This is the word of the Lord.

• PSALM 39 •

℟ (1 Co 11: 26b) **Proclaim the death of the Lord until he comes.**

You do not ask for sacrifice and offerings,
  but an open ear.
You do not ask for holocaust and victim.
  Instead, here am I. ℟

In the scroll of the book it stands written
  that I should do your will.
My God, I delight in your law
  in the depth of my heart. ℟

Your justice I have proclaimed
  in the great assembly.
My lips I have not sealed;
  you know it, O LORD. ℟

O let there be rejoicing and gladness
for all who seek you.
Let them ever say: "The LORD is great"
who love your saving help. ℟

Alleluia, alleluia! God loved the world so much that he gave his only Son;/ everyone who believes in him has eternal life. Alleluia!

● *Not even in Israel have I found faith like this.* ●

A reading from
the holy Gospel according to Luke 7: 1-10

WHEN JESUS HAD COME to the end of all he wanted the people to hear, he went into Capernaum. A centurion there had a servant, a favourite of his, who was sick and near death. Having heard about Jesus he sent some Jewish elders to him to ask him to come and heal his servant. When they came to Jesus they pleaded earnestly with him. "He deserves this of you," they said, "because he is friendly towards our people; in fact, he is the one who built the synagogue." So Jesus went with them, and was not very far from the house when the centurion sent word to him by some friends: "Sir," he said, "do not put yourself to trouble; because I am not worthy to have you under my roof; and for this same reason I did not presume to come to you myself; but give the word and let my servant be cured. For I am under authority myself, and have soldiers under me; and I say to one man: Go, and he goes; to another: Come here, and he comes; to my servant: Do this, and he does it." When Jesus heard these words he was astonished at him and, turning round, said to the crowd following him, "I tell you, not even in Israel have I found faith like this." And when the

messengers got back to the house they found the servant in perfect health.
This is the Gospel of the Lord.

PRAYER OVER THE GIFTS

Lord, be pleased with this sacrifice we present
in honour of John Chrysostom,
for we gather to praise you as he taught us.
Grant this through Christ our Lord.

COMMUNION ANTIPHON

You have not chosen me; I have chosen you. Go and bear fruit that will last. (Jn 15: 16)

PRAYER AFTER COMMUNION

God of mercy, may the sacrament we receive
in memory of John Chrysostom
make us strong in your love
and faithful in our witness to your truth.
We ask this in the name of Jesus the Lord.

MEDITATION OF THE DAY

Our Faith and Christ's Action

The liturgical service takes place on earth, but it belongs to the realm of heavenly realities. In fact it was not instituted by a human being or an angel, but by the Spirit himself, so that those who are still living in the flesh should think of performing the service of angels.

O what mercy, O what love of God for human beings! Christ who is seated with the Father in highest heaven is at that moment grasped by the hands of all and does not hesitate to give himself to anyone who wants to embrace him and be bound to him.

He whom the eyes of faith perceive is possessed by everyone.

You remember how Elijah was surrounded by a great crowd and had in front of him the victim for sacrifice placed on the stone (see 1 K 18). Everyone stood stock still. The silence was complete. Only the prophet raised a prayer. Suddenly from heaven came down fire on the victim. It was a marvellous spectacle that filled everyone with amazement.

Here, however, something much more than a marvellous spectacle is unfolded. Something is happening that is greater than any marvel. Here the priest draws down not fire but the Holy Spirit himself.

SAINT JOHN CHRYSOSTOM

Saint John Chrysostom († 407) was a famed preacher and commentator on Scripture.

Prayer for the Evening

Let us take up God's word in prayer and praise!

Glory be to the Father… Alleluia!

HYMN

Metre: 66 84 D
This hymn can be sung to the tune used for *The God of Abraham Praise*

The pilgrim church of God,
We mount the narrow way,
We tread the path that Jesus trod,
His call to obey:
To whom God sent his Son,
On whom the Spirit came,
Who in the faith of Christ are one
And in his name.

His word of life divine
Shall light and truth impart,
And with immortal wisdom shine
For mind and heart.
So may we live and grow,

This grace upon us poured,
With hearts and minds alike to know
And serve the Lord.

PSALM 118 41-48

Son of man, I have appointed you as sentry to the House of Israel. Whenever you hear a word from me, warn them in my Name. (Ezk 3: 17)

A faithful bishop of the pilgrim Church, Saint John Chrysostom suffered exile and hardship as a result of his courage in calling the powerful to task for their sins.

Lord, let your love come upon me,
the saving help of your promise.
And I shall answer those who taunt me
for I trust in your word.

Do not take the word of truth from my mouth
for I trust in your decrees.
I shall always keep your law
for ever and ever.

I shall walk in the path of freedom
for I seek your precepts.
I will speak of your will before kings
and not be abashed.

Your commands have been my delight;
these I have loved.
I will worship your commands and love them
and ponder your statutes.

Glory be to the Father…

Word of God Galatians 6: 1

EVEN IF A PERSON is caught in some transgression, you who are spiritual should correct that one in a gentle spirit, looking to yourself, so that you also may not be tempted.

Do not take the word of truth from my mouth. (Ps 118: 43)

CANTICLE OF MARY (Text, back cover A)

Let the message of Christ, in all its richness, find a home with you. Teach each other, and advise each other, in all wisdom. (Col 3: 16)

INTERCESSIONS

God's word of freedom is his gift of love, for which great teachers and preachers have given their lives. In remembrance of Saint John Chrysostom, let us pray:

℟ Lord, let your love come upon us!

You sent your only Son, the living Word, to call the world to conversion of heart:
– grant us ears to hear and hearts to live according to your word. ℟

You have sent prophets and saints to call your people to faithfulness:
– grant us always courageous preachers of your word. ℟

You have sent wise and holy teachers to instruct your people:
– inspire young people to take up the study of your word as a task for life. ℟

Personal intentions

Our Father…

May the Lord rescue us from all evil attempts on us and bring us safely to his heavenly kingdom. Amen. (cf. 2 Tm 4: 18)

MARIAN ANTIPHON (Text, page 23)

SAINTS
OF TODAY AND YESTERDAY

I beseech you, O most sweet Lord Jesus Christ, that your passion be to me a source of strength whereby I may be fortified, protected, and defended.

SAINT CURONOTUS
Priest and Martyr († before 400)

Curonotus was a priest who was tortured and beheaded for his faith in Iconium (Konya, Turkey). The particular era in which he suffered is uncertain. Traditionally Curonotus has been commemorated on September 12.

SAINT AEMILIANUS
Bishop († c. 380)

Aemilianus is the earliest bishop of the French see of Valence known to history. His name is recorded in connection with a synod convened in Valence in 347. Aemilianus served with a reputation for great sanctity. The bishop of Vercelli, Italy, Saint Eusebius, counted Aemilianus among his friends. Aemilianus died around 380 after an episcopate of over thirty years.

When my pride, profiting by some moment of inattention, starts to build its castles in the air, and tries to make me soar aloft, I will make it a rule to think of these three places: Gethsemane, the house of Caiaphas, Calvary.

Blessed John XXIII

[TUESDAY, SEPTEMBER 14]
The Triumph of the Cross

Prayer for the Morning

Behold the wood of the cross,
on which has hung our salvation: come, let us adore!
(cf. Veneration of the Cross/Good Friday)

Glory be to the Father, and to the Son, and to the Holy Spirit, as it was in the beginning, is now, and ever shall be, world without end. Amen. Alleluia!

HYMN **Metre: 10 10 and refrain**

℟ Lift high the cross, the love of Christ proclaim,
Till all the world adore his sacred Name.

Led on their way by this triumphant sign,
The hosts of God in conquering ranks combine. ℟

O Lord, once lifted on the glorious tree,
As thou hast promised, draw the world to thee. ℟

So shall our song of triumph ever be:
Praise to the Crucified for victory. ℟

PSALM 91 **2-7, 9**

As for me, the only thing I can boast about is the cross of our Lord Jesus Christ, through whom the world is crucified to me, and I to the world. (Ga 6: 14)

The cross, instrument of torture and death, raised aloft as a sign of glory, continues to confound the wisdom of this world. God's work of salvation stands human expectations on their head: humility is exaltation, wounds are healing, death is life.

It is good to give thanks to the Lord,
to make music to your name, O Most High,

to proclaim your love in the morning
and your truth in the watches of the night,
on the ten-stringed lyre and the lute,
with the murmuring sound of the harp.

Your deeds, O Lord, have made me glad;
for the work of your hands I shout with joy.
O Lord, how great are your works!
How deep are your designs!
The foolish man cannot know this
and the fool cannot understand.
But you, Lord, are eternally on high.

Glory be to the Father…

Word of God 1 Corinthians 1: 20-25

WHERE ARE the philosophers now? Where are the scribes? Where are any of our thinkers today? Do you see now how God has shown up the foolishness of human wisdom? If it was God's wisdom that human wisdom should not know God, it was because God wanted to save those who have faith through the foolishness of the message that we preach. And so, while the Jews demand miracles and the Greeks look for wisdom, here are we preaching a crucified Christ; to the Jews an obstacle that they cannot get over, to the pagans madness, but to those who have been called, whether they are Jews or Greeks, a Christ who is the power and the wisdom of God. For God's foolishness is wiser than human wisdom, and God's weakness is stronger than human strength.

Christ humbled himself,/ becoming obedient to death,/ even death on a cross. (cf. Ph 2: 8)

CANTICLE OF ZECHARIAH (Text, back cover B)
But God raised him high/ and gave him the name/ which is above all other names. (Ph 2: 9)

INTERCESSIONS

To Christ our Lord most high, we pray:

℟ We adore you, O Christ, and we bless you because, by your holy cross, you have redeemed the world!

You emptied yourself and took the condition of a slave to set us free: ℟

You became obedient even unto death to deliver us from the fruits of disobedience: ℟

You arose from the dead to raise us out of the shadow of death into endless light: ℟

Personal intentions

Our Father…

Lord Jesus Christ, by your death on the cross, you triumphed over sin and death. Raise our fallen world to the glory no human wisdom can expect, who live and reign with the Father and the Holy Spirit, one God for ever and ever. Amen.

MASS

Feast of the Triumph of the Holy Cross

The Triumph of the Cross consists in the fact that "the event of the cross and Resurrection abides and draws everything toward life" (CCC 1085). We exalt Christ's cross whenever we freely take it up, filled with the certainty that the ultimate meaning and fulfillment which we crave in life comes to us through this unending event. "With the cross we are freed from the restraint of the enemy and we clutch on to the strength of salvation" (Saint Theodore the Studite). For salvation means escape from our own inability. At the same time, "we cannot produce or give any other fruit," writes Saint Catherine of Siena, "but the fruit we have taken from the tree of life." No wonder that "the sign of the cross makes kings of all those reborn in Christ" (Saint Leo the Great).

ENTRANCE ANTIPHON

We should glory in the cross of our Lord Jesus Christ, for he is our salvation, our life and our resurrection; through him we are saved and made free. (See Ga 6: 14)

GLORIA ———————————— **page 450**

OPENING PRAYER

God our Father,
in obedience to you
your only Son accepted death on the cross
for the salvation of mankind.
We acknowledge the mystery of the cross on earth.
May we receive the gift of redemption in heaven.
We ask this through our Lord Jesus Christ, your Son,
who lives and reigns with you and the Holy Spirit,
one God, for ever and ever.

● *If anyone was bitten by a serpent, he looked at the bronze serpent and lived.* ●

A reading from the Book of Numbers 21: 4b-9

ON THE WAY THROUGH the wilderness the people lost patience. They spoke against God and against Moses, "Why did you bring us out of Egypt to die in this wilderness? For there is neither bread nor water here; we are sick of this unsatisfying food."

At this God sent fiery serpents among the people; their bite brought death to many in Israel. The people came and said to Moses, "We have sinned by speaking against the LORD and against you. Intercede for us with the LORD to save us from these serpents." Moses interceded for the people, and the LORD answered him, "Make a fiery serpent and put it on a standard. If anyone is bitten and looks at it, he shall live." So Moses fashioned a bronze serpent which he put on a standard, and if anyone was bitten by a serpent, he looked at the bronze serpent and lived.

• PSALM 77 •

℟ (see 7b) **Never forget the deeds of the Lord.**

Give heed, my people, to my teaching;
  turn your ear to the words of my mouth.
I will open my mouth in a parable,
  and reveal hidden lessons of the past. ℟

When he slew them then they would seek him,
  return and seek him in earnest.
They would remember that God was their rock,
  God the Most High their redeemer. ℟

But the words they spoke were mere flattery;
  they lied to him with their lips.
For their hearts were not truly with him;
  they were not faithful to his covenant. ℟

Yet he who is full of compassion
  forgave them their sin and spared them.
So often he held back his anger
  when he might have stirred up his rage. ℟

● *He humbled himself, therefore God raised him high.* ●

A reading from
the Letter of Saint Paul to the Philippians 2: 6-11

The state of Jesus Christ was divine, yet he did not cling to his equality with God but emptied himself to assume the condition of a slave and became as men are; and being as all men are, he was humbler yet, even to accepting death, death on a cross. But God raised him high and gave him the name which is above all other names so that all beings in the heavens, on earth and in the underworld, should bend the knee at the name of Jesus and that every tongue should acclaim Jesus Christ as Lord, to the glory of God the Father.
This is the word of the Lord.

Alleluia, alleluia! We adore you, O Christ, and we bless you;/ because by your cross you have redeemed the world. Alleluia!

● *The Son of Man must be lifted up.* ●

A reading from
the holy Gospel according to John 3: 13-17

Jesus said to Nicodemus: "No one has gone up to heaven except the one who came down from heaven, the Son of Man who is in heaven; and the Son of Man must be lifted up, as Moses lifted up the serpent in the desert, so that everyone who believes may have eternal life in him.

"Yes, God loved the world so much that he gave his only Son, so that everyone who believes in him may not be lost but may have eternal life. For God sent his Son into the world not to condemn the world, but so that through him the world might be saved."
This is the Gospel of the Lord.

PRAYER OVER THE GIFTS

Lord,
may this sacrifice once offered on the cross
to take away the sins of the world
now free us from our sins.
We ask this through Christ our Lord.

PREFACE OF THE EXALTATION OF THE CROSS

Father, all-powerful and ever-living God,
we do well always and everywhere to give you thanks.

You decreed that man should be saved through the wood of the cross.
The tree of man's defeat became his tree of victory;
where life was lost, there life has been restored
through Christ our Lord.

Through him the choirs of angels
and all the powers of heaven
praise and worship your glory.
May our voices blend with theirs
as we join in their unending hymn: **Holy…**

Or:

PREFACE OF THE PASSION OF THE LORD I

Father, all-powerful and ever-living God,
we do well always and everywhere to give you thanks.

The suffering and death of your Son
brought life to the whole world,
moving our hearts to praise your glory.
The power of the cross reveals your judgement on this world and the kingship of Christ crucified.

We praise you, Lord,
with all the angels and saints in their song of joy: **Holy…**

COMMUNION ANTIPHON

When I am lifted up from the earth, I will draw all men to myself, says the Lord. (Jn 12: 32)

PRAYER AFTER COMMUNION

Lord Jesus Christ,
you are the holy bread of life.
Bring to the glory of the resurrection
the people you have redeemed by the wood of the cross.
We ask this through Christ our Lord.

SOLEMN BLESSING OR PRAYER OVER THE PEOPLE

May almighty God keep you from all harm
and bless you with every good gift.
Amen.

May he set his Word in your heart
and fill you with lasting joy.
Amen.

May you walk in his ways,
always knowing what is right and good,
until you enter your heavenly inheritance.
Amen.

May almighty God bless you,
the Father, and the Son, and the Holy Spirit.
Amen.

MEDITATION OF THE DAY

The Glory of the Cross

It is in the light of Calvary that we can see what it means for us to confess our poverty and our helplessness and to renounce the attempt to overcome them on our own. It is there that we accept our suffering and turn it into a compassion with all the pains that people bear, bundled together as they are in the suffering of Christ. It is there that we discover and fortify our charitable yearning for all righteousness to be revealed, while at the same time tempering it with a deep and comprehensive mercy, which we know we need ourselves and which we hope to share with all people. And so we come imperceptibly to see everything more purely in the light of God's seeing of all that he has made, and so we come to be able at least to whisper the truth of the infinite peace of God's will even in the midst of the storms and contentions of life in this world... It is the cross and only the cross that provides a constant point of reference in the chaos of our world, because there is all our poverty and helplessness and pain, all our yearning and all our mutual injustice, taken up into the stillness of God's everlasting love and made into the instrument and revelation of his unchanging will.

FATHER SIMON TUGWELL, O.P.

Father Simon Tugwell is a Dominican priest, the author of several books on theology and spirituality, and a member of the Dominican Historical Institute.

Prayer for the Evening

Holy is God! Holy and strong! Holy and immortal!
Come, let us adore!

Glory be to the Father, and to the Son, and to the Holy Spirit, as it was in the beginning, is now, and ever shall be, world without end. Amen. Alleluia!

HYMN Metre: LM

This hymn can be sung to the tune used for *Praise God from Whom All Blessings Flow*

Behold, behold the glorious wood
Upon which hung our only good;
It bore him up in offering,
The Lamb whose praise the angels sing.

Behold against the black of night,
The doorway to eternal light

Stands open now: the narrow way
Invites us in to endless day.

All glory be to him who died,
All honour to the Crucified,
Who lives and reigns eternally,
With Father, Spirit: One in Three.

CANTICLE OF PETER 1 P 2: 21-24

When I am lifted up from the earth, I shall draw all men to myself. (Jn 12: 32)

The key to this feast lies in the last line of this canticle: Christ's suffering was hideous, his death dreadful, but by his wounds, we were healed. The wounds borne by Christ risen and glorified are visible signs of suffering and death transformed into channels through which the grace of God flows out to lift the world from darkness to light.

Christ suffered for you,
and left you an example
to have you follow in his footsteps.

He did no wrong;
no deceit was found in his mouth.
When he was insulted,
he returned no insult.

When he was made to suffer,
he did not counter with threats.
Instead he delivered himself up
to the One who judges justly.

In his own body
he brought your sins to the cross,
so that all of us, dead to sin,
could live in accord with God's will.

By his wounds, you were healed.

Word of God

Romans 6: 8-11

BUT WE BELIEVE that having died with Christ we shall return to life with him: Christ, as we know, having been raised from the dead will never die again. Death has no power over him any more. When he died, he died, once for all, to sin, so his life now is life with God; and in that way, you too must consider yourselves to be dead to sin but alive for God in Christ Jesus.

Although he was Son, he learnt to obey through suffering. (He 5: 8)

CANTICLE OF MARY (Text, back cover A)

Death, where is your victory?/ Death, where is your sting? (1 Co 15: 55)

INTERCESSIONS

To the Lord who is enthroned in glory we pray:

℟ We adore you, O Christ, and we bless you because, by your holy cross, you have redeemed the world!

You suffered for us and now you live for ever to make intercession for us: ℟

You were insulted for our sake and now you reign for ever in glory: ℟

You were delivered up for us and now you are raised up for ever upon the throne that is yours at the right hand of the Father: ℟

Personal intentions

Our Father…

Peace to all who are in Christ. Amen. (cf. 1 P 5: 14)

MARIAN ANTIPHON (Text, page 23)

[WEDNESDAY, SEPTEMBER 15]

Our Lady of Sorrows

Prayer for the Morning

On this feast of the Blessed Virgin Mary, let us give praise and thanks to God!

Glory be to the Father, and to the Son, and to the Holy Spirit, as it was in the beginning, is now, and ever shall be, world without end. Amen. Alleluia!

HYMN

Metre: LM
This hymn can be sung to the tune used for *The Glory of These Forty Days*

Beneath the cross the Mother kept
Bleak vigil under darkened skies.
Upon the cross her Son hung nailed,
Stabbed through by crowds of hostile eyes.

"And your own soul a sword shall pierce,"
The old man in the Temple said,
The Spirit's sword, the word of God –
God's word be done, was all she said.

Upon the cross the Saviour died;
Beneath, the Mother bowed her head;
Above, the storm broke harsh and wild –
God's word be done, was all she said.

A soldier came and thrust him through;
The blood and water proved him dead.
They laid his body in her arms –
God's word be done, was all she said.

At vigil's end, the Crucified
Arose from death her glorious Lord.

O Father, Son, and Spirit, God,
We praise and magnify your Word.

PSALM 39 6-9

You will need endurance to do God's will and gain what he has promised. (He 10: 36)

God's word cut deeply into Mary's life: it cut away all the ordinary hopes a young woman might have for her future, for her family life, for her child. Yet she accepted with a courageous consent that anticipates and mirrors the obedience of her Son "even to accepting death, death on a cross." (cf. Ph 2: 8)

How many, O Lord my God,
are the wonders and designs
that you have worked for us;
you have no equal.
Should I proclaim and speak of them,
they are more than I can tell!

You do not ask for sacrifice and offerings,
but an open ear.
You do not ask for holocaust and victim.
Instead, here am I.

In the scroll of the book it stands written
that I should do your will.
My God, I delight in your law
in the depth of my heart.

Glory be to the Father…

Word of God Lamentations 2: 18-19

CRY ALOUD, THEN, to the Lord,/ groan, daughter of Sion;/ let your tears flow like a torrent,/ day and night;/ give yourself no relief,/ grant your eyes no rest.

Up, cry out in the night-time,/ in the early hours of darkness;/ pour your heart out like water/ before the Lord./ Stretch out your hands to him/ for the lives of your children.

So even those whom God allows to suffer must trust themselves to the constancy of the creator and go on doing good. (1 P 4: 19)

CANTICLE OF ZECHARIAH **(Text, back cover B)**

My heart is pierced within me. (Ps 108: 22)

INTERCESSIONS

Through the intercession of the Blessed Virgin Mary, let us pray:

℟ Have pity, Lord, have pity.

For all parents who bear and raise children in poverty and exile: ℟

For all parents who grieve the loss of a child before birth: ℟

For all parents who suffer over their children's life choices: ℟

For all parents who mourn the death of a child: ℟

Personal intentions

Our Father…

God our Father, the Blessed Virgin Mary took part in her Son's redemptive suffering for love of you and for the sake of the world. Through her intercession, may all your Church's suffering bear saving fruit in Christ our Lord. Amen.

MASS

(Today, the Gospel of the memorial of Our Lady of Sorrows is obligatory. However, for the first reading and the psalm, one can choose between the texts of the Wednesday of the Twenty-Fourth Week in Ordinary Time, pages 75-77, or those of the memorial, pages 74-75.)

Our Lady of Sorrows

Memorial

● *The Blessed Virgin was born to be the Mother of God. From the first moment of Mary's immaculate presence in her mother's womb, Our Lady has led us to her Son. From the cross, Christ commands, "Behold, your mother." As the Saviour's dying gift to us, Jesus leads us back to Mary. For we need the maternal closeness of the Sorrowful Mother to sustain us when overcome by the terrifying trials of life. Through Mary's compassionate presence at the cross, that event – as it recurs in our life – becomes more deeply human, filling us with the courage to face life's sufferings, certain in the secure embrace of divine providence. Whenever Mary loves us, she gives us Jesus. By obeying the Lord in our devout beholding of the Mother of God, we give Mary the chance to speak her Yes to the "annunciation" uttered from the cross: "Behold, your son."* ●

ENTRANCE ANTIPHON

Simeon said to Mary: This child is destined to be a sign which men will reject; he is set for the fall and the rising of many in Israel; and your own soul a sword shall pierce. (Lk 2: 34-35)

OPENING PRAYER

Father,
as your Son was raised on the cross,
his mother Mary stood by him, sharing his sufferings.
May your Church be united with Christ
in his suffering and death

and so come to share in his rising to new life,
where he lives and reigns with you and the Holy Spirit,
one God, for ever and ever.

● *He learnt to obey and he became the source of eternal salvation.* ●

A reading from the Letter to the Hebrews 5: 7-9

DURING HIS LIFE on earth, Christ offered up prayer and entreaty, aloud and in silent tears, to the one who had the power to save him out of death, and he submitted so humbly that his prayer was heard. Although he was Son, he learnt to obey through suffering; but having been made perfect, he became for all who obey him the source of eternal salvation.
This is the word of the Lord.

PSALM 30

℟ (17) **Save me, O Lord, in your love.**

In you, O LORD, I take refuge;
let me never be put to shame.
In your justice, set me free,
hear me and speedily rescue me. ℟

Be a rock of refuge for me,
a mighty stronghold to save me,
for you are my rock, my stronghold.
For your name's sake, lead me and guide me. ℟

Release me from the snares they have hidden
for you are my refuge, Lord.
Into your hands I commend my spirit.
It is you who will redeem me, Lord. ℟

But as for me, I trust in you, Lord,
  I say, "You are my God."
My life is in your hands, deliver me
  from the hands of those who hate me. ℟

How great is the goodness, LORD,
  that you keep for those who fear you,
that you show to those who trust you
  in the sight of men. ℟

Or:

Wednesday of the Twenty-Fourth Week in Ordinary Time

● *There are three things that last: faith, hope and love, and the greatest of these is love.* ●

A reading from the first Letter of Saint Paul to the Corinthians 12: 31-13: 13

BE AMBITIOUS for the higher gifts. And I am going to show you a way that is better than any of them.

If I have all the eloquence of men or of angels, but speak without love, I am simply a gong booming or a cymbal clashing. If I have the gift of prophecy, understanding all the mysteries there are, and knowing everything, and if I have faith in all its fulness, to move mountains, but without love, then I am nothing at all. If I give away all that I possess, piece by piece, and if I even let them take my body to burn it, but am without love, it will do me no good whatever.

Love is always patient and kind; it is never jealous; love is never boastful or conceited; it is never rude or selfish; it does not take offence, and is not resentful. Love takes no pleasure in other people's sins but delights in the truth; it is always ready to excuse, to trust, to hope, and to endure whatever comes.

Love does not come to an end. But if there are gifts of prophecy, the time will come when they must fail; or the gift of languages, it will not continue for ever; and knowledge – for this, too, the time will come when it must fail. For our knowledge is imperfect and our prophesying is imperfect; but once perfection comes, all imperfect things will disappear. When I was a child, I used to talk like a child, and think like a child, and argue like a child, but now I am a man, all childish ways are put behind me. Now we are seeing a dim reflection in a mirror; but then we shall be seeing face to face. The knowledge that I have now is imperfect; but then I shall know as fully as I am known.

In short, there are three things that last: faith, hope and love; and the greatest of these is love.
This is the word of the Lord.

PSALM 32

℟ (12) Happy the people the Lord has chosen as his own.

Give thanks to the LORD upon the harp;
with a ten-stringed lute sing him songs.
O sing him a song that is new,
play loudly, with all your skill. ℟

For the word of the LORD is faithful,
and all his works are to be trusted.
The LORD loves justice and right
and fills the earth with his love. ℟

They are happy, whose God is the LORD,
the people he has chosen as his own.

May your love be upon us, O LORD,
as we place all our hope in you. ℟

[Our Lady of Sorrows]

STABAT MATER

(Sequence)

At the cross her station keeping,
Stood the mournful Mother weeping,
Close to Jesus to the last.

Through her heart, his sorrow sharing,
All his bitter anguish bearing,
Now at length the sword had passed.

Oh, how sad and sore distressed
Was that Mother highly blessed
Of the sole-begotten One.

Christ above in torment hangs;
She beneath beholds the pangs
Of her dying glorious Son.

Is there one who would not weep,
'Whelmed in miseries so deep,
Christ's dear Mother to behold?

Can the human heart refrain
From partaking in her pain,
In that Mother's pain untold?

Bruised, derided, cursed, defiled,
She beheld her tender child,
All with bloody scourges rent.

For the sins of his own nation
Saw him hang in desolation,
Till his spirit forth he sent.

O you Mother, font of love!
Touch my spirit from above,
Make my heart with yours accord.

Make me feel as you have felt;
Make my soul to glow and melt
With the love of Christ ourLord.

Holy Mother, pierce me through;
In my heart each wound renew
Of my Saviour crucified.

Let me share with you his pain,
Who for all my sins was slain,
Who for me in torments died.

Let me mingle tears with you,
Mourning him who mourned for me,
All the days that I may live:

By the cross with you to stay,
There with you to weep and pray,
Is all I ask of you to give.

Virgin of all virgins best,
Listen to my fond request:
Let me share your grief divine.

Let me, to my latest breath,
In my body bear the death
Of that dying Son of yours.

Wounded with his every wound,
Steep my soul till it has swooned
In his very Blood away.

Be to me, O Virgin, nigh,
Lest in flames I burn and die,
In his awful judgement day.

Christ, when you shall call me hence,
Be your Mother my defence,
Be your cross my victory.

While my body here decays,
May my soul your goodness praise,
Safe in paradise with you.
Amen. (Alleluia.)

Alleluia, alleluia! Happy is the blessed Virgin Mary;/ who, without dying, won the palm of martyrdom/ beneath the Cross of the Lord. Alleluia!

● *Christ above in torment hangs; she beneath beholds the pangs of her dying glorious Son. (*Stabat Mater*).* ●

A reading from
the holy Gospel according to John 19: 25-27

NEAR THE CROSS of Jesus stood his mother and his mother's sister, Mary the wife of Clopas, and Mary of Magdala. Seeing his mother and the disciple he loved standing near her, Jesus said to his mother, "Woman, this is your son." Then to the disciple he said, "This is your mother." And from that moment the disciple made a place for her in his home.
This is the Gospel of the Lord.

Or:

● *A sword will pierce your own soul.* ●

A reading from
the holy Gospel according to Luke 2: 33-35

AS THE FATHER AND MOTHER of Jesus stood wondering at the things that were being said about him, Simeon

blessed them and said to Mary his mother, "You see this child: he is destined for the fall and for the rising of many in Israel, destined to be a sign that is rejected – and a sword will pierce your own soul too – so that the secret thoughts of many may be laid bare."
This is the Gospel of the Lord.

PRAYER OVER THE GIFTS

God of mercy,
receive the prayers and gifts we offer
in praise of your name
on this feast of the Virgin Mary.
While she stood beside the cross of Jesus
you gave her to us as our loving mother.
Grant this through Christ our Lord.

PREFACE OF THE BLESSED VIRGIN MARY I OR II

COMMUNION ANTIPHON

Be glad to share in the sufferings of Christ! When he comes in glory, you will be filled with joy. (1 P 4: 13)

PRAYER AFTER COMMUNION

Lord,
hear the prayers
of those who receive the sacraments of eternal salvation.
As we honour the compassionate love of the Virgin Mary, may we make up in our own lives
whatever is lacking in the sufferings of Christ
for the good of the Church.
We ask this in the name of Jesus the Lord.

MEDITATION OF THE DAY

The Sorrowful Mother

In the Crucified One the soul that dies is divided from the spirit of mission which is breathed out with bowed head and given up to the Father and to the

Church: in the Mother who shares his suffering, whose "soul magnifies the Lord" and whose "spirit rejoices in God my Saviour" (Lk 1: 46-47), the sword pierces between praise and rejoicing: the rejoicing is borne away with the spirit to God, while the soul remains behind and, when the body is taken down from the cross, can only utter the assent of praise with a sigh in the most profound darkness, in the utmost weakness.

It is here and nowhere else that sinners – whether oppressors or the weeping oppressed – can find refuge. As Claudel has written:

> "For the poor man there is no firm friend unless he finds someone poorer than himself. So come, my oppressed sister, and behold Mary... Behold her who is there, without complaint as without hope, like a poor man who has found someone poorer, and both contemplate each other in silence."

It is the greater suffering that hides and thereby consoles: not with soothing words, not with promises that things will get better, but simply because the more profound pain as such goes on giving praise and only now does so adequately, just as from a broken jar of ointment comes a stronger aroma.

It remains an impenetrable mystery how this temporal precipitous distress of a Mother shares in and is involved in the eternal praise of her transfiguration. Her heart remains as open as that of her Son, who is continually offering his heart's blood in the Eucharistic meal: "My blood is drink indeed, and he who does not drink it has no life in him." One should not place far from that of her Son the Mother's heart pierced by the sword, the heart that offers itself to all the poor as one yet poorer, even if its openness is only to be understood as pointing to the eternal openness of his heart to the Father. "I am the door," he says; she only says: "I am the handmaid, do whatever he tells you."

FATHER HANS URS VON BALTHASAR

Father von Balthasar († 1988) was an eminent Swiss Catholic theologian who wrote prodigiously.

Prayer for the Evening

Through the Blessed Virgin Mary,
let us give thanks and praise to God our Saviour!

Glory be to the Father, and to the Son, and to the Holy Spirit, as it was in the beginning, is now, and ever shall be, world without end. Amen. Alleluia!

HYMN Metre: 88 7

At the cross her station keeping,
Stood the mournful mother weeping,
Where he hung, the dying Lord:

Bowed with anguish, deeply grieved,
For her soul, of joy bereaved,
Felt the sharp and piercing sword.

Deep the woe of her affliction,
When she saw the crucifixion
Of her ever-glorious Son.

PSALM 56 2-6

All you who pass by the way,/ look and see:/ is any sorrow like the sorrow that afflicts me? (Lm 1: 12)

Saint Augustine called this psalm a description of Christ's passion. Mary suffered with her Son's suffering, was pierced with his piercing, and was taken up into his glory. As the image of her Son, she is the image of redeemed humanity, the image of God restored and made perfect through Christ.

Have mercy on me, God, have mercy
for in you my soul has taken refuge.
In the shadow of your wings I take refuge
till the storms of destruction pass by.

I call to God the Most High,
to God who has always been my help.
May he send from heaven and save me
and shame those who assail me.

May God send his truth and his love.

My soul lies down among lions,
who would devour the sons of men.
Their teeth are spears and arrows,
their tongue a sharpened sword.

O God, arise above the heavens;
may your glory shine on earth!

Glory be to the Father…

Word of God John 19: 32-34

CONSEQUENTLY the soldiers came and broke the legs of the first man who had been crucified with him and then of the other. When they came to Jesus, they found he was already dead, and so instead of breaking his legs one of the soldiers pierced his side with a lance; and immediately there came out blood and water.

I am the handmaid of the Lord.
Let what you have said be done to me. (Lk 1: 38)

CANTICLE OF MARY (Text, back cover A)

Now a great sign appeared in heaven: a woman, adorned with the sun, standing on the moon, and with the twelve stars on her head for a crown. (Rv 12: 1)

INTERCESSIONS

For all those who live the mystery of the cross in our day, let us pray:

℟ O God, send help from heaven and save your people!

For all families driven from their homes by poverty and war:
– grant them one day the joy of return. ℟

For all those dying in shame and disgrace:
– grant them the comfort of your love through the presence of Mary. ℟

For all those buried by strangers in anonymous graves:
– raise them to the heavenly kingdom where all rejoice in a new name. ℟

Personal intentions

Our Father…

May the God of peace be with you all! Amen. (Rm 15: 33)

MARIAN ANTIPHON (Text, page 23)

SAINTS
OF TODAY AND YESTERDAY

O Mary, Mother of mercy, pray for me now.

SAINT MATERNUS
Bishop (4th century)

Maternus is the earliest bishop of Cologne, Germany, of whom there is a trustworthy historical record. During Maternus' episcopate, a Catholic bishop of North Africa named Caecilian was targeted by the bishops of a puritanical and schismatic sect of heretics known as Donatists. The adherents of Donatism, asserting that the validity of a sacrament was conditional upon the virtue of the minister, set up their own separate hierarchy, claiming that only the Donatists constituted the one true Church. The Donatist bishops lodged a protest against Caecilian with the Roman Emperor Constantine I, asking him to have Caecilian tried by bishops from Gaul (France and Germany). The emperor, who a short time earlier had abolished the empire's anti-Christian laws, granted their request. Maternus was one of three bishops chosen to act as judges at this trial. He and his fellow judges handed down a unanimous decision totally exonerating their fellow Catholic prelate Caecilian.

Consider how love draws all the pains,
all the torments, all the sufferings, all the sorrows,
the wounds, the passion, the cross,
and even the death of our Redeemer
into the heart of his most holy Mother.
Saint Francis de Sales

Thursday, September 16

The first day of the Papal visit

Scotland

When Pope Benedict arrives at Edinburgh airport, he travels to the Palace of Holyrood. At the beginning of his State Visit, Pope Benedict will be welcomed by Her Majesty The Queen and HRH The Duke of Edinburgh. This will be followed by a State Reception at which the Holy Father will meet with other members of the Royal Family and prominent members of British society. Later the Holy Father will travel through the centre of Edinburgh in the Popemobile.

Later the Holy Father will travel to Glasgow and to Bellahouston Park where he will celebrate an open-air Mass in the evening. The Mass is a moment to celebrate and affirm Catholic faith in Scotland and the contribution the Catholic Church has made to the development of education in Scotland.

After the Mass Pope Benedict will travel by plane from Glasgow to London. During the time of the Papal Visit Pope Benedict will reside at the Apostolic Nunciature in Wimbledon, which our present Nuncio often describes as "the Pope's house".

Programme

10.30: Arrival of Pope Benedict XVI at Edinburgh Airport

11.00: State Welcome and Audience with HM Queen Elizabeth II at the Palace of Holyrood

11.45: State Reception

12.30: Popemobile journey through central Edinburgh

15.45: Motorcade to Bellahouston Park, Glasgow

16.45: Pope Benedict XVI presides at the celebration of Mass

20.00: Departure from Glasgow Airport

21.10: Arrival at London Heathrow Airport. Transfer to the Apostolic Nunciature

THE CHURCH IN SCOTLAND

Right Rev Mgr John McIntyre
Dr Mary McHugh

The Catholics of Scotland come from many different ancestries and traditions. Besides Scots there will be those who highlight the contribution of the migrant, including Irish, Italian, Lithuanian, Polish, Filipino and others. However, a decisive moment in laying the foundations of the Scottish Catholic Church was the marriage of the Scots king Malcolm Canmore in c.1070 to the Saxon princess Margaret. The Church that she found in Scotland acknowledged its debt to the saints of the 4th-7th centuries, such as Ninian at Whithorn, Columcille (Columba) at Iona, and Kentigern at Glasgow. Formed originally on the Irish model dominated by monastic centres, the Scottish Church in Margaret's day, although orthodox in belief and conscious of itself as part of western Christendom, was by European standards unstructured and attached to its indigenous customs. Margaret, and the kings of Scots throughout the Middle Ages, brought to Scotland the civilising and evangelising influences of the great European orders of monks and later of friars. To Margaret and her sons is also attributed the medieval diocesan system. Particularly in the time of Wallace and Bruce, the Church became associated with Scotland's drive for independent nationhood. By the end of the 12th century the papacy had declared the Scottish Church a "special daughter" of the Holy See, precluding English claims to ecclesiastical overlordship. Yet it was only in the early 15th century that two archdioceses were created, St Andrews in 1472, followed by Glasgow in 1492. The same century saw the foundation of three Scottish universities, St Andrews, Glasgow, and Aberdeen, with papal approval and patronage.

By the 16th century the relationship between the Church, the crown, and the papacy was being compromised by the usurping by Scottish kings of Church income and the rights of appointment to high Church positions. This tension came to a head in 1560, when a Scottish parliament made Calvinist belief and practice the law of the land. It was not simply a matter of religion, or of the corrosive criticism of the scandalous lives of some parish clergy and bishops. Politics also played a part, especially the identification of Catholicism with domination by France, the compromising policies and later unpopularity of Mary Queen of Scots, and the comprehensive victory, after her flight, of those whose power was bound up with the new religious order.

After the religious and political upheavals of the 16th century, Scotland came to be regarded by the Church as a missionary territory. From 1598 to 1621, Catholics in Scotland were nominally subject to the English archpriests. The establishment in 1622 by Pope Gregory XV of the Sacred Congregation for the Propagation of the Faith (Propaganda Fide) was soon followed, in England, by the appointment of the first vicar-apostolic, William Bishop, in 1623. However, Scottish priests reminded Pope Gregory XV of the late 12th-century Papal bull "*Cum Universi*" which had declared the Scottish Church subject only to the Holy See. Thus in 1653, a Scottish Catholic Mission was created and in 1727, this was divided into Highland and Lowland districts and, a century later it was divided again into Eastern, Western, and Northern districts. In 1868-69, Charles Eyre was appointed with the twin task of restoring harmony within the western district, and of preparing for the re-establishment of a diocesan hierarchy in Scotland. On March 4, 1878, under Pope Leo XIII, this was achieved and the rule of vicars-apostolic ended with the creation of six Sees, and the appointment of diocesan bishops. In 1947-48 two further dioceses, Motherwell and Paisley, were added to create the eight dioceses we have today.

From the late 18th century onwards, a steadily increasing number of Catholics arrived in the industrial cities and counties of Scotland, particularly from Ireland as well as from the Scottish Highlands and Islands. Their arrival transformed the geographical profile of post-Reformation Scottish Catholicism moving it away from its former strongholds in the western Highlands and islands, and the northeast. Glasgow after all had not figured prominently in the post-Reformation history of the Scottish Catholic community, apart from the martyrdom of John Ogilvie in 1615. This changing profile was also reflected in the addition of Edinburgh to the medieval diocesan title of St Andrews. During the 19th and 20th centuries, other immigrants would arrive, from Italy, Lithuania, and Poland.

This growing Catholic urban population created a continuing need for more priests, parishes, churches, and schools. The sixteenth-century Council of Trent had established the seminary system to improve clerical training. From 1714 with the opening of a seminary at Loch Morar, and particularly with the establishment of Scalan in 1717, it was possible for priests to train in Scotland. The gift of the manor house and estate of John Menzies of Pitfodels enabled the opening, in 1829, of the seminary at Blairs. Post-reformation seminaries also existed at Rome, in Spain, and in France (until 1793).

Many parishes began with a building which served a dual function, as both chapel and school. However, permanent, and recognisable churches were also erected, the earliest of these being St Gregory's at Preshome (established 1788-1790). As well as providing and maintaining churches, a priest in 19th-century Scotland also served as manager of his parochial school, a situation which continued until the passing of the Education (Scotland) Act in 1918. The 1918 Act enabled the Catholic voluntary sector, by then struggling under a myriad of demands, to accept the opportunity provided to fully enter the Scottish education system. In the 19th and 20th centuries, religious orders also made a significant contribution to education by helping to staff the parochial schools and establish Catholic colleges for teacher-training. Parishes also fulfilled social and economic roles, including the promotion of parish savings banks, and even football teams.

The presence into the twentieth century of religious orders such as the Franciscans and Dominicans are tangible links with the medieval past. Today hospices and care services continue the long tradition, again dating back to medieval times, of concern for the most disadvantaged in the community. Succeeding generations benefit from what has gone before, and still build upon it.

In more recent times the Church in Scotland, while continuing to be enriched by the vision of the Second Vatican Council, has suffered with the rest of the Western Church from a lessening of practising membership and of vocations to the priesthood and religious life, and from the pressure of an increasingly secularised society. But there are still many things to take pride in – the quality of our schools both in the state and private sector, our parish communities lively in faith, and the readiness with which our bishops and others speak out in defence of Christian values. We are happy to be Scots and to be Catholic, and rejoice to welcome our Pope.

HOLYROOD ABBEY AND PALACE

The palace of Holyrood house, where the Holy Father will be received by the Queen, is Her Majesty's official residence in Scotland, and is used for a variety of official engagements. Its origins can be traced back to 1128, when the Abbey of Holyrood was founded by King David I for the Canons of Saint Augustine, and also to house his late mother's relic of the Holy Rood (Holy Cross). The ruined nave of the 12th- and 13th-century abbey church can still be seen. At the other end of what became the Royal Mile stood the Castle within which Saint Margaret's chapel, also built by David I, can still be visited.

When attending Parliaments and Councils monarchs preferred to live within the abbey guesthouse, or other royal lodgings within the abbey precinct, rather than in the bleak Castle. By the mid-15th century Edinburgh was emerging as Scotland's capital and, in keeping with this new status, in 1501 a building described as the King's Palace at Holyrood was commenced by James IV. Both the Abbey and the palace witnessed many great events in history including the marriage of King James IV to Margaret Tudor, sister of Henry VIII. The palace was also the residence of Mary, Queen of Scots after her return from France, and of James VI before he acceded to the throne of England in 1603. It was also the base for Bonnie Prince Charlie for some time during the 1745 uprising. Although the palace suffered through times of neglect, it also underwent periodic reconstruction and refurbishment under various monarchs who wished to preserve their connection with Scotland.

by Dr Mary McHugh and Rev Gerald Sharkey

The Relationship Between the Scottish Crown and the Church

Dr Mary McHugh
Rev Anthony Gallagher

The relationship between the Church and the Scottish crown is long, and best discerned in a variety of ancient sources. Adomnan's *Life of Saint Columba* (d. 597) speaks of the saint anointing Aidan, the King of Argyll, c.574. One of the oldest recorded Scottish documents is a charter by King David I in 1127 to the Church of Saint Cuthbert. David (d.1153) and his mother Saint Margaret (d.1093) have long been accepted by generations as saints because of their concern for the poor and their interest and involvement in religious matters.

Throughout the Middle Ages churchmen often served in the office of Chancellor, the chief minister of the Crown in Scotland. Bishop Lamberton of St Andrews, and Bishop Wishart of Glasgow became noted supporters of Robert Bruce during the Wars against England. One of Robert Bruce's chancellors, Bernard de Linton, who was also Abbot of Arbroath, is usually credited as being the person who drafted the Declaration of Arbroath in 1320 in an attempt to convince the Pope of the legitimacy and acceptance of Bruce's kingship.

Occasionally, Scotland and her monarchs received indications of papal esteem, and spiritual encouragement. William the Lyon (d. 1214) is reputed to have received both a sword and a Golden Rose from the Pope. James III (d. 1488) also received the Golden Rose. His son, James IV (d. at Flodden in 1513), received various papal gifts, including a Golden Rose and, it is claimed that Pope Alexander VI also presented him with a silver-gilt sceptre. In 1507, James IV received a blessed sword and a hat. Both the sceptre and the sword form part of the Honours of Scotland today.

Nevertheless, the relationship between Scots crown and Church could be ambivalent. The monarch did not always act as the protector of the Church that the papal gifts might imply. In the 1530s, King James V used the religious and political upheavals of the time to access the revenues of the Church in Scotland allegedly for the protection and defence of the realm, and also to assist with creating a College of Justice.

In the centuries after the Reformation Parliament of 1560, the relationship between the Catholic community and the crown became uncertain. Some Catholics, such as the Innes family, supported the exiled Stewart dynasty. However, Jacobitism never became the official policy of the Scottish Catholic community. As Britain found herself at war, first with the American colonies and then with revolutionary France, the Government came to accept that to equate religion with political loyalty was false. It was perfectly possible to be a good Catholic and a good citizen.

A succession of Catholic Relief Acts, from 1793 and continuing into the 20th century dismantled the penal laws. After 1829, it became lawful for persons professing the Roman Catholic religion to elect and be elected members to serve in Parliament for Scotland. From the middle of the 19th century, the Catholic community in Scotland was able to access Privy Council grants to support Catholic education. By the 1930s, when the Stewart tomb in Saint Peter's Basilica was restored, the royal family contributed to the costs, and agreed to the original tombstones finding a home in the Scots College in Rome, where they still remain.

Scots Catholics now play their part in all aspects of government and society. The reign of Queen Elizabeth II has seen progress continue; and has also witnessed the spread of the ecumenical movement and a search for understanding and healing of historic divisions. During her reign the present Queen has visited the Vatican three times. On her state visit in 1980, which also paved the way for the pastoral visit of Pope John Paul II to the United Kingdom in 1982, the Queen expressed her support for the growing movement of unity between the Christian Churches throughout the world and her wish that all would be enabled to see more clearly those truths which both unite and divide us in a new and constructive light. This present visit by Pope Benedict XVI, the first ever papal State visit to the United Kingdom, marks another step in this journey.

The Importance of the Mass

Fr Allen Morris

Pope Benedict comes to the United Kingdom at the invitation of the Monarch and her government. This Papal visit is therefore quite different from the pastoral visit of Pope John Paul in 1982. Then the focus was on the Pontiff's meeting with the Catholic faithful and centred on the celebration of the Sacraments. This visit, a State visit, gives more emphasis to the Holy Father's meeting with the Monarch, the Government and his address to our society at large.

Even so three of the major events of this visit are the celebrations of Mass, the Eucharist, with the Catholic faithful in Glasgow, London and Birmingham, and another, the Prayer Vigil in Hyde Park, has a strongly Eucharistic focus. It is opportune to remember why the Mass matters so much to Catholics, indeed to all Christians.

The Anglican liturgist Gregory Dix wrote: "At the heart of the Mass is the Eucharistic action, a thing of an absolute simplicity – the taking, blessing, breaking and giving of bread and the taking, blessing and giving of a cup of wine and water, as these were first done with their new meaning by a young Jew before and after supper with His friends on the night before He died. He had told His friends to do this henceforward with the new meaning for the *anamnesis* (memory) of Him, and they have done it always since. Was ever another command so obeyed? For century after century, spreading slowly to every continent and country and among every race on earth, this action has been done, in every conceivable human circumstance, for every conceivable human need from infancy and before it to extreme age." (*The Shape of the Liturgy.*)

The Mass may have been the fault line along which many of the crises in Church unity have rumbled, leading sometimes to tragic upheavals and separation of Christian from Christian. But it remains the primary and indispensable source from which the faithful seek to derive the true Christian spirit, be they Catholic, Orthodox, Protestant or Anglican. It is this primary source because in essence it is here that the Christian most regularly and persuasively encounters Jesus Christ, truly present to draw us deeper into the Communion of life with him, and through our sharing in the Spirit, with the Father of all.

Dix focuses on the action that informs the shape of the Liturgy of the Eucharist, the second principal part of the Mass. It is preceded by another principal part of the Mass: the Liturgy of the Word. Here Christ speaks in and through the words of Scripture to those gathered in his name, sanctifying us, challenging and encouraging us to embrace the ways of holiness.

It is only then that, fortified by the nourishment served from the Table of the Word, that we move to the altar where the Church, the Body of Christ, joins with Jesus Christ its Head, in offering his Sacrifice of Praise to the Father. This Sacrifice offered once and for all by Jesus on the Cross of Calvary is re-presented by the Church united with him at its every celebration of the Mass. In its liturgy the Church is present once more to the Paschal

Mystery of Christ's Passion, Death and Resurrection by which it is freed from sin and freed for life.

This Sacrifice, this loving self-offering by Jesus is then made available to the Church in a most intimate way in the invitation to receive Holy Communion. The gifts of bread and wine offered at the altar, have now become through grace, and in a fashion which defies our senses, his Body and Blood. The Catholic faithful are invited to eat and drink the Saviour of the World, that he might live in us and we live, more faithfully, in him.

In the Mass the Church inevitably looks back to the saving events which gave her birth, but that remembering of the past is enriched in her celebration by a new and present encounter with the living Lord. Mass is not about nostalgia but a re-energising for life now. It is often said that Christians go to Mass (simply) in order to be sent away again. The name of the final part of the liturgy, the dismissal, gives the whole action its name, "Mass". The Latin for the dismissal, *missio*, is also the origin of the word "mission", and at the end of the Mass we are reminded of the mission which belongs to us all: to continue the work of bringing the light and healing of the Gospel of Jesus Christ to the world.

Pope Benedict has sought to draw out still more clearly this dimension of our worship in a text provided for new English translation of the Roman Missal: "Go in peace, glorifying the Lord by your life". The sign of the authenticity of our worship is to be the way in which the holiness of God is made manifest in the ordinariness of our daily lives made sacred by the way we live them.

SAINT NINIAN

Little is known for certain about the life and ministry of Saint Ninian. Tradition suggests to us that he was a Briton, born during the 4th century, perhaps in Northern England. He may have travelled to Rome to learn more about the faith, and been welcomed by Pope Saint Damasus (366-384) and after lengthy studies, ordained priest and bishop by Pope Saint Siricius (384-399). It is said that he knew Saint Martin of Tours. He returned home and settled in southern Scotland, in Galloway, at Whithorn, where he founded his mission. There he built his church, called "Candida Casa" or White House – perhaps a whitewashed stone building. He worked among his own people, the Britons of the border regions and also among the Picts, in the modern Lothian region and in Fife, so is called the apostle to these groups. As the first known bishop working in Scotland, he occupies a very special place in our religious history.

Saint Ninian,
first to preach the Good News of Christ in our land,
hear our prayers and present them to the Lord,
whom you served so faithfully.
Gain for us a new outpouring of the Holy Spirit,
abundant vocations to the priesthood and religious life,
deeper faith in God's merciful love,
stronger love for God and for our neighbour,
a renewal of the Christian life in our nation.
May we imitate your fidelity to the call of Christ and your passion to share the truth He brought us, and so also be found worthy to share the heavenly reward. Amen.

Rev Gerald Sharkey

[CELEBRATION OF THE HOLY EUCHARIST
Feast of Saint Ninian of Galloway
Bellahouston Park, Glasgow]

GATHERING IN PRAYER – HYMNS

How Lovely on the Mountains

1. How lovely on the mountains are the feet of him
who brings good news, good news,
announcing peace, proclaiming news of happiness:
Our God reigns.

2. You watchmen, lift your voices joyfully as one,
shout for your king, your king!
See eye to eye, the Lord restoring Sion:
Our God reigns

3. Wasteplaces of Jerusalem, break forth with joy!
We are redeemed, redeemed.
The Lord has saved and comforted his people.
Our God reigns

4. Ends of the earth, see the salvation of our God!
Jesus is Lord, is Lord!
Before the nations, he has bared his holy arm
Our God reigns

5. How lovely on the mountains are the feet of him
who brings good news, good news,
announcing peace, proclaiming news of happiness:
Our God reigns

Hail Redeemer

1. Hail, Redeemer, King divine!
Priest and Lamb, the throne is thine,
King, whose reign shall never cease,
Prince of everlasting peace.

℟ Angels, saints and nations sing:
"Praised be Jesus Christ, our King;
Lord of life, earth, sky and sea,
King of love on Calvary."

2. King whose name creation thrills,
rule our minds, our hearts, our wills,
till in peace each nation rings
with thy praises, King of kings.

3. King most holy, King of truth,
guide the lowly, guide the youth;
Christ the King of glory bright,
be to us eternal light.

4. Shepherd-King, o'er mountains steep,
homeward bring the wandering sheep,
shelter in one royal fold
states and kingdoms, new and old.

CHOIR *My Dearest Lord: Prayer of Columba*

Words of verse 2 and music Catherine Walker.

My dearest Lord, be thou a bright flame before me,
be thou a guiding star above me,
be thou a smooth path beneath me,
be thou a kindly shepherd behind me,
today and ever more, today and ever more.

When Christ our Lord

E.M. Barrett.

1. When Christ our Lord to Andrew cried:
"Come, thou, and follow me,"
the fisher left his net beside the Sea of Galilee.
To teach the truth the Master taught,
to tread the path he trod
was all his will and thus he brought
unnumbered souls to God.

2. When Andrew's hour had come, and he
was doomed, like Christ to die,
he kissed his cross exultingly,
and this his noble cry:
"O noble cross! O precious wood!
I long have yearned for thee;
uplift me to my only good
who died on thee for me."

3. Saint Andrew now in bliss above,
thy fervent prayers renew
that Scotland yet again may love
the faith, entire and true;
that I the cross allotted me
may bear with patient love! '
Twill lift me, as it lifted thee,
to reign with Christ above.

CHOIR **_To Christ the Seed_**

Words: Traditional.

To Christ the seed,
to Christ the sheaves,
so into God's barns
may we all be brought.

To Christ the sea,
to Christ the fish,
so into God's nets
may we all be caught.

From birth to growth,
from growth to age,
may your two arms, O Christ,
fold us around.

From age to death,
from death to new birth,
in the palace of grace may we be found.

City of God

1. Awake from your slumber! Arise from your sleep!
A new day is dawning for all those who weep.
The people in darkness have seen a great light.
The Lord of our longing has conquered the night.

℟ Let us build the city of God,
may our tears be turned into dancing!
For the Lord, our light and our love,
has turned the night into day.

2. We are sons of the morning, we are daughters of day.
The one who has loved us has brightened our way.
The Lord of all kindness has called us to be
a light for his people to set their hearts free.

3. O city of gladness, now lift up your voice!
Proclaim the good tidings that all may rejoice!

Ninian of Galloway

Text by Rt Rev J. McHardy; Music by by F. Duffy (*Candida Casa*).

1. Ninian of Galloway,
homage we fondly pay
and tribute bring;
Saint by our Church proclaimed,
Scotland's apostle named.
Thy praise we sing, thy praise we sing.

2. Born of our Scottish race,
God led thee forth by grace,
to find in Rome
that pearl so richly priced,
that faultless creed of Christ,
and bear it home, and bear it home.

3. Softly the Christian morn
dawned o'er the lone Whithorn

like kindly sun;
Nobly thy loyal band,
led by thy sure command,
our kingdom won. Our kingdom won.

4. Where once thy footsteps trod,
unquenched, the fires of God
await thy hand;
renew thy fervent care.
Tender to God our prayer
to bless our land, to bless our land.

As the Pope Makes his Way Through the Park

Amazing Grace (played by Strathclyde Police Pipe Band)

My Soul Proclaims

My soul proclaims the Lord my God,
my spirit sings his praise!
He looks on me, he lifts me up,
and gladness fills my days.

All nations now will share my joy,
his gifts he has outpoured;
his little one he has made great;
I magnify the Lord.

For those who love his holy name,
his mercy will not die.
His strong right arm puts down the proud
and lifts the lowly high.

He fills the hungry with good things,
the rich he sends away.
The promise made to Abraham
is filled to endless day.

Magnificat, magnificat,
magnificat, praise God!
Praise God, praise God,
praise God, praise God,
magnificat, praise God!

All People that on Earth do Dwell
William Kethe, based on Ps 99.

All people that on earth do dwell,
sing to the Lord with cheerful voice;
him serve with fear, his praise forth tell,
come ye before him and rejoice.

The Lord, ye know, is God indeed,
without our aid he did us make;
we are his folk, he doth us feed
and for his sheep he doth us take.

O enter then his gates with praise,
approach with joy his courts unto;
praise, laud and bless his name always,
for it is seemly so to do.

For why? the Lord our God is good:
his mercy is for ever sure;
his truth at all times firmly stood,
and shall from age to age endure.

To Father, Son and Holy Ghost,
the God whom heaven and earth adore,
from men and from the angel-host
be praise and glory evermore.

Organ Voluntary

MOTET - *As His Holiness vests* — *Locus Iste*
Bruckner

This place was made by God,
a priceless sacrament;
beyond reproach.

Locus iste a Deo factus est,
inestimabile sacramentum;
irreprehensibilis est.

SILENT PREPARATION FOR MASS

ENTRANCE PROCESSION

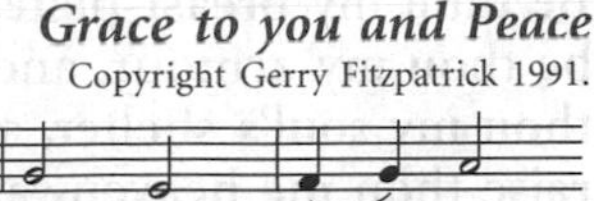

Grace to you and Peace

Copyright Gerry Fitzpatrick 1991.

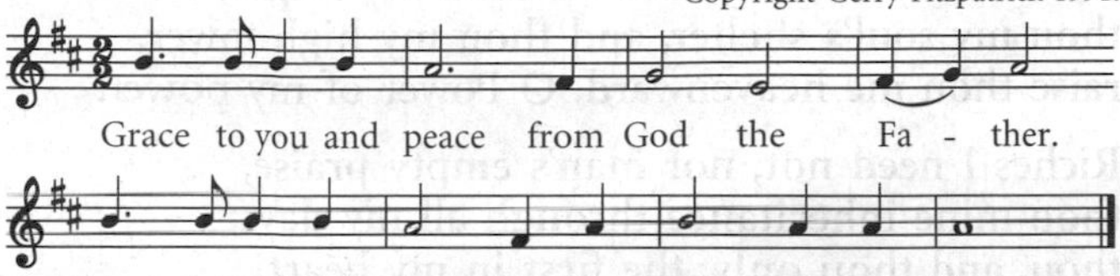
Grace to you and peace from God the Fa - ther.
Grace to you and peace from the Lord Je - sus Christ.

The Choir sings the above refrain and all repeat.

Choir:

**To all the people, chosen as the friends of God,
called to goodness like him who came to give us life
and hope.**

All: Grace to you and peace…

Choir:

**I am the shepherd of Israel,
I know my own and my own know me.
I seek the lost and bring back the strayed,
I bind up the cripple, strengthen the weak.
I am the shepherd of Israel,
I know my own and my own know me.**

All: Grace to you and peace…

Be thou my vision

Words: Irish 8th century, tr. Mary Byrne versified by Eleanor Hull.

**Be thou my vision, O Lord of my heart,
naught be all else to me save that thou art;
thou my best thought in the day and the night;
waking or sleeping, thy presence my light.**

**Be thou my wisdom, be thou my true word,
I ever with thee and thou with me, Lord;**

thou my great Father, and I thy true son;
thou in me dwelling, and I with thee one.

Be thou my breast-plate, my sword for the fight,
be thou my armour, and be thou my might,
thou my soul's shelter, and thou my high tower,
raise thou me heavenward, O Power of my power.

Riches I need not, nor man's empty praise,
thou mine inheritance through all my days;
thou, and thou only, the first in my heart,
high King of heaven, my treasure thou art!

High King of heaven when battle is done,
grant heaven's joy to me, O bright heaven's sun;
Christ of my own heart, whatever befall,
still be my vision, O Ruler of all.

Welcome

The Archbishop of Glasgow, the Most Reverend Mario Conti, welcomes his Holiness to Scotland and to the United Kingdom.

Introductory Dialogue

✠ Pope: In the name of the Father, and of the Son, and of the Holy Spirit.

All: **Amen.**

✠ Pope: The grace of our Lord Jesus Christ and the love of God and the fellowship of the Holy Spirit be with you all.

All: **And also with you.**

The Penitential Act

✠ Pope: As we prepare to celebrate the mystery of Christ's love, let us acknowledge our failures and ask the Lord for pardon and strength.

All: **I confess to almighty God, and to you my brothers and sisters, that I have sinned through my own**

fault, in my thoughts and in my words, in what I have done and in what I have failed to do; and I ask the Blessed Mary, ever virgin, all the angels and saints, and you, my brothers and sisters, to pray for me to the Lord, our God.

✠ **Pope:** **May almighty God have mercy on us, forgive us our sins, and bring us to everlasting life.**

All: **Amen.**

Kyrie (Missa de Angelis)

CANTOR, THEN ALL:
Ky-ri - e e - lé - i - son.
CANTOR, THEN ALL:
Chri- ste e - lé - i - son.
CANTOR:
Ky- ri - e e - lé - i - son.
ALL:
Ky- ri - e
e - lé - i - son.

Gloria

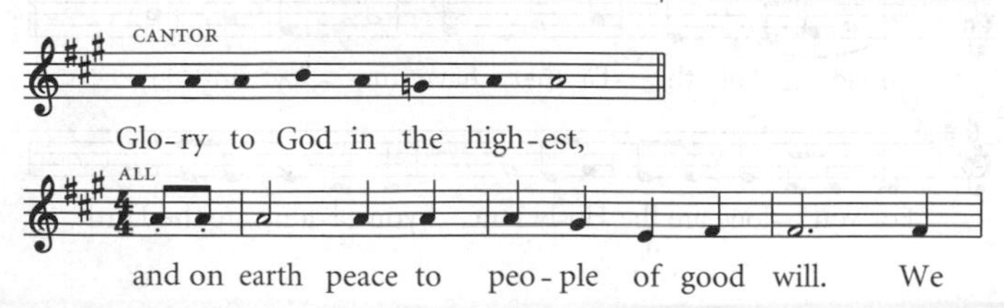
CANTOR
Glo- ry to God in the high- est,
ALL
and on earth peace to peo - ple of good will. We

praise you, we bless you, we a -
dore you, we glo - ri-fy you,
We give you thanks for your great glo - ry, Lord God,
hea-ven-ly King, O God, al - migh-ty Fa - ther.
Lord Je - sus Christ, On - ly Be-got-ten Son,
Lord God, Lamb of God, Son of the Fa-ther, you
take a - way the sins of the world, have mer - cy on
us; you take a - way the sins of the world, re -
ceive our prayer; you are seat-ed at the right
hand of the Fa-ther, have mer - cy on us.
For you a-lone are the Ho-ly One, you a-lone are the Lord,

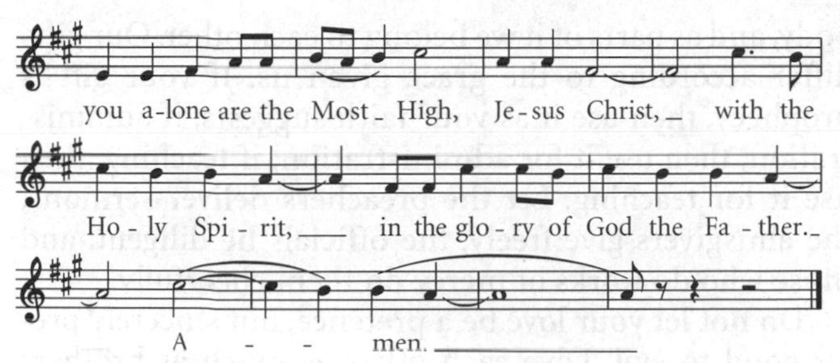
you a-lone are the Most_ High, Je-sus Christ,_ with the
Ho-ly Spi-rit,___ in the glo-ry of God the Fa-ther._
A - - men.

Collect

✠ **Pope:** **Lord our God,**
you brought the Picts and Britons
to a knowledge of the faith
through the teaching of Saint Ninian, the bishop:
in your goodness, listen to our prayers:
grant that we who have received from him
the light of your truth
may remain strong in faith and active in works of charity.
We ask this though our Lord, Jesus Christ, your Son,
who lives and reigns with you and the Holy Spirit,
one God, for ever and ever.

All: **Amen.**

• Liturgy of the Word •

A reading from
the letter of St Paul to the Romans **12:3–13**

IN THE LIGHT of the grace I have received I want to urge each one among you not to exaggerate his real importance. Each of you must judge himself soberly by the standard of the faith God has given him. Just as each of our bodies has several parts and each part has a separate function, so all of us, in union with Christ, form one body, and as parts of it we belong to each other. Our gifts differ according to the grace given us. If your gift is prophecy, then use it as your faith suggests; if administration, then use it for administration; if teaching, then use it for teaching. Let the preachers deliver sermons, the almsgivers give freely, the officials be diligent, and those who do works of mercy do them cheerfully.

Do not let your love be a pretence, but sincerely prefer good to evil. Love each other as much as brothers should, and have a profound respect for each other. Work for the Lord with untiring effort and with great earnestness of spirit. If you have hope, this will make you cheerful. Do not give up if trials come; and keep on praying. If any of the saints are in need you must share with them; and you should make hospitality your special care.

This is the word of the Lord.
Thanks be to God.

• PSALM 22 •

His good-ness shall fol-low me al-ways
to the end of my days.
Gerry Fitzpatrick

The Lord is my shepherd: there is nothing I shall want.
Fresh and green are the pastures
where he gives me repose.
Near restful waters he leads me
to revive my drooping spirits. ℟

In truth he guides me along the right path,
if I should walk in the valley of darkness

no evil would I fear.
You are there with your crook and staff,
with these you give me comfort. ℟

You have prepared a banquet for me
in the sight of my foes.
My head you have anointed with oil,
my cup is overflowing. ℟

Goodness and kindness shall surely follow me
all the days of my life.
In the Lord's own house shall I dwell forever,
forever and ever. ℟

Gospel Acclamation

Gerry Fitzpatrick

Al - le - lu - ia, al - le - lu - ia.
Al - le - lu - ia, al - le - lu - ia.

Alleluia. Falbhaibh is teagaisgibh a h-uile cinneadh,
tha mise maille ribh gu deireadh an t-saoghail.
Go make disciples of all the nations.
***I am with you to the end of time.* Alleluia.**

Fosgail ar cridhe, a' Thighearna,
's gun gabh sinn ri briathran do Mhic.
Open our hearts, Lord, open our hearts, Lord,
***That we may hear the words of your Son.* Alleluia.**

Deacon: The Lord be with you
All: **And also with you**

Deacon: A reading from the holy Gospel according to Luke
All: **Glory to you, Lord**

A reading from
the holy Gospel according to Luke **10:1–9**

THE LORD APPOINTED seventy-two others and sent them out ahead of him, in pairs, to all the towns and places he himself was to visit. He said to them, 'The harvest is rich but the labourers are few, so ask the Lord of the harvest to send labourers to his harvest. Start off now, but remember, I am sending you out like lambs among wolves. Carry no purse, no haversack, no sandals. Salute no one on the road. Whatever house you go into, let your first words be, "Peace to this house!" And if a man of peace lives there, your peace will go and rest on him; if not, it will come back to you. Stay in the same house, taking what food and drink they have to offer, for the labourer deserves his wages; do not move from house to house. Whenever you go into a town where they make you welcome, eat what is set before you. Cure those in it who are sick, and say, "The Kingdom of God is very near to you."'

This is the Gospel of the Lord.
Praise to you, Lord Jesus Christ

Homily

Prayer of the Faithful

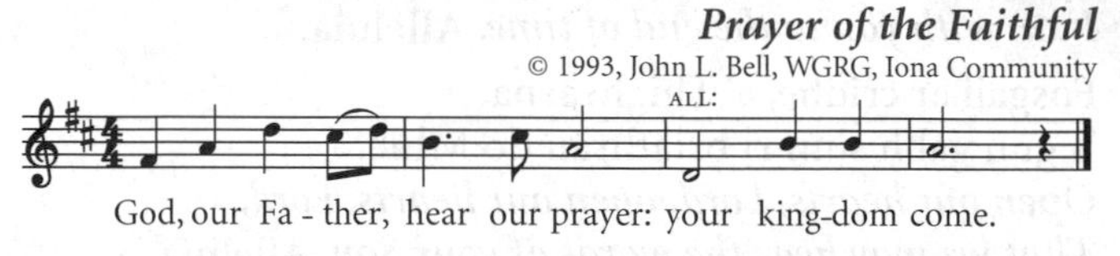

ALL:
God, our Fa - ther, hear our prayer: your king-dom come.

• Liturgy of the Eucharist •

Celtic Invocation

Christ be near at eith - er hand, Christ be -

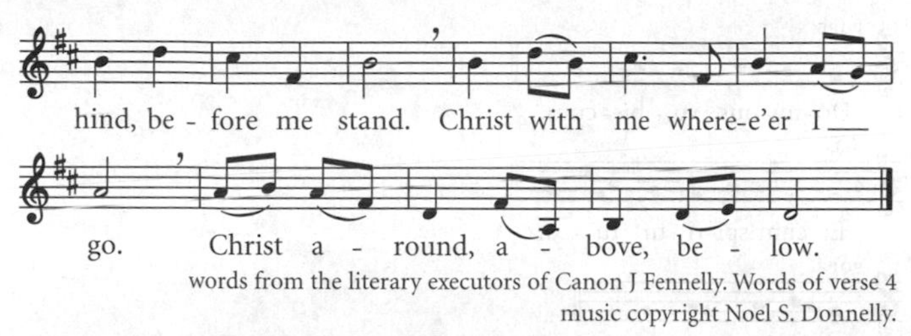

hind, be - fore me stand. Christ with me where-e'er I
go. Christ a - round, a - bove, be - low.

words from the literary executors of Canon J Fennelly. Words of verse 4
music copyright Noel S. Donnelly.

2. Christ be in my heart and mind.
Christ within my soul enshrined,
Christ control my wayward heart.
Christ abide and ne'er depart.

3. Christ my life and only way.
Christ my lantern night and day.
Christ be my unchanging friend.
Guide and shepherd to the end.

4. Praise the Father, source of all love!
Praise the Son, who reigns above!
Praise Holy Spirit, comfort in need!
Praise on our lips, in our hearts and our deeds!

✠ **Pope:** Pray, my brothers and sisters, that our sacrifice may be acceptable to God, the almighty Father.

All: **May the Lord accept the sacrifice at your hands for the praise and glory of his name, for our good, and the good of all his Church.**

Prayer over the Gifts

✠ **Pope:** Lord,
accept the gifts your people offer you
on this feast of Saint Ninian.
may these gifts bring us
your help for which we long.
We ask this through Christ our Lord.

All: **Amen.**

POPE
Dó-mi-nus vo - bís-cum.
ALL
Et cum spí-ri-tu tu - o.
POPE
Sur - sum cor - da.
ALL
Ha-bé - mus ad Dó-mi-num.
POPE
Grá-ti - as a - gá - mus Dó-mi-no De - o nos-tro.
ALL
Di - gnum et iu - stum est.

Preface

Father, all-powerful and ever-living God, we do well always and everywhere to give You thanks.

You give the Church this feast in honour of Saint Ninian; you inspire us by his holy life, instruct us by his preaching, and give us Your protection in answer to his prayers.

We join the angels and the saints as they sing their unending hymn of praise:

Vere dignum et iustum est, æquum et salutáre, nos tibi semper et ubíque grátias ágere: Dómine, sancte Pater, omnípotens ætérne Deus: per Christum Dóminum nostrum.

Quia sic tríbuis Ecclésiam tuam sancti Niniani festivitáte gaudére, ut eam exémplo piæ conversatiónis corróbores, verbo prædicatiónis erúdias, gratáque tibi supplicatióne tueáris.

Et ídeo, cum Angelórum atque Sanctórum turba, hymnum laudis tibi cánimus, sine fine dicéntes:

Sanctus

CANTOR, THEN ALL
Ho - ly, Ho - - ly, Ho - ly
Lord God of Hosts. Heav'n and
CANTOR, THEN ALL
earth are full of your glo - ry. Ho - san -
na, ho - san - na, ho - san - na in the high - est. Ho -
high - est. Bless - ed is he who comes in the name of the
Lord. Ho - san - na, ho - san - na, ho -
CANTOR, THEN ALL
san - na, ho - san - na, ho - san -
na, ho - san - na in the high - est, ho- high - est.

Eucharistic Prayer II

Vere Sanctus es, Dómine, fons omnis sanctitátis. Hæc ergo dona, quæsumus, Spíritus tui rore sanctífica, ut nobis Corpus et ✠ Sanguis fiant Dómini nostri Iesu Christi.

Lord you are holy indeed, the fountain of all holiness. Let your Spirit come upon these gifts to make them holy, so that they may become for us the body ✠ and blood of our Lord, Jesus Christ.

Before he was given up to death, a death he freely accepted, he took bread and gave you thanks. He broke the bread, gave it to his disciples, and said: TAKE THIS ALL OF YOU, AND EAT IT: THIS IS MY BODY WHICH WILL BE GIVEN UP FOR YOU. *When supper was ended, he took the cup. Again he gave you thanks and praise, gave the cup to his disciples, and said:* TAKE THIS, ALL OF YOU AND DRINK FROM IT: THIS IS THE CUP OF MY BLOOD, THE BLOOD OF THE NEW AND EVERLASTING COVENANT. IT WILL BE SHED FOR YOU AND FOR ALL SO THAT SINS MAY BE FORGIVEN. DO THIS IN MEMORY OF ME.

The Mystery of Faith.

Qui cum Passióni voluntárie traderétur, accépit panem et grátias agens fregit, dedítque discípulis suis, dicens: ACCÍPITE ET MANDUCÁTE EX HOC OMNES: HOC EST ENIM CORPUS MEUM, QUOD PRO VOBIS TRADÉTUR.

Símili modo, postquam cenátum est, accípiens et cálicem íterum tibi grátias agens dedit discípulis suis, dicens: ACCÍPITE ET BÍBITE EX EO OMNES: HIC EST ENIM CALIX SÁNGUINIS MEI NOVI ET ÆTÉRNI TESTAMÉNTI, QUI PRO VOBIS ET PRO MULTIS EFFUNDÉTUR IN REMISSIÓNEM PECCATÓRUM. HOC FÁCITE IN MEAM COMMEMORATIÓNEM.

Mystérium fídei.

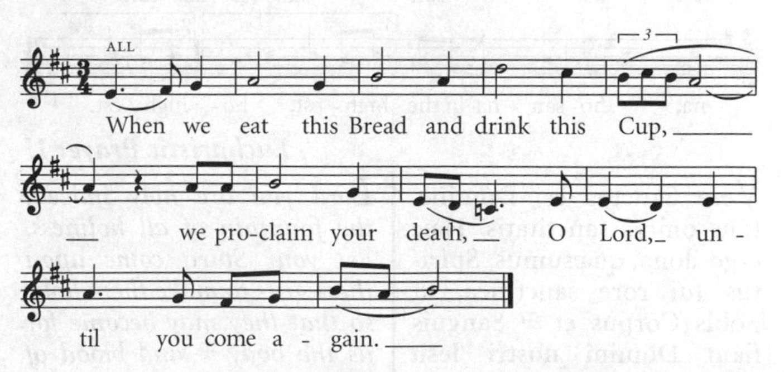

ALL
When we eat this Bread and drink this Cup, we pro-claim your death, O Lord, un - til you come a - gain.

Mémores ígitur mortis et resurrectiónis eius, tibi, Dómine, panem vitæ et cálicem salútis offérimus, grátias agéntes quia nos dignos habuísti astáre coram te et tibi ministráre.
Et súpplices deprecámur ut Córporis et Sánguinis Christi partícipes a Spíritu Sancto congregémur in unum.
Recordáre, Dómine, Ecclésiæ tuæ toto orbe diffúsæ, ut eam in caritáte perfícias una cum Papa nostro Benedicto et me indigno famulo et univérso clero.
Meménto étiam fratrum nostrórum, qui in spe resurrectiónis dormiérunt, omniúmque in tua miseratióne defunctórum, et eos in lumen vultus tui admítte.
Omnium nostrum, quæsumus, miserére, ut cum beáta Dei Genetríce Vírgine María, beátis Apóstolis et ómnibus Sanctis, qui tibi a sæculo placuérunt, ætérnæ vitæ mereámur esse consórtes, et te laudémus et glorificémus per Fílium tuum Iesum Christum.

In memory of his death and resurrection, we offer you, Father, this life-giving bread, this saving cup. We thank you for counting us worthy to stand in your presence and serve you.
May all of us who share in the body and blood of Christ be brought together in unity by the Holy Spirit.
Lord, remember your Church throughout the world; make us grow in love, together with Benedict our Pope, me, your unworthy servant, and all the clergy.
Remember our brothers and sisters who have gone to their rest in the hope of rising again; bring them and all the departed into the light of your presence.
Have mercy on us all; make us worthy to share eternal life with Mary, the virgin Mother of God, with the apostles, and with all the saints who have done your will throughout the ages. May we praise you in union with them, and give you glory through your Son, Jesus Christ.

The Doxology and the Great Amen

POPE
Per ipsum, et cum ipso, et in ip - so,
est tibi Deo Patri omnipoténti,
in unitáte Spí-ri-tus San-cti,
om-nis ho-nor et gló-ri-a
ALL
per ómnia saé-cu-la sae-cu-ló-rum. A - men.

• Communion Rite •

✠ **Pope: Praeceptis salutaribus moniti, et divina institutione formati, audemus dicere:**

Let us pray with confidence to the Father in the words our Saviour gave us:

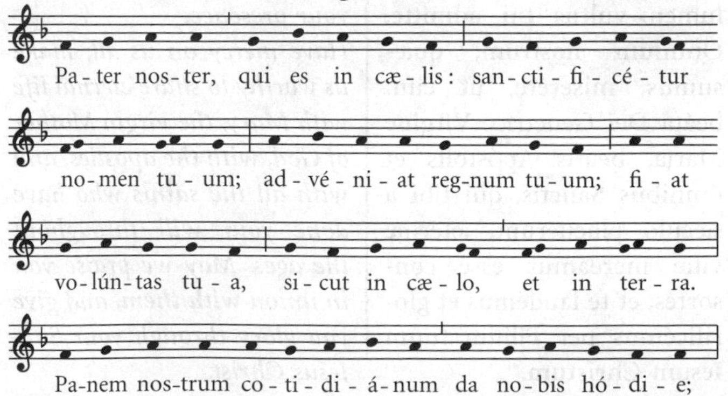
Pa-ter nos-ter, qui es in cæ-lis: san-cti-fi-cé-tur
no-men tu-um; ad-vé-ni-at reg-num tu-um; fi-at
vo-lún-tas tu-a, si-cut in cæ-lo, et in ter-ra.
Pa-nem nos-trum co-ti-di-á-num da no-bis hó-di-e;

et di - mí - te no - bis dé - bi - ta nos - tra,
si - cut et nos di - mít - ti - mus de - bi - tó - ri - bus nos - tris;
et ne nos in - dú - cas in ten - ta - ti - ó - nem;
sed lí - be - ra nos a ma - lo.

Our Father,
who art in heaven
hallowed be thy name.
Thy kingdom come,
Thy will be done
on earth as it is in heaven.
Give us this day our daily bread
and forgive us our trespasses
as we forgive those who trespass against us.
And lead us not into temptation,
but deliver us from evil.

✠ **Pope:** Deliver us, Lord, from every evil
and grant us peace in our day.
In your mercy, keep us free from sin
and protect us from all anxiety,
as we wait in joyful hope
for the coming of our Saviour, Jesus Christ.

All: **For the kingdom, the power, and the glory are yours, now and for ever. Amen.**

✠ **Pope:** Lord, Jesus Christ, you said to your apostles: I leave you peace, my peace I give you. Look not on our sins, but on the faith of your Church, and

grant us the peace and unity of your kingdom,
where you live for ever and ever.

All: **Amen.**

✠ **Pope:** The peace of the Lord be with you always.

All: **And also with you.**

Deacon: Let us offer each other the sign of peace.

Lamb of God

ALL
Lamb of God, you take a - way the sins of the world,
CANTOR
have mer - cy on us,
ALL
have mer - cy on us.
3
ALL
Lamb of God, you take a - way the sins of the world,
CANTOR
have mer - cy on us,
ALL
have mer - cy on us.
ALL
Lamb of God, you take a - way the sins of the world,
CANTOR, THEN ALL
1.
2.
grant us peace.

✠ **Pope:** This is the Lamb of God who takes away the sins of the world. Happy are those who are called to his supper:

All: **Lord, I am not worthy to receive you, but only say the word and I shall be healed.**

DURING THE DISTRIBUTION OF HOLY COMMUNION

Take and Eat

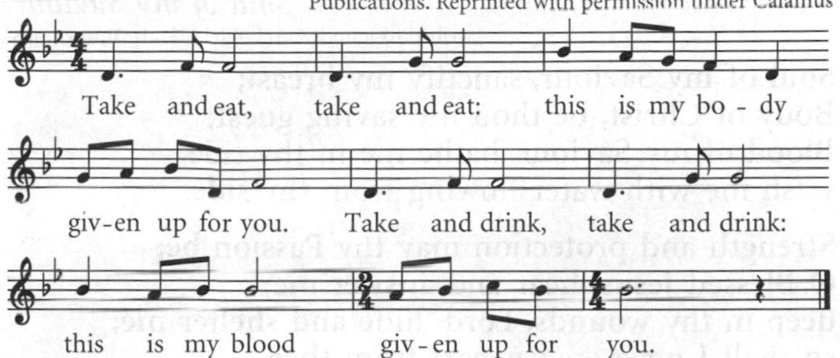

Take and eat, take and eat: this is my bo - dy
giv-en up for you. Take and drink, take and drink:
this is my blood giv-en up for you.

I am the Word that spoke and light was made;
I am the seed that died to be re-born;
I am the bread that comes from heav'n above;
I am the vine that fills your cup with joy.

I am the way that leads the exile home;
I am the truth that sets the captive free;
I am the life that raises up the dead;
I am your peace, true peace my gift to you.

I am the Lamb that takes away your sin;
I am the gate that guards you night and day;
you are my flock, you know the shepherd's voice;
you are my own, your ransom is my blood.

I am the corner-stone that God has laid;
a chosen stone and precious in his eyes;
you are God's dwelling place, on me you rest;
like living stones, a temple for God's praise.

I am the light that came into the world;
I am the light that darkness cannot hide;
I am the morning star that never sets;
lift up your face, in you my light will shine.

I am the first and last, the Living One;
I am the Lord that died that you might live;

I am the bridegroom, this my wedding song;
you are my bride, come to the marriage feast.

Soul of my Saviour

Ascribed to John XX11(1249-1334), tr Anonymous

Soul of my Saviour, sanctify my breast;
Body of Christ, be thou my saving guest;
Blood of my Saviour, bathe me in thy tide,
wash me with water flowing from thy side.

Strength and protection may thy Passion be;
O Blessed Jesus, hear and answer me;
deep in thy wounds, Lord, hide and shelter me;
so shall I never, never part from thee.

Guard and defend me from the foe malign;
in death's dread moments make me only thine;
call me and bid me come to thee on high,
when I may praise thee with thy saints for aye.

Seed, Scattered and Sown

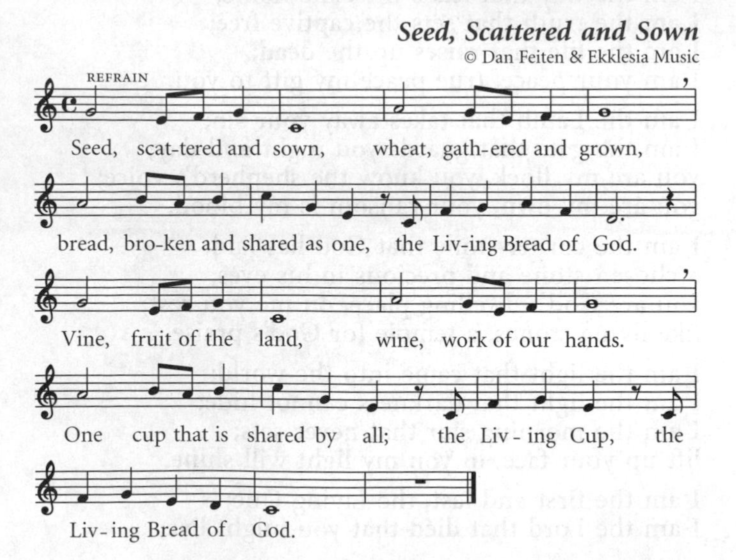

REFRAIN
Seed, scat-tered and sown, wheat, gath-ered and grown,
bread, bro-ken and shared as one, the Liv-ing Bread of God.
Vine, fruit of the land, wine, work of our hands.
One cup that is shared by all; the Liv - ing Cup, the
Liv - ing Bread of God.

1. Is not the bread we break a sharing in our Lord?
Is not the cup we bless the blood of Christ outpoured?

2. The seed which falls on rock will wither and will die.
The seed within good ground will flower and have life.

3. As wheat upon the hills was gathered and was grown.
So may the church of God be gathered into one.

COMMUNION MOTET

Ave, verum corpus natum de Maria Virgine, Vere passum immolatum in Cruce pro homine, Cujus latus perforatum unda fluxit sanguine, Esto nobis praegustatum in mortis examine. O clemens, O pie, O Dulcis Jesu fili Mariae.	*Hail, true Body, born of the Virgin Mary, who truly suffered, sacrificed on the Cross for mankind, whose pierced side flowed with water and blood: be for us a foretaste [of heaven] in the trial of death. O merciful, O kind, O sweet Jesus, Son of Mary.*

IN HONOUR OF BLESSED MARY MCKILLOP

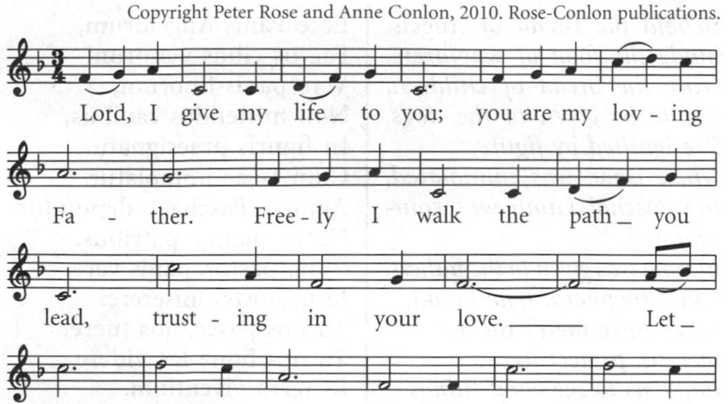
Lord, I give my life _ to you; you are my lov - ing
Fa - ther. Free - ly I walk the path _ you
lead, trust - ing in your love. ______ Let _
your will be my will; let my will be

yours. In trust draw me close to
you, the Fa - ther my soul a - dores.

2. Lord, I seek to do your work,
touching the world with your kindness.
Gladly I share your cross of pain,
trusting in your love.
Let your will be my will, let my will be yours.
In trust draw me close to you.
The Saviour my soul adores.

3. Lord, I long for you alone,
you are the treasure I yearn for.
You are the breath which brings me life,
trusting in your love.
Let your will be my will, let my will be yours.
In trust draw me close to you.
The Spirit my soul adores.

COMMUNION MOTET

Behold the Bread of Angels,	Ecce Panis Angelorum,
made the food of wayfarers,	Factus cibus viatorum
truly the bread of children,	Vere panis filiorum,
not to be given to the dogs.	Non mittendus canibus.
Presignified by figure,	In figuris praesignatur,
when Isaac was immolated,	Cum Isaac immolatur,
the Paschal Lamb was commanded,	Agnus Paschae deputatur,
manna was given to the fathers.	Datur manna patribus.
Good shepherd, true bread,	Bone pastor, panis vere,
Jesus, have mercy on us:	Jesu, nostri miserere:
feed us, protect us,	Tu nos pasce, nos tuere,
make us to see good things	Tu nos bona fac videre
in the land of the living.	In terra viventium.

Tu qui cuncta scis et vales, Qui nos pascis hic mortales: Tuos ibi commensales, Coheredes et sodales Fac sanctorum civium. Amen.	*Thou who knowest and willest all things, who feeds us mortals by this: make thine own to be partakers of, co-heirs and citizens in that holy city of saints. Amen.*

Do làmh, a Chrìosda

Na faclan: Dòmhnall Iain MacDhòmhnaill Am fonn: Iseabail T. Dhòmhnallach
New composition by Donald John MacDonald, Peninerine. Melody Ishbel T. MacDonald. Hymn book Seinnibh Dhan Tighearna.

Do làmh, a Chrìosda, bi leinn an comhnaidh Ar sìol gu fàs thu ar gàrradh ròsan; Ar foghar buair Thu, ar cruach dhan eòrna Nad shaibhlean biodhmaid aig crìch ar beò-bhith.	*Your hand, O Lord, be with us always You are our growth seed, our rose garden; Our plentiful harvest, our barley mound May we be in your barns at our life's end.*
Ar n-oiteag chùbhraidh, ar driùchd na Màigh Thu, Ar cala dìdein an tìmean gàbhaidh, Ar grunndan iasgaich, ar biadh, ar sàth Thu, Nad lìontaibh biodhmaid aig ìre bàis dhuinn.	*You are our fragrant breeze, our May dew, Our safe harbour in stormy times, Our fishing grounds, our food, our satisfaction, May we be in your nets at the moment of our death.*
Nar làithean leanabais biodh t'ainm-sa beò dhuinn, Nar làithean aosda do ghaol biodh còmh' rinn, Tro neòil ar dubh'rachd ar cùrsa treòraich, Tro shiantan dùr, gu reul-iùil ar dòchais.	*In our childhood days, may your name be alive to us. In our declining days, may your love be with us, Through our dark clouds, direct our course, Through dark storms, to the guiding star of our hope*

Death is not the end for us,
but a new growth -
O fill us with your grace, be close to us forever;
And when the moment comes at the end of our time,
youthful May will replace dark winter.

Cha chrìoch am bàs dhuinn
ach fàs às ùr dhuinn
O lìon led ghràs sinn, gu bràth bi dlùth dhuinn;
'S nuair thig an t-àm oirnn
aig ceann ar n-ùine,
'S e òg-mhìos Mhàigh bhios an aite Dùdlachd.

Where True Love is Dwelling

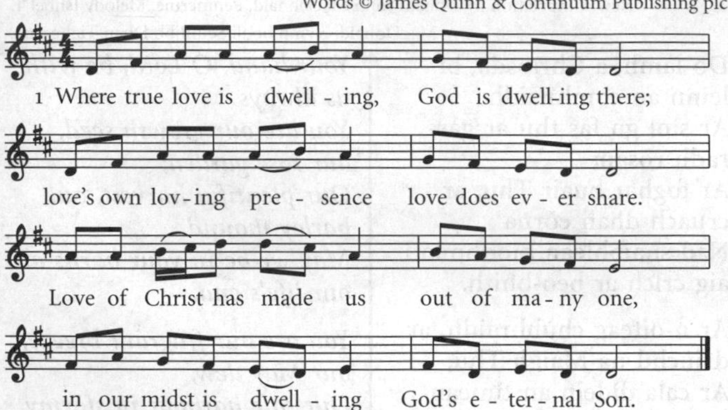
1 Where true love is dwell - ing, God is dwell-ing there;
love's own lov - ing pre - sence love does ev - er share.
Love of Christ has made us out of ma - ny one,
in our midst is dwell - ing God's e - ter - nal Son.

Give him joyful welcome, love him and revere,
cherish one another with a love sincere.
As in Christ we gather discord has no part;
ours is but one spirit but one mind and heart.

Bitterness now ended, let there be accord;
always with us dwelling be our God and Lord.
May we share the vision with the saints on high,
of Christ's matchless glory when we come to die.

Joy of all the blessed, be our heavenly prize;
dwell with us forever, Lord of Paradise!
Where true love is dwelling, God is dwelling there;
love's own loving presence love does ever share.

God to Enfold You

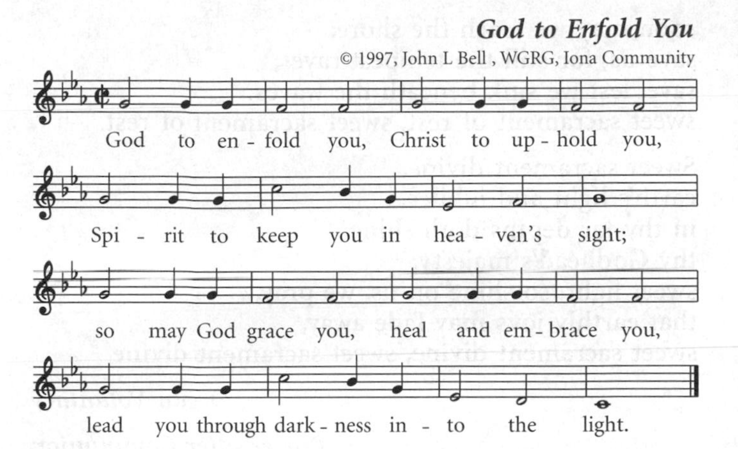
God to en - fold you, Christ to up - hold you,
Spi - rit to keep you in hea - ven's sight;
so may God grace you, heal and em - brace you,
lead you through dark - ness in - to the light.

Sweet Sacrament Divine

Francis Stanfield 1835-1914

Sweet sacrament divine,
hid in thy earthly home,
lo! round thy lowly shrine,
with suppliant hearts we come;
Jesus, to thee our voice we raise,
in songs of love and heartfelt praise,
sweet sacrament divine, sweet sacrament divine.

Sweet sacrament of peace,
dear home of every heart,
where restless yearnings cease,
and sorrows all depart,
there in thine ear all trustfully
we tell our tale of misery,
sweet sacrament of peace, sweet sacrament of peace.

Sweet sacrament of rest,
Ark from the ocean's roar,
within thy shelter blest

soon may we reach the shore;
save us, for still the tempest raves;
save, lest we sink beneath the waves.
sweet sacrament of rest, sweet sacrament of rest.

Sweet sacrament divine,
earth's light and jubilee,
in thy far depths doth shine
thy Godhead's majesty;
sweet light, so shine on us, we pray,
that earthly joys may fade away,
sweet sacrament divine, sweet sacrament divine

Organ Voluntary

Prayer after Communion

✠ **Pope:** Lord our God,
You give us the holy body and blood
of your Son.
May the salvation we celebrate
be our undying hope.
Grant this through Christ our Lord.

All: Amen.

• Concluding Rites •

POPE
Dó-mi-nus vo-bís-cum.
ALL
Et cum spí-ri-tu tu-o.
POPE
Sit nomen Dómini be-ne-díc-tum.
ALL
Ex hoc nunc et usque in saé-cu-lum.

POPE
Adiutórium nostrum in nómine Dó-mi-ni.
ALL
Qui fecit caelum et ter-ram.
POPE
Benedícat vos om-ni-pó-tens De-us: Pa-ter, et Fí-li-us,
et Spí-ri-tus San-ctus.
ALL
A-men.
DEACON
I-te, mis-sa est.
ALL
De-o grá-ti-as.
God, we praise you
1 God, we praise you, God, we bless you, God, we name you
sov' - reign Lord! Migh - ty King whom an - gels wor - ship,
Fa - ther by your Church a-dored. All cre - a - tion
shows your glo - ry, heav'n and earth draw near your throne,
sing-ing 'Ho-ly, ho-ly, ho-ly', Lord of hosts and God a-lone.

True apostles, faithful prophets,
saints who set the world ablaze.
Martyrs, once unknown, unheeded,
join one growing song of praise,
while your Church on earth confesses
one majestic Trinity:
Father, Son, and Holy Spirit,
God, our hope eternally.

Jesus Christ, the king of glory,
everlasting Son of God.
Humble was your virgin mother,
hard the lonely path you trod.
By your cross is sin defeated,
hell confronted face to face,
heaven opened to believers,
sinners justified by grace.

Christ, at God's right hand victorious,
you will judge the world you made;
Lord, in mercy help your servants
for whose freedom you have paid:
Raise us up from dust to glory,
guard us from all sin today;
king enthroned above all praises,
save your people, God, we pray.

Words from Te Deum, Christopher Idle. Published by Jubilate Hymns

Strathclyde Police Pipe band plays to conclude the Mass.

Acknowledgements: With thanks to Glasgow City Council for the use of Bellahouston Park and for supporting the visit to the City; Hayes & Finch Ltd for providing much of what is needed for the Liturgy; Neil Reid (Marble Mason) for Sanctuary Furniture; John Felix (Carpenter) for Sanctuary Furniture; Allen Organs for the use of the organ; University of Strathclyde for assistance with plans and drawings; DF Concerts for event and site management.

Friday, September 17

The second day of the Papal visit

England

On the second day of the Papal visit, Pope Benedict goes to St Mary's University College, Twickenham, where the focus of his visit will be first on education. He will meet for prayer with representatives of religious congregations – particularly those who have a charism for education and a history of education – and then go to meet about 3,000 young people (schoolchildren, students) to celebrate Catholic education. Catholic schools across England, Scotland and Wales have been invited to join this meeting by television and through the internet, and so to share this moment of celebration and prayer at the beginning of a new academic year.

Towards the end of the morning the Holy Father will meet with religious leaders and people of religious faith from across the United Kingdom. His meeting will provide the opportunity to explore the importance of religion and belief across the breadth of British society.

Later in the day, Pope Benedict will meet with the Archbishop of Canterbury and each will deliver a short address before the Anglican and Roman Catholic diocesan bishops of England and Wales.

The Holy Father next goes to Westminster Hall where he has been invited to deliver an Address to British society. From there Pope Benedict goes to Westminster Abbey to meet other Church leaders and to join with them in the celebration of Evening Prayer.

His visit will begin with a prayer for peace at the tomb of the Unknown Soldier and conclude with a moment of prayer and reflection at the shrine of Saint Edward the Confessor.

By custom the Holy Father never attends official dinners, and so after evening prayer he will return to the Apostolic Nunciature. By custom a State Banquet is one of the ways in which the State conducts a State Visit, and so an official dinner will take place in Lancaster House hosted by senior ministers for the members of the Papal entourage.

Programme

10.00: Pope Benedict arrives at St Mary's University College, Twickenham. Prayer with representatives of religious congregations in St Mary's Chapel.

10.15: Celebration of Catholic Education with children and students (including presentation of John Paul II Institute for Sport).

11.30: Gathering with Religious Leaders and People of Faith, St Mary's College, Twickenham.

12.30: Pope Benedict returns to the Apostolic Nunciature.

16.00: Pope Benedict meets with the Archbishop of Canterbury at Lambeth Palace in the presence of Anglican and Catholic diocesan bishops of England, Wales and Scotland.

17.00: Popemobile to Westminster Hall.

17.10: Pope Benedict delivers an *Address to British Society* at Westminster Hall.

18.00: Popemobile to Westminster Abbey.

18.15: Celebration of Evening Prayer in Westminster Abbey, beginning with a Prayer for peace at the Tomb of the Unknown Soldier and concluding with a time of prayer at the Shrine of Saint Edward the Confessor.

19.30: Pope Benedict returns to the Apostolic Nunciature.

20.15: Her Majesty's Government hosts an Official Dinner for the Papal Entourage in honour of Pope Benedict XVI at Lancaster House.

The Church in England

Fr Gerard Skinner

A 4th-century writer from a far off country was adamant that "Even the British Isles have felt the power of the Word, for there too churches and altars have been erected: there too... men may be heard discussing points of Scripture, with different voices, but not with different belief." Even before Pope Gregory the Great sent Saint Augustine and his band of Roman monks in 596, faith in Jesus Christ as proclaimed by the successors of Saint Peter had existed in the British Isles. But with the arrival of Saint Augustine's mission in 597, a new evangelisation took root and became firmly established through cathedrals and monasteries, parish churches and above all through holy men and women tirelessly toiling for the greater glory of God.

Britain was to become known as the "Isle of Saints" through the lives and witness of martyrs such as Saints Alban, Julius and Aaron (3rd century), Boniface, the apostle of Germany (d.754) and Thomas of Canterbury (d.1170); monks and nuns such as Saint David (6th century), the Northumbrian historian Bede the Venerable (d.735), and the wise Hilda (d.680), Abbess of Whitby; saints who were kings such as Edward the Confessor (d.1066), or scholars such as Edmund of Abingdon (d.1175). Great shrines, hugely popular destinations for pilgrimages, were built to celebrate the lives of the saints and enable pilgrims to pray near their relics.

By the end of the 8th century the Anglo-Saxons had begun to express their loyalty to the Pope as the Bishop of Rome by sending each year a voluntary donation to Rome. This was called the *Denarius Sancti Petri* (the Alms of St Peter), but is better known today as Peter's Pence – a collection taken today throughout the world. From 1154 until 1159 Peter's Pence supported the work of the only English Pope, Adrian IV, who was born in Hertfordshire.

The English were renowned for devotion to the Blessed Virgin Mary, and England was known as the "Dowry of Mary". The poor and princes devoutly made their way on pilgrimage to the Marian shrine of Walsingham – King Henry VIII being the last English king to pray at the shrine.

The subsequent breaking of unity with the successors of Saint Peter led not only to the destruction of so many churches and monasteries but also to the systematic crushing of a whole way of life for ordinary men and women. For many the monasteries had been their very source of employment or shelter and a lively centre of local communities.

A tragic loss of life accompanied the Reformation – many Catholics and Protestants were brutally executed. The most famous of the martyrs are Saint John Fisher, the Bishop of Rochester, and his friend Saint Thomas More, Lord Chancellor of England, who died saying "I die the king's good servant, but God's first." Throughout the turbulence of the 16th and 17th centuries many died for their faith. It is striking that amongst the lists of the Catholic English and Welsh martyrs can be found men and women from every walk of life: mothers like Saint Margaret Clitherow, priest's housekeepers like Saint Anne Line, nobility like Saint Philip Howard or Blessed Margaret Pole, and scholars such as Saint Edmund Campion.

Forced underground by penal laws, the Catholic Church in England and Wales continued to care for souls. In 1688 Blessed Pope Innocent XI decided to divide the Catholics in England and Wales into four districts, each with a bishop (a Vicar Apostolic) who was directly responsible to the Pope for the pastoral care of his area. Despite the great difficulties involved in travelling long distances and ministering whilst remaining undetected, the Vicars Apostolic were remarkably successful in laying firm foundations for the time when Catholics would once again be free to worship publicly. The legal freedom to be a Catholic came about slowly, with the Papists Act of 1778 giving Catholics the right to own and inherit property and to join the army. The Catholic Relief Act of 1791 allowed the opening of Catholic churches, so long as they were registered. In the following years the arrival of thousands of French refugees fleeing the French revolution and the support of the Pope for Britain during the Napoleonic wars led to a slow change in public opinion. This made possible the Catholic Emancipation Act of 1829 that gave Catholics almost equal rights to any other British citizen, including the right to vote and to hold most public offices.

Finally in 1850 Blessed Pope Pius IX established a system of Catholic Dioceses in England and Wales, the former Vicars Apostolic becoming the bishops of the newly re-established Catholic hierarchy. The following year, at Oscott College, Birmingham, a recent convert piest preached to the First Synod of Westminster one of the most famous sermons in the English language. The preacher, Fr John Henry Newman, declared that with the restoration of the Catholic hierarchy was the "coming of a Second Spring", a new time of abundant growth for the Catholic Church in England and Wales.

Newman's words proved to be prophetic. Between 1850 and 1950 thousands of newly built cathedrals, churches, schools, convents, monasteries, hospitals, care homes and colleges opened, built from the gifts of the whole Catholic community, a testimony to their living Faith. Catholicism was once again making a public and striking contribution to English society as a whole, particularly in the field of education. The following fifty years were marked by the canonisation of forty of the English and Welsh martyrs. Pope John Paul II beatified eighty-five more martyrs in 1987 and during the Jubilee of AD 2000 declared Saint Thomas More the Patron Saint of statesmen and politicians.

In 1982 Pope John Paul II became the first Pope to visit the United Kingdom. He came seeking to strengthen the faith of the flock with which he was entrusted. The Seven Sacraments formed the programme for his journey throughout England, Scotland and Wales.

Pope Benedict XVI comes by contrast on a State visit at the invitation of the Queen and her Government. His visit is rich with historical resonance. He addresses British society in Westminster Hall, the place where Saint Thomas More was sentenced to death in 1535. He will preside over the first ever Beatification to take place in this country when he beatifies Cardinal John Henry Newman – the first Englishman who was not a martyr to be beatified in over six hundred years. Above all Pope Benedict will witness to the gift of faith in God and to the hope and love offered by the Gospel of Jesus Christ, the Pope praying that once again it may be said that "the British Isles have felt the power of the Word".

The Place of Religious in the Church

Conference of Religious

Religious men and women commit their lives entirely to God and express this through a vowed life within community and in self-giving service to others. They are "resurrection-people" of love, hope and encouragement to one another and the wider society. Their role within the Church has been to act as witnesses of God's love, by living out gospel values to the highest level. "I am the Resurrection – I have come so that you may have life and have it abundantly" (John 10:10).

Throughout history their founders, male and female, have responded to the great needs and crises of society. They turned them into opportunities for evangelisation, for renewal, for rebirth. Their inspiration fuelled a succession of movements of religious and social renewal:

❋ the early monastic communities with their challenge to radical embracing of the teaching of Christ;

❋ the influence of the Benedictine communities in sustaining order and faith at the time of the demise of the Latin Roman Empire;

❋ the Cistercians in the 12th century;

❋ the new forms of religious life instituted by Sts Dominic and Francis in the 13th century;

✻ the innovative Sisters of Charity and Sisters of Mercy responding to the 'cry of the poor';

✻ the birth of a rich variety of teaching and nursing congregations of religious men and women in France in the aftermath of the French Revolution and in response to the urban poverty which was a consequence of the Industrial Revolution;

✻ the ecumenical monastic community of Taizé, witnessing to a gospel shared by the Churches;

✻ the Secular Institutes and the new Orders of the 21st century.

Whether monastic or ministerial in their mode of life, and what ever their charism, all religious congregations are united in being Christ centred, bearing witness to the "body of Christ" within the Church; and acting as a "leaven for good in a hurting world". They seek to show how gospel values can be applied and re-interpreted to the needs of the contemporary world.

The ministry undertaken by religious over the past fifty years has had a profound impact on the fabric of society. It has been expressed in education, healthcare, the ministry of prayer, of pastoral work, of supporting parish communities. Religious have been instrumental in preparing so many people for their relationship with God. Their outreach includes refugees, asylum seekers and minority groups, prisoners, victims of trafficking and the homeless. There is a strong commitment to the justice and peace movement, to preserving the integrity of creation and to custodial care for the environment.

In their ministerial role Religious meet the needs of multicultural, multi-faith communities as well as facing the growth of secularism. These challenges are faced together by Religious in the development of increased collaborative, and networking initiatives, providing strength and support through unity.

At a Mass celebrating the Golden Jubilee of the Conference of Religious Archbishop Vincent Nichols paid tribute to the contribution of religious:

“There are not many people who will not have a word of thanks for the love and support they have received from the religious, especially religious women, either as children or in old age.

“So we rejoice in their past and we are thankful for the present, for the goodness that is here, which is God’s gift and is so tangible. We look to the future not knowing what it holds, but confident that if we are faithful then the Lord will never turn his gracefulness and his generosity from us. If we can be eloquent in putting before people heroic love – then they will follow – they will follow”.

[PRAYER WITH RELIGIOUS (WITH CHARISM IN EDUCATION) Twickenham]

OPENING CHANT

Veni Sancte Spiritus

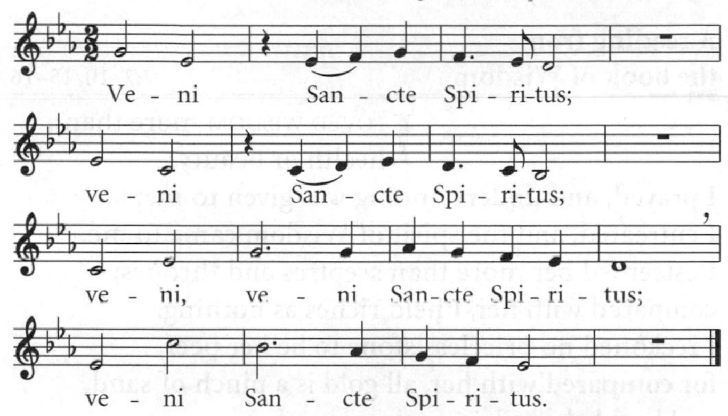
Ve - ni San - cte Spi - ri-tus;
ve - ni San - cte Spi - ri-tus;
ve - ni, ve - ni San-cte Spi - ri - tus;
ve - ni San - cte Spi - ri - tus.

Greeting of the Holy Father by a religious

Sign of the Cross and Greeting

✠ **Pope:** In the name of the Father, and of the Son,
and of the Holy Spirit.
All: Amen.
✠ **Pope:** Peace be with you.
All: And also with you.

Opening prayer

✠ **Pope:** God of all knowledge,
whose wisdom unfolds for us
the meaning of the world in which we live,
be the inspiration and the end of all our efforts
to know, learn, and teach.

Through the seeds of inquiry and wonder
which you have implanted,
may we continue to grow in your wisdom.
Grant this through our Lord Jesus Christ, your Son,
who lives and reigns with you in the unity of the
Holy Spirit,
God for ever and ever.

A reading from the book of Wisdom 7:7–10. 15–16

I LOVED WISDOM more than
health or beauty.
I prayed, and understanding was given to me;
I entreated, and the spirit of Wisdom came to me.
I esteemed her more than sceptres and thrones;
compared with her, I held riches as nothing.
I reckoned no priceless stone to be her peer,
for compared with her, all gold is a pinch of sand,
and beside her silver ranks as mud.
I loved her more than health or beauty,
preferred her to the light,
since her radiance never sleeps.
May God grant me to speak as he would wish
and express thoughts worthy of his gifts,
since he himself is the guide of Wisdom,
since he directs the sages.
We are indeed in his hand, we ourselves and our words,
with all our understanding, too, and technical knowledge.
This is the word of the Lord.
Thanks be to God.

SUNG RESPONSE

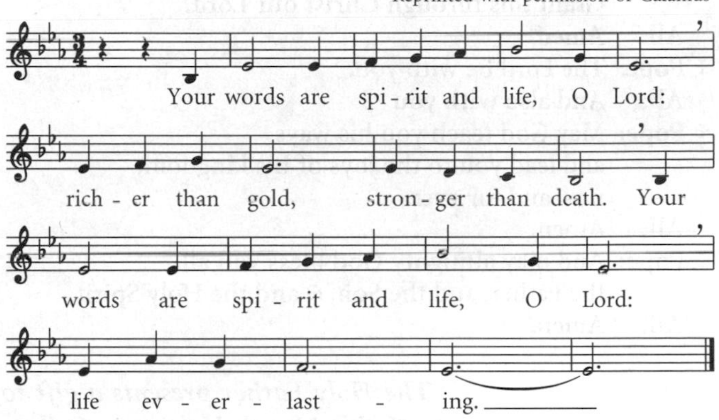
Your words are spi - rit and life, O Lord:
rich - er than gold, stron - ger than death. Your
words are spi - rit and life, O Lord:
life ev - er - last - ing.

Short address by Pope Benedict

Lord's Prayer

✠ **Pope:** Jesus taught us to call God our Father,
and so we have the courage to say:
Our Father…

Prayer and Blessing

✠ **Pope:** Lord God,
in your wisdom and love
you surround us with the mysteries of the universe.
In times long past you sent us your prophets
to teach your laws
and to bear witness to your undying love.
You sent us your Son
to teach us by word and example
that true wisdom comes from you alone.
Send your Spirit upon those you have called
to share their knowledge with gentle patience

and endeavour always to bring the truth
to eager minds.
Grant this through Christ our Lord.

All: Amen.

✠ **Pope:** The Lord be with you.

All: And also with you

✠ **Pope:** May God teach you his ways
and lead you to the joys of his kingdom,
now and for ever.

All: Amen.

✠ **Pope:** And may almighty God bless you all,
the Father, and the Son, ✠ and the Holy Spirit.

All: Amen.

The Holy Father presents a gift to
Saint Mary's University College

FINAL HYMN — ***Lord, you give the great commission***

Text by Jeffrey Rowthorn © 1978, Hope Publishing Co.
Reprinted with permission of Calamus
Tune: by Cyril V Taylor (1907-1991).

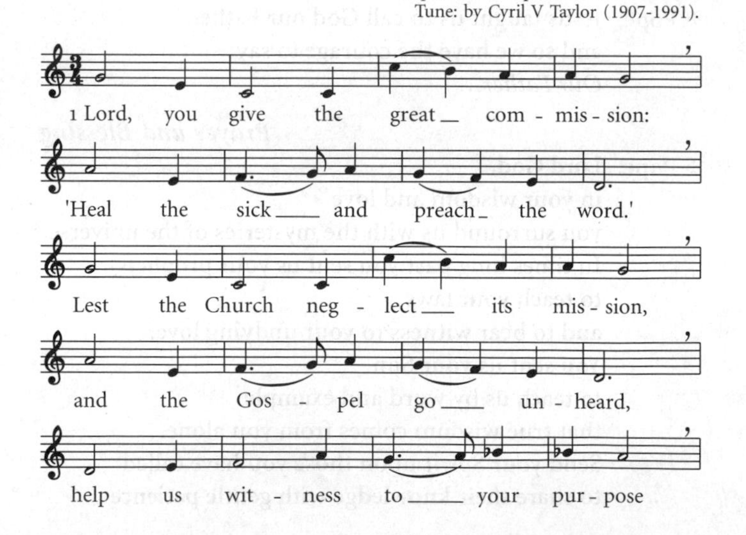
1 Lord, you give the great_ com - mis - sion:
'Heal the sick___ and preach_ the word.'
Lest the Church neg - lect___ its mis - sion,
and the Gos - pel go___ un - heard,
help us wit - ness to___ your pur - pose

with re - newed in - te - gri - ty;
With the Spi - rit's gifts em - power us
for the work of mi - ni - stry.

2. Lord, you call us to your service:
'In my name baptise and teach.'
That the world may trust your promise,
life abundant meant for each,
give us all new fervour,
draw us closer in community;
With the Spirit's gifts empower us
for the work of ministry.

3. Lord, you show us love's true measure;
'Father, what they do, forgive.'
Yet we hoard as private treasure
all that you so freely give.
May your care and mercy lead us
to a just society;
With the Spirit's gifts empower us
for the work of ministry.

4. Lord, you bless with words assuring:
'I am with you to the end.'
Faith and hope and love restoring,
may we serve as you intend,
and, amid the cares that claim us,
hold in mind eternity;
With the Spirit's gifts empower us
for the work of ministry.

CATHOLIC EDUCATION IN ENGLAND AND WALES

The Catholic Education Service
For England and Wales

The Church was arguably the first provider of schools and universities in England. Following the Reformation in the 16th century, the Catholic Church's role as a provider of public education went largely underground until the 1800s. In 1847 the Catholic Poor School Committee was established, which focused on the promotion of Catholic primary education. This was followed by the re-establishment of the Catholic hierarchy in England and Wales in 1850. Because the Church has always viewed education as vital to the formation and development of the whole person, it put the setting up of Catholic schools for the Catholic community ahead of building churches, often using its schools in those early days as the place for worship for the parish. In 1905 the Catholic Education Council was established as the overarching organisation to promote Catholic Education in England and Wales on behalf of the Catholic Bishops (this later became the Catholic Education Service for England and Wales).

Catholic schools continued to be established throughout the late nineteenth and early twentieth century, which, at a time when state involvement in education was still very limited, meant that Catholic parents from underprivileged backgrounds were nevertheless able to send their children to school. Service to those who are amongst the most disadvantaged in our society has also always been central to the mission of Catholic education. Many Catholic schools were established in the 19th century to meet the needs of poor Catholic immigrants from Ireland and that mission remains strong today, with Catholic schools frequently receiving the disadvantaged from the new immigrant populations from across the world. Catholic dioceses today remain conscious of their responsibility to meet the needs of established local Catholic families, Catholic traveller children and Catholic immigrants from other parts of the world, especially Eastern Europe and parts of Africa, Latin America and South East Asia.

In 1944 the educational landscape across England and Wales changed forever with the passing of the Education Act 1944 (also known as the "Butler Act"). This act promised "secondary education for all" and increased the school leaving age to 15, meaning that all children from the post-war generation received a minimum of 10 years of education.

Under the Butler Act, Catholic schools became "voluntary aided" schools. This meant that they became part of the state system of education, whilst retaining their distinctively Catholic ethos through various legal protections which continue to apply to Catholic schools to this day. The agreement between Church and State meant that the funding of Catholic schools was shared by the Catholic foundations of the schools (in most cases the dioceses or religious orders) and by the government. Today, the Catholic Church contributes around £20 million every year towards the capital costs of its schools.

In 2010, there are over 2300 Catholic schools across England and Wales (Catholic schools make up approximately 10% of the total number of schools nationally). The universality of the Catholic Church means that these schools are the most ethnically diverse of all maintained schools in England and are on a par with other schools in terms of social inclusivity criteria. Ofsted data shows that Catholic schools excel academically and pastorally, and are consistently rated better than other maintained schools in terms of what Ofsted describe as the school's "overall effectiveness".

The Church is also involved in higher education in England through its three university colleges (St Mary's in Twickenham, Newman College in Birmingham and Leeds Trinity) and one joint Anglican-Catholic university (Liverpool Hope). This continues the long-established involvement of the Church in higher education in England, which dates back to at least the 13th century. Prior to the Reformation, the Church played a major role in the development of Oxford and Cambridge Universities.

Following the restoration of the Catholic hierarchy, the Bishops' intention to establish schools meant that teacher training became a priority. With this in mind, a number of teacher training colleges were established (St Mary's, established in 1850, is one of the oldest). Some of these teacher training colleges have now been subsumed into larger universities, and others have expanded to become university colleges and universities in their own right. Thus, higher education in the Catholic tradition continues to flourish.

Through its involvement in primary and secondary education, the Catholic Church currently educates over 800,000 pupils across England and Wales, in addition to the thousands of students involved in Catholic higher education. As such its stake in education is not only deeply embedded in our country's history, through its continued collaboration with the state via the dual system, but is something that the Church continues to place an enormously high priority on in 2010.

[CELEBRATION OF CATHOLIC EDUCATION]

SIYAHAMBA – WE ARE WALKING IN THE LIGHT OF GOD

Sign of the Cross and Greeting

✠ **Pope:** In the name of the Father, and of the Son, and of the Holy Spirit.
All: **Amen.**
✠ **Pope:** Peace be with you.
All: **And also with you.**

A student of St Mary's University College introduces Bishop Malcolm McMahon OP, Bishop of Nottingham and Chairman of the Catholic Education Service of England and Wales, who formally welcomes the Holy Father.

A variety of songs and symbolic actions follow which represent the rich diversity of traditions and dimensions of education in the United Kingdom and beyond.

Litany of Commitment

The assembly repeats each line after the reader:

Primary student: God has made me for his own – R
God wants me to do his work – R

Teacher: God has given me a special place in his world – R
God has given me a mission – R

Governor: God has made me a link in a chain – R
God asks me to work together with those who do good – R

Diocesan Education Officer:
I want to do God's work – R
I want to do what is good – R

Secondary student: I want to be his angel of peace – R
I shall speak his word wherever I am – R

University Teacher: I will keep his commandments – R
I trust my God because he knows what he is doing – R

Vote of thanks from a young person

Address by The Holy Father

The Lord's Prayer

Pope Benedict invites those present and all following on television or on the internet to join together in praying the Our Father:

Our Father,
who art in heaven,
hallowed be thy name.
Thy kingdom come.
Thy will be done,
on earth as it is in heaven.
Give us this day our daily bread
and forgive us our trespasses,
as we forgive those who trespass against us.
And lead us not into temptation,
but deliver us from evil.

Apostolic Blessing

✠ **Pope:** The Lord be with you.
All: And also with you.

✠ **Pope:** May the Lord bless you and keep you.
All: Amen.

✠ Pope: May his face shine upon you,
and be gracious to you.
All: Amen.

✠ Pope: May he look upon you with kindness,
and give you his peace.
All: Amen.

✠ Pope: May almighty God bless you, the Father ✠,
and the Son ✠, and the Holy ✠ Spirit.
All: Amen.

Recessional Hymns

Fill Your Hearts

Timothy Dudley-Smith, © Oxford University Press.

Fill your hearts with joy and gladness,
sing and praise your God and mine!
Great the Lord in love and wisdom,
might and majesty divine!
He who framed the starry heavens
knows and names them as they shine.

Praise the Lord, his people, praise him!
wounded souls his comfort know;
those who fear him find his mercies,
peace for pain and joy for woe;
humble hearts are high exalted,
human pride and power laid low.

Praise the Lord for times and seasons,
cloud and sunshine, wind and rain;
spring to melt the snows of winter
till the waters flow again;
grass upon the mountain pastures,
golden valleys thick with grain.

Fill your hearts with joy and gladness,
peace and plenty crown your days;
love his laws, declare his judgments,
walk in all his words and ways;
he the Lord and we his children--
praise the Lord, all people, praise!

Tell Out, My Soul
Timothy Dudley-Smith, © Oxford University Press.

Tell out, my soul, the greatness of the Lord!
Unnumbered blessings give my spirit voice;
tender to me the promise of his word;
in God my Saviour shall my heart rejoice.

Tell out, my soul, the greatness of his Name!
Make known his might, the deeds his arm has done;
his mercy sure, from age to age to same;
his holy Name--the Lord, the Mighty One.

Tell out, my soul, the greatness of his might!
Powers and dominions lay their glory by.
Proud hearts and stubborn wills are put to flight,
the hungry fed, the humble lifted high.

Tell out, my soul, the glories of his word!
Firm is his promise, and his mercy sure.
Tell out, my soul, the greatness of the Lord
to children's children and for evermore!

THE CATHOLIC CHURCH AND THE 2012 OLYMPICS

With less than two years to go, the 2012 Olympic and Paralympic Games will see thousands of people visiting London and other cities across England, Scotland and Wales for the world's largest sporting event.

The Catholic bishops of England and Wales are encouraging the Church's engagement at the heart of the 2012 Games in every way possible (www.catholic2012.com). The Scottish bishops are also preparing the Catholic community to play as great a role as possible in the 2014 Commonwealth Games in Glasgow. Engagement is happening primarily through the ecumenical endeavour *More Than Gold* (www.morethangold.org.uk) which offers many ways to show support for, and to get involved with, the Games.

Engagement is also being encouraged at school, parish and diocesan levels. The Games provide an opportunity for the UK's Catholic family to welcome every nation to our shores between July and September 2012.

The legacy of the Games, especially for young people, is also in the minds of the bishops and during his visit Pope Benedict launches the UK's *John Paul II Foundation for Sport* as a foundation that will serve as both a resource and servant of the world of sport, drawing on the inspiration of Pope John Paul that sport embodies what it is to be fully alive as human beings and to display the glory of God.

Dialogue between the Catholic Church and other religions in Britain

Peter Fleetwood

Britain's history as a seafaring nation, its colonial past and its strong economic links with so many parts of the world partly explain the arrival of many migrants over the centuries, many of whom have brought with them strong and proud religious traditions, so the art of dialogue is well established here. Immigration from the Indian sub-continent brought communities of Hindus, Sikhs and Muslims, which are well established around London, Bristol, Cardiff, the West Midlands and the industrial towns of Lancashire and Yorkshire. Shared values – for example, a respect for the sacredness of life – often bring Catholics close to members of the other major religions.

But there is inevitably a shadow side; in straitened economic circumstances, caricatures of other people's cultures and religions can create misunderstandings and sometimes even lead to violence. So there is a practical need for religious leaders to encourage their fellow-believers to be more aware of their neighbours' religious beliefs and traditions.

The Catholic Church in every diocese is involved in "inter-faith" organisations, and the same is true at the national level. In England and Wales, the Bishops' Conference's Committee for Relations with Other Religions operates a network of diocesan representatives involved in dialogue with other religions, and over the years the Committee has published about 30 leaflets and booklets to help people discover more about other religions.

In the spring of 2010, the Bishops published a teaching document entitled *Meeting God in Friend and Stranger: fostering mutual respect and understanding between the religions*, which reminds all Catholics that they are called by their baptism to engage in dialogue with others, and specifically with people of other religions. The document stresses that this dialogue is not limited to academics, but takes place where everyday life is shared in an atmosphere of respect and openness. Current government directives on education place great emphasis on the need for "Community Cohesion", and all schools are required to prove that they are making children aware of it. There is no doubt that the government's concern has grown out of a new awareness of the significance of religion since September, 2001, but it means that positive relationships between the adherents of different religions are being encouraged throughout society.

The part played by the Churches in this area is generally welcomed, and *Meeting God in Friend and Stranger* will potentially add depth to a discussion that often tends to "equalise" all religions; indeed, the document stresses that, although motivations for dialogue may be different, there is every reason for Catholics, particularly at a local level, to be involved. *Meeting God in Friend and Stranger* is realistic in its recognition that the road of dialogue is a long one, but it also lists many positive initiatives and examples of good practice all over England and Wales. Pope Benedict is visiting countries where dialogue is urgently needed, but where the Catholic Church at every level remains firmly committed to it.

> "From one ancestor he made all nations to inhabit the whole earth, and he allotted the times of their existence and the boundaries of the places where they would live, so that they would search for God and perhaps grope for him and find him – though indeed he is not far from each one of us."
>
> Acts of the Apostles 17: 26-27.

The search for unity

Mgr Andrew Faley

I pray not only for these (you have given me), but also for those who through their teaching will come to believe in me. May they all be one just as, Father, you are in me and I am in you, so that they also may be in us, so that the world may believe it was you who sent me. (John 17: 20ff)

Christ's prayer to his Father is the kindly light in the search for the unity of the Church. God stirs in us the desire for unity, which is as human as it is Divine. It is a desire that causes Christians to reach out to each other, and to all people: it is at the heart of the mission of the Church. Whichever way you approach Christian belief, you come to the same truth: that Jesus Christ, the Word made flesh, in whom divinity and humanity are perfectly united, is the source and heart of all unity.

In Jesus Christ, God invites all people and all creation into union with himself. In Jesus Christ, the Church serves this activity, which is measurable in its effects, changing and challenging in its outcomes, hindered by weakness and sin, but never overcome. This is the Communion of the Church to which all Christians belong. This is the new People of God, the Church.

Yet the Church on earth is divided. In our country the consequence of the Reformation of the 15th and 16th centuries and other historical events which fragmented the Church are still with us. At the same time Christian churches in the United Kingdom have become renowned for the quality of relationship between them and their sustained commitment in working for unity. Even so the ecumenical journey towards the full unity of the Church is not and has not been an easy one. It has had its high as well as its low points and the experience of journeying together continues to challenge each church to be true to itself as well as open to the truth of the other.

During this Papal visit Pope Benedict will participate in Evening Prayer in Westminster Abbey, accompanied by the Archbishop of Canterbury and many other Christian leaders including Catholic, Orthodox and Anglican Bishops and leaders of the Free Churches and other Christian traditions. This time of prayer, in which Christians across our nation will also take part, itself demonstrates the journey that the Christian churches have taken from being strangers to one another, to becoming true friends and pilgrims. The very place of celebration with its profound place in the history of the Church in the United Kingdom, and its close association with the Monarchy, is an expression of how close the churches have grown towards each other in recent years on their pilgrimage towards what Jesus prayed for.

Some of the first words spoken by Pope Benedict following his election confirmed his personal commitment to the full unity of the Church. He said:

> "Peter's current Successor takes on as his primary task the duty to work tirelessly to rebuild the full and visible unity of all Christ's followers. This is his ambition, his impelling duty." (Initial Message of Pope Benedict XVI, April 20, 2005.)

Over the past fifty years, the Catholic Church in the United Kingdom has committed itself to the same goal. At the same time as trying achieve a theological consensus and working towards a visible unity between the churches, these churches have together worked to better serve the needs of the poor and the outcast in modern society. In this way, the degrees of unity that have been achieved are intimately bound to the mission of the Church to the world.

The growth in friendly relations and understanding between churches, especially over the past fifty years, and the development of ecumenical life that is now taken for granted, is a precious gift of God. It is often our human tendency to want quick fixes, and to fall into apathy if they are not achieved. But the ecumenical journey in our countries shows that true Christian unity will only come about by patient prayer, and deepening and genuine understanding and love. Called to be one by Jesus Christ, the churches continue to discern in their cooperation what it is that unites and what needs to be understood in what still divides.

Over these years, Christians in our countries have learned what it means to move from cooperation to commitment. This requires a change of heart and a trust in believing that God is always greater, and that his gifts can always surprise us. In growing closer to each other through God's grace, Christians are learning how to value the gifts that the other brings, rather than relying on what it is they have to offer. In this way, the path towards full unity opens out to new ways of knowing and loving, not for ourselves alone, but for the sake of the world that the Church is sent to serve.

The Evening Prayer in Westminster Abbey is a celebration of Christian faith for the sake of the world which the Church serves, in Christ's name. As such, it is also an expression of true commitment to the search for unity, and to deep spiritual conversion, which means a change of heart and mind for all Christians. Pope John Paul II spoke of this repeatedly throughout his ministry and Pope Benedict calls us to the same conversion. Like all conversion, it is beyond our powers and can only be achieved by the graciousness of God. It is a measure of this abiding graciousness of God that Christians are gathered with Pope Benedict and other Christian leaders in Westminster Abbey in prayerful faith and enduring hope.

WESTMINSTER HALL

Almost one thousand years of the Nation's history are contained within the ancient walls of Westminster Hall at the Palace of Westminster. The tall grey walls of the hall give little away today of the pomp and ceremony of the past.

Built for William Rufus the Hall was completed in time for him to celebrate Whitsun on May 29, 1099. The new hall was to provide a place for feasting and for the entertainment of foreign heads of state on a prodigious scale. On the dais at the southern end, the king's throne behind the table faced down the length of the hall; here new monarchs were seated for the coronation breakfast at which they received the acclamation by the peers. From the 12th century onwards, following the service in Westminster Abbey, the hall was also used for the coronation banquets of every monarch from King Richard I (1189) until King George IV (1821). The close ties between Church and State have continued to be maintained at Westminster for centuries.

Westminster Hall was gradually appropriated by the judiciary, with the first judges sitting there by 1178. It was the place in which the English legal system was developed over several centuries. The king's council, or Curia Regis, developed over time to include three common law courts: the exchequer, the common pleas and the king's (or queen's) bench. The hall witnessed many great state trials including those of King Charles I (1649) and Sir Thomas More (1535) who were tried for treason, subsequently found guilty and executed. Thomas More was canonised by Pius XI in 1935, the 400th anniversary of his death. The courts continued to sit inside, or adjacent to the Hall, until 1883.

A major remodelling of the hall in the Gothic style took place between 1394 and 1401. Stone towers were added to the north façade to give the entrance greater prominence and the walls were raised by 2 feet – the master mason was Henry Yevele. Inside the hall the string course decoration beneath the windows bears the arms and symbols of the king who commissioned it, Richard II, the chained White Hart and the Helm, together with the arms of Edward the Confessor. Over 600 tons of oak were brought for the creation of a new and spectacular roof by the king's master carpenter, Hugh Herland. The hammer beam construction was a masterpiece of medieval English carpentry and design which succeeded in spanning at high level the full interior space of the hall – 73 metres (239.5 feet) in length by 21 metres (67.5 feet) in width.

Thirteen roof trusses were made in total, and almost certainly represent Christ and the twelve Apostles, the authority of the holy judges represented by the king on earth. The carved angels at the end of each hammer beam hold shields bearing the coat of arms of the king.

The Hall has been used for the Lying in State of monarchs and queen consorts since King Edward VII, and of two great statesmen, William Ewart Gladstone (1898) and Sir Winston Churchill (1965). Here too addresses to Parliament have been given by Her Majesty the Queen and, among others, President Mandela of South Africa.

WESTMINSTER ABBEY

Not only is Westminster Abbey steeped in more than a thousand years of British history, it has a key and developing contemporary role in the centre of national life, and as a place of welcome and prayer for millions of worshippers and visitors. Benedictine monks first settled on the site in the middle of the 10th century, establishing a tradition of Christian community life that continues to this day. The venue for the coronation of our monarchs since 1066, it is the final resting place of seventeen of them. The present church, begun in 1245, is one of the most important Gothic buildings in the country; with the shrine of the medieval saint Edward the Confessor at its heart. A treasure-house of centuries of art, it has become the place where some of the most significant people and events in the nation's history are remembered.

The daily and communal life of Westminster Abbey revolves around Morning and Evening Prayer and the Eucharist, to which special services are added to mark significant occasions. Its mission, overseen by the Dean and Chapter, is to serve God as a "school of the Lord's service" (as St Benedict described community life) by offering daily and public worship; to serve the Sovereign by daily prayer and by a ready response to requests; to serve the nation by fostering true religion within national life, maintaining a close relationship with Parliament; and to serve pilgrims and all other visitors by a tradition of hospitality. Here the Pope will share with Christians from across the United Kingdom and from a wide variety of denominations in the Abbey's tradition of daily prayer.

SHRINE OF ST EDWARD

The chapel containing the shrine of Saint Edward the Confessor (king 1042-66) lies beyond the high altar at the spiritual and architectural focal point of Westminster Abbey. The king's body was buried in 1066 in front of the high altar, but Edward was declared a saint in 1161 and, two years later, the first shrine was erected. The present shrine, made by workmen from Italy in the Cosmati style of the pavement that surrounds both the high altar and the shrine, was part of Henry III's rebuilt church. On October 13, 1269, Saint Edward's body was brought to its new resting place – and that date is celebrated by the Church each year as his feast. Above the decorated stone base was a gold feretory containing the saint's coffin, with an adjustable canopy. The Shrine was dismantled after the dissolution of the monastery in 1540 but reassembled in 1556 with much of the decoration damaged. The saint's body now lies in a hollow in the top of the stone base under a wooden canopy. The Archbishop of Canterbury and the Pope will join the long tradition of pilgrims praying at this holy place.

A SERVICE OF EVENING PRAYER

Westminster Abbey

in the presence of

His Holiness Pope Benedict XVI

and

His Grace The Archbishop of Canterbury

• The Arrival •

His Holiness The Pope and His Grace The Archbishop of Canterbury are received at the Great West Door by The Dean and Chapter of Westminster.

The Very Reverend Dr John Hall, Dean of Westminster, welcomes His Holiness The Pope to The Collegiate Church of St Peter in Westminster and invites His Holiness to pray at the Grave of the Unknown Warrior.

The Pope says a Prayer for Peace:

> **Lord God, you hold both heaven and earth in a single peace. Let the design of your great love shine on the waste of our anger and sorrow, and give peace to your Church, peace among nations, peace in our homes, and peace in our hearts, in Jesus Christ our Lord. Amen.**

Leaders of the Churches in the British Isles are presented to The Pope.

The Pope and The Archbishop retire to the Jericho Parlour to vest, during which the Choir of Westminster Abbey sings and the Procession of Church Leaders moves to places in the Sacrarium.

• The Opening Rite •

CHOIR

**The glory of the Lord has risen upon us.
Let us rejoice and sing God's praise for ever.
Glory be. Alleluia.**

HYMN

Westminster Abbey, 205 NEH - Latin, c7th–8th c. - trans. J. Mason Neale (1818-1866).

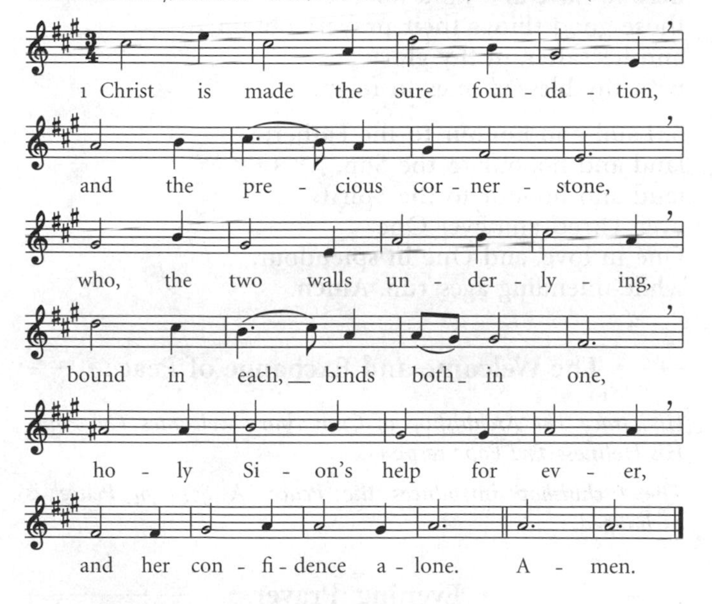

1 Christ is made the sure foun - da - tion,
and the pre - cious cor - ner - stone,
who, the two walls un - der - ly - ing,
bound in each, binds both in one,
ho - ly Si - on's help for ev - er,
and her con - fi - dence a - lone. A - men.

**2. All that dedicated city,
dearly loved by God on high,
in exultant jubilation
pours perpetual melody,
God the One, in threefold glory,
singing everlastingly**

3. To this temple, where we call thee,
come, O Lord of hosts, today;
with thy wonted loving-kindness,
hear thy people as they pray;
and thy fullest benediction
shed within its walls for ay.

4. Here vouchsafe to all thy servants
gifts of grace by prayer to gain;
here to have and hold for ever,
those good things their prayers obtain,
and hereafter, in thy glory,
with thy blessèd ones to reign.

5. Laud and honour to the Father;
laud and honour to the Son,
laud and honour to the Spirit,
ever Three, and ever One,
One in love, and One in splendour,
while unending ages run. Amen.

• The Welcome and Exchange of Peace •

His Grace The Archbishop of Canterbury welcomes The Pope.
His Holiness The Pope responds.

The Archbishop introduces the Peace. A Sign of Peace is exchanged.

• Evening Prayer •

CHOIR: PSALM 138

I will give thanks unto thee, O Lord, with my whole heart: even before the gods will I sing praise unto thee.

I will worship toward thy holy temple, and praise thy name, because of thy loving-kindness and truth: for thou hast magnified thy name, and thy Word, above all things.

When I called upon thee, thou heardest me: and enduedst my soul with much strength.

All the kings of the earth shall praise thee, O Lord: for they have heard the words of thy mouth.

Yea, they shall sing in the ways of the Lord: that great is the glory of the Lord.

For though the Lord be high, yet hath he respect unto the lowly: as for the proud, he beholdeth them afar off.

Though I walk in the midst of trouble, yet shalt thou refresh me: thou shalt stretch forth thy hand upon the furiousness of mine enemies, and thy right hand shall save me.

The Lord shall make good his loving-kindness toward me: yea, thy mercy, O Lord, endureth for ever; despise not then the works of thine own hands.

Glory be to the Father, and to the Son: and to the Holy Ghost; as it was in the beginning, is now, and ever shall be: world without end. Amen.

A reading from the Letter to the Philippians 2:5–11

LET THE SAME MIND be in you that was in Christ Jesus, who, though he was in the form of God, did not regard equality with God as something to be exploited, but emptied himself, taking the form of a slave, being born in human likeness. And being found in human form, he humbled himself and became obedient to the point of death – even death on a cross. Therefore God also

highly exalted him and gave him the name that is above every name, so that at the name of Jesus every knee should bend, in heaven and on earth and under the earth, and every tongue should confess that Jesus Christ is Lord, to the glory of God the Father.

HYMN

Hereford 431 NEH — Charles Wesley (1707–1788).

1 O thou_ who cam - est from_ a - bove_
the fire_ ce - les - tial to_ im - part,_
kin - dle a flame_ of_ sa - cred love_
on the_ mean al - tar of_ my heart!

2. There let it for thy glory burn
with inextinguishable blaze,
and trembling to its source return
in humble prayer, and fervent praise.

3. Jesus, confirm my heart's desire
to work, and speak, and think for thee;
still let me guard the holy fire,
and still stir up thy gift in me.

4. Ready for all thy perfect will,
my acts of faith and love repeat,
till death thy endless mercies seal,
and make the sacrifice complete.

A reading from
the Gospel according to St Mark 10:35–45

JAMES AND JOHN, the sons of Zebedee, came forward to him and said to him, 'Teacher, we want you to do for us whatever we ask of you.' And he said to them, 'What is it you want me to do for you?' And they said to him, 'Grant us to sit, one at your right hand and one at your left, in your glory.' But Jesus said to them, 'You do not know what you are asking. Are you able to drink the cup that I drink, or be baptized with the baptism that I am baptized with?' They replied, 'We are able.' Then Jesus said to them, 'The cup that I drink you will drink; and with the baptism with which I am baptized, you will be baptized; but to sit at my right hand or at my left is not mine to grant, but it is for those for whom it has been prepared.' When the ten heard this, they began to be angry with James and John. So Jesus called them and said to them, 'You know that among the Gentiles those whom they recognise as their rulers lord it over them, and their great ones are tyrants over them. But it is not so among you; but whoever wishes to become great among you must be your servant, and whoever wishes to be first among you must be slave to all. For the Son of Man came not to be served but to serve, and to give his life as a ransom for many.'

After the proclamation of the Gospel, The Archbishop and The Pope venerate the St Augustine (or Canterbury) Gospels, the volume of the Gospels brought to Canterbury from Rome by St Augustine in the 6th Century.

The Pope and The Archbishop exchange Addresses.

The Choir sings Magnificat during which The Dean venerates with incense the Altar and the Church Leaders.

MAGNIFICAT

Charles Villiers Stanford (1852-1924).

My soul doth magnify the Lord: and my spirit hath rejoiced in God my Saviour.

For he hath regarded: the lowliness of his handmaiden.

For behold, from henceforth: all generations shall call me blessed.

For he that is mighty hath magnified me: and holy is his Name.

And his mercy is on them that fear him: throughout all generations.

He hath shewed strength with his arm: he hath scattered the proud in the imagination of their hearts.

He hath put down the mighty from their seat: and hath exalted the humble and meek.

He hath filled the hungry with good things: and the rich he hath sent empty away.

He remembering his mercy hath holpen his servant Israel: as he promised to our forefathers, Abraham and his seed, for ever.

Glory be to the Father, and to the Son: and to the Holy Ghost;

As it was in the beginning, is now, and ever shall be: world without end. Amen.

Bidding Prayers

Let us bless the Lord:	or	Lord, hear us:
thanks be to God.		**Lord, graciously hear us**

Our Father,
Who art in heaven
Hallowed be thy name.

Thy kingdom come,
Thy will be done
On earth as it is in heaven.
Give us this day our daily bread
And forgive us our trespasses
As we forgive those who trespass against us.
And lead us not into temptation,
But deliver us from evil.

For thine is the kingdom, the power,
and the glory, for ever and ever. Amen.

ANTHEM

Maurice Duruflé (1902-1986): Antiphon at the foot-washing, Maundy Thursday.

Ubi caritas et amor, Deus ibi est. Congregavit nos in unum Christi amor. Exsultemus et in ipso jucundemur. Timeamus et amemus Deum vivum. Et ex corde diligamus nos sincero. Amen.

Where charity and love are, there is God. The love of Christ has brought us together into one flock. Let us rejoice and let us be glad in that love. Let us fear and love the living God; and let us love one another from a pure heart. Amen.

— • Prayers at the shrine of Saint Edward • —

The Archbishop says a Prayer for the Church and the nations:

Lord God, ruler of heaven and earth, in your mercy grant the increase of peace and justice in this our nation and in the community of nations. Bless all who witness to the gospel's call in the public life of our countries; and strengthen the Church's vision of your eternal kingdom, so that we may with courage and persistence serve the common good, and hold before all men and women the challenge and the promise of your righteousness. In the name of Jesus, our Servant and our King. **Amen.**

The Pope says a Prayer for the Unity of the Church:

Lord, hear the prayers of your people, and bring the hearts of believers together in your praise and in common sorrow for their sins. Heal the divisions among Christians; that we may rejoice in the perfect unity of your Church, and move together as one to eternal life in your kingdom. Grant this through our Lord Jesus Christ, your Son, who lives and reigns with you and the Holy Spirit, one God, for ever and ever. Amen.

• The Concluding Rite •

HYMN

Michael 333 NEH Robert Bridges (1844-1930) / Herbert Howells (1892-1983).

1 All my hope on God _ is __ found - ed;
he doth still my trust __ re - new.
Me through change and chance he gui - deth,
on - ly good and on - ly true.
God un - known, he a - lone
calls my heart _ to be __ his own.

2. Daily doth th'Almighty giver
bounteous gifts on us bestow;
his desire our soul delighteth,
pleasure leads us where we go.
Love doth stand at his hand;
joy doth wait on his command.

3. Still from man to God eternal
sacrifice of praise be done,
high above all praises praising
for the gift of Christ his Son.
Christ doth call one and all:
ye who follow shall not fall.

The Archbishop and The Pope jointly pronounce the Blessing:

May God the Holy Trinity make you strong in faith and love, defend you on every side, and guide you in truth and peace; and the blessing of almighty God, the Father, the Son, and the Holy Spirit, be among you and remain with you always. Amen.

The Procession moves to the west end of the church.

The bells of the Abbey Church are rung.

The service was sung by The Choir of Westminster Abbey, conducted by James O'Donnell, Organist and Master of the Choristers. The organ was played by Robert Quinney, Sub-Organist.

(The full text of this Order of Service can be downloaded from the Westminster Abbey website at www.westminster-abbey.org.)

OFFICIAL DINNER

On the evening of September 17, 2010, the UK Government will host a dinner for the *Seguito*, the official delegation from the Holy See accompanying the Pope. It will be held at Lancaster House in central London and will be a working dinner, offering an opportunity for discussion of areas where the UK Government and the Holy See share interests and goals. The Holy See and the UK Government work closely together on a wide range of issues. These include support for international development and an end to poverty; better access to education in developing countries; tackling climate change and helping developing countries to deal with its impacts; preventing and resolving conflict; and finding ways to encourage disarmament.

Saturday, September 18

The third day of the Papal visit

England

The first part of the third day of the visit begins at Westminster Cathedral. There, in Archbishop's House, Pope Benedict XVI will meet the Prime Minister and other senior politicians, including the Leader of the Opposition. Following this the Holy Father celebrates Mass in Westminster Cathedral, a Mass in honour of the Precious Blood (the dedication of the Cathedral). Immediately following the Mass the Holy Father will greet young people from all the parishes of England and Wales and Scotland, gathered in the piazza of the Cathedral. Returning to the Cathedral he will bless a new mosaic of Saint David which is to be installed there, and will offer a greeting to the people of Wales.

During the afternoon Pope Benedict will visit St Peter's Residence, Vauxhall, a residence for the elderly, and then will return north of the Thames to take part in a Prayer Vigil in Hyde Park.

Programme

09.00: Courtesy calls from the Prime Minister, Deputy Prime Minister and Acting Leader of the Opposition.

10.00: Pope Benedict XVI presides at the celebration of Mass in Westminster Cathedral.

- Greeting of young people in the Piazza of Westminster Cathedral.
- Greeting to the people of Wales with prayer at the Statue of Our Lady of the Taper and blessing of the mosaic of Saint David.

17.00: Pastoral Visit to St Peter's Residence, Vauxhall.

18.15: Popemobile journey through London to Hyde Park.

18.30: Pope Benedict XVI participates in Evening Prayer Vigil in Hyde Park.

19.45: Pope Benedict returns to the Apostolic Nunciature.

The Catholic Church and the British Government

HE Mr Francis Campbell
Her Majesty's Ambassador to the Holy See

The Catholic Church plays a unique role on the world stage. Globally and locally it is active whether through delivering health and education services at the grassroots level, or lobbying world leaders on important global issues such as climate change and conflict resolution. This global presence gives the Catholic Church a unique position in the fight against poverty.

The Holy See has an unusually large global reach because the Catholic Church has over 1.15 billion adherents (17.5% of the world's population, including over 10% of the UK population). It reaches into every corner of the planet through its 500,000 priests, 800,000 sisters/nuns, 219,655 parishes. The Holy See has serious influence in as many countries as are in the Commonwealth, a privileged status as interlocutor with the two other Abrahamic faiths – Islam and Judaism – and two generations of intense experience in inter-faith dialogue and many centuries of co-existence. The Holy See is one of the world's oldest organisations with a continuous history from the period of the Emperor Constantine in the 4th century AD.

The UK and the Holy See

The Crown's first resident ambassador was sent to the Pope in 1479, making the embassy to the Holy See the UK's oldest embassy. John Shirwood was appointed by King Edward IV as the first resident Ambassador to the Holy See. Formal diplomatic relations between the Crown and the Holy See were interrupted in 1536. Formal diplomatic links were restored in 1553, but ceased again in 1559 until they were restored in 1914. However, unofficial ties between the UK and the Holy See were maintained through much of the 18th and 19th centuries: for example, Lord Odo Russell was the UK's unofficial Minister to the Holy See from 1858 to 1870. The United Kingdom re-established formal resident diplomatic relations with the Holy See in 1914.

Today the UK and Holy See are actively engaged in many areas of international policy. The Holy See is a crucial partner to the international community in the area of international development and a key ally in making progress on many of the Millennium Development Goals. The Catholic Church is reckoned to be the world's second largest international development body after the UN. Caritas Internationalis is a Vatican body which brings together some 160 national Catholic Aid agencies under a single umbrella (including CAFOD in England and Wales and SCIAF in Scotland). More than 50% of the hospitals in Africa are operated under the auspices of faith-based organisations, with the Catholic Church in

Africa being responsible for nearly one quarter of all health care provision. The Catholic Church is one of biggest global health providers. It runs 5,246 hospitals, 17,530 dispensaries, 577 leprosy clinics, 15,208 houses for the elderly, chronically ill and people with physical and learning disabilities worldwide. Catholic Church agencies provide a quarter of all HIV care in Africa. In education too, the Catholic Church provides around 12 million school places in Sub Saharan Africa each year, thereby offering educational opportunities to many millions of young people to help them out of poverty.

The Pope regularly writes to world leaders ahead of crucial G8 and G20 summits, reminding them not to forget the plight of the poor in the developing world. And in November 2006 he bought the first Immunisation Bond, which was an initiative led by the UK. To date, the Bond has raised over $1.6 billion to spend on health and immunisation programmes in 70 of the world's poorest countries. The funds raised will prevent 5 million child deaths between 2006 and 2015, and more than 5 million future adult deaths by protecting more than 500 million children in campaigns against measles, tetanus and yellow fever.

On efforts to tackle climate change, the Holy See is a key ally of the United Kingdom. The Vatican City State is at the forefront of international efforts to become carbon-neutral and to tackle climate change. Pope Benedict's

2009 Encyclical *Caritas in Veritate* focused strongly on environmental issues, calling on the international community to counter mistreatment of the environment, to work to ensure that the costs of exploiting resources are borne by those who incur them, not by future generations, and stressing that the protection of the environment and the climate requires full international co-operation, including with the weakest regions of the world.

The Vatican City State is offsetting its emissions through the planting of trees and installing of solar panels on the Vatican's rooftops. It also recently announced plans to build Europe's largest solar farm on 740 hectares to the north of Rome, which would produce enough energy to power over 40,000 homes and so exceed the EU's renewable energy targets.

On disarmament, the Holy See played a crucial role in achieving the international consensus required to agree a Treaty on Cluster Munitions in 2008. Over 100 states have now signed up to the Treaty, with the Holy See among the first to do so. More recently, in 2009 the Holy See played an important role in encouraging 153 states to support a UN General Assembly Resolution on moving ahead with an Arms Trade Treaty.

The Holy See is in a unique position to help the international community eradicate poverty, tackle conflict, address Climate Change and build strong communities.

WESTMINSTER CATHEDRAL

Westminster Cathedral – the Metropolitan Cathedral of the Most Precious Blood – is the mother church of the Catholic Church in England and Wales. Thus it is the focal point for major occasions in the life of the Church, both nationally and within the Archdiocese of Westminster.

The Cathedral is also the seat of the Archbishop of Westminster. Cardinal Nicholas Wiseman was the first, appointed at the Restoration of the Hierarchy in 1850. His successors have included Cardinals Arthur Hinsley, John Carmel Heenan, George Basil Hume, and Cormac Murphy-O'Connor. Archbishop Vincent Nichols was installed as eleventh Archbishop of Westminster on May 21 2009.

The building of the Cathedral owes much to the energy and vision of Cardinal Herbert Vaughan, the third Archbishop of Westminster. The first stone was laid in 1895; the fabric was completed and the first regular celebrations of Mass and the Divine Office held in 1903; and the Cathedral celebrated the centenary of the consecration earlier this year.

The architectural masterwork of John Francis Bentley, the Cathedral is built in an early Christian Byzantine style – an approach which allowed the structure to be erected in a comparatively short time. The vision for the interior, envisaged from the outset of the Cathedral's planning, is one of rich decoration in mosaic and marble. While future generations will have plenty of scope to play their part in bringing this dream to fruition, much has already been achieved: there are already over 120 different varieties of marble, brought from 24 different countries, installed in the Cathedral. Many of the side-chapels have been adorned with mosaic decoration, the most recent being St Joseph's Chapel in 2006; smaller mosaics of St Anthony and St David have been installed this year, and plans exist for further decoration.

Westminster Cathedral is known not solely for its architecture, but as a community of faith, welcoming many thousands through its doors each week. Many come to receive the Sacraments: to attend Mass, or as parishioners participating in the various sacramental programmes. A particular ministry is exercised in the confessional: for over forty hours a week, a priest is available to celebrate the Sacrament of Reconciliation with many who come to find pardon and peace from God in the Cathedral. Others come simply to find the peace and stillness which is still to be enjoyed at quieter times of day, a valuable commodity indeed among the noise and business of central London.

The Cathedral Choir is justifiably world-famous. It was the wish of Cardinal Vaughan that the dignity of the building should be matched by the nobility of the liturgy and the best of music – an aim shared by Sir Richard Terry, the first Master of Music, and nurtured by those who have followed him over the decades, and who together have established the choral tradition at Westminster Cathedral as amongst the finest in the world. The choir is well-known for its recordings and has toured extensively, but its focus remains the celebration of Mass and the Divine Office. Much of the music sung by the boys and men of the choir each day is that of English and continental Renaissance composers, now in the mainstream of choral repertoire because of the foresight of Terry and his successors in reviving these once-forgotten masterpieces; music from across the centuries in a variety of styles, including contemporary works commissioned specially for Westminster Cathedral choir, are also regularly sung.

The visit of Pope John Paul II to the Cathedral in 1982 is commemorated by a stone set at the foot of the steps into the sanctuary. Much has occurred between the last Papal Visit and the visit of Pope Benedict XVI: the Cathedral has had its hundredth birthday, the decoration is considerably more complete, two more Archbishops have taken their places as successors of Cardinal Wiseman. But the mission and purpose of the Cathedral remains unchanged. And that purpose was well expressed by the late Cardinal Hume when he wrote, 'The remarkable creation which is Westminster Cathedral exists to help us search for God and to offer him worship. It is a home for all. It is a place where we meet Christ, and, in and through Him, gain strength and courage to take another step along the road to God.'

Fr Alexander Master

CELEBRATION OF THE HOLY EUCHARIST
Votive Mass of the Precious Blood
Westminster Cathedral

HYMN DURING PROCESSION OF BISHOPS

Tune: Diedemata (George Elvey, 1816-1893) - Words: Matthew Bridges (1800-1894).

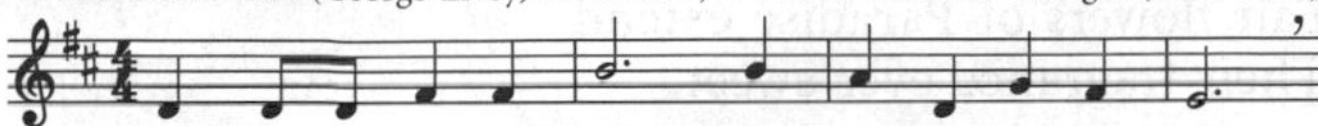
Crown him with ma- ny crowns, The Lamb up- on his throne.

Hark,how the hea-venly an - them drowns All mu-sic but its own:

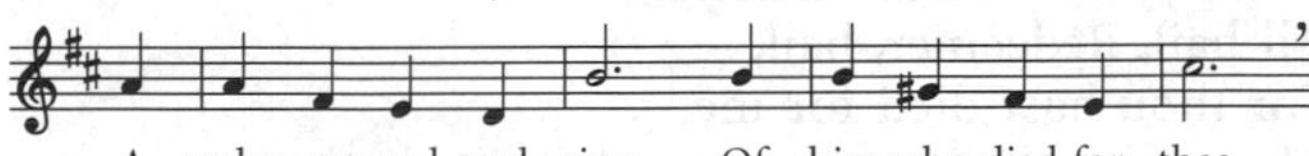
A - wake, my soul, and sing Of him who died for thee,

And hail him as thy match-less King Through all e - ter- ni - ty.

2. Crown him the Virgin's Son,
The God incarnate born,
Whose arm those crimson trophies won
Which now his brow adorn:
Fruit of the mystic Rose,
As of that Rose the Stem;
The Root whence mercy ever flows,
The Babe of Bethlehem.

3. Crown him the Lord of love:
Behold his hands and side,
Rich wounds yet visible above
In beauty glorified:
No angel in the sky
Can fully bear that sight,
But downward bends his burning eye
At mysteries so bright.

4. Crown him the Lord of peace,
Whose power a sceptre sways
From pole to pole, that wars may cease,
Absorbed in prayer and praise:
His reign shall know no end,
And round his piercèd feet
Fair flowers of Paradise extend
Their fragrance ever sweet.

5. Crown him the Lord of heaven,
One with the Father known,
And the blest Spirit through him given
From yonder triune throne:
All hail, Redeemer, hail,
For thou hast died for me,
Thy praise shall never, never fail
Throughout eternity.

INTROIT

Worthy is the Lamb who was slain is to receive strength and divinity, wisdom and power and honour: to him be glory and power forever.

V. O God, give your judgment to the king, to a king's son your justice.

Dignus est Agnus, qui occisus est, accipere virtutem, et divinitatem, et sapientiam, et fortitudinem, et honorem. Ipsi gloria et imperium in sæcula sæculorum.
V. Deus, iudicium tuum Regi da: et iustitiam tuam Filio Regis.

Introductory Dialogue

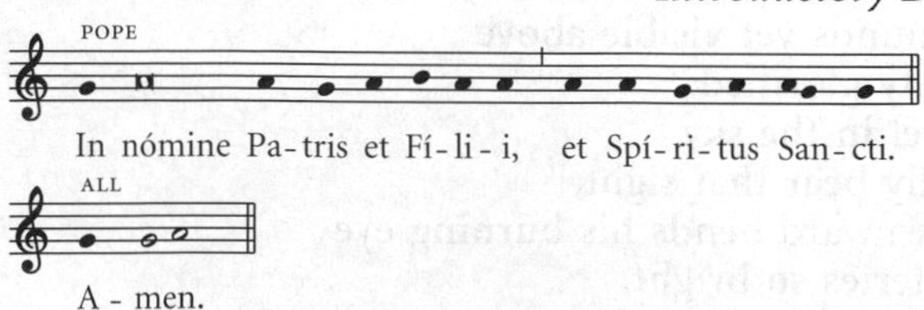

POPE
In nómine Pa-tris et Fí-li-i, et Spí-ri-tus San-cti.
ALL
A - men.

POPE
Pax vo-bis.
ALL
Et cum spí-ri-tu tu-o.

The Penitential Act

✠ **Pope:** My brothers and sisters, to prepare ourselves to celebrate the sacred mysteries, let us call to mind our sins.

All: I confess to almighty God, and to you my brothers and sisters, that I have sinned through my own fault, in my thoughts and in my words, in what I have done and in what I have failed to do; and I ask the Blessed Mary, ever virgin, all the angels and saints, and you, my brothers and sisters, to pray for me to the Lord, our God.

✠ **Pope:** May almighty God have mercy on us, forgive us our sins, and bring us to everlasting life. **Amen.**

Kyrie

Mass for five voices, William Byrd (1540-1623).

Kyrie eleison, Christe eleison, Kyrie eleison.
Lord have mercy, Christ have mercy, Lord have mercy.

Gloria

Mass for five voices, William Byrd (1540-1623).

Gloria in excelsis Deo… *Glory to God in the highest…*

Collect

✠ **Pope:** Father,
by the blood of your own Son
you have set all men free and saved us from death.
Continue your work of love within us,
that by constantly celebrating the mystery of our salvation
we may reach the eternal life it promises.

We ask this through our Lord Jesus Christ, your Son,
who lives and reigns with you and the Holy Spirit,
one God, for ever and ever

All: Amen.

• Liturgy of the Word •

A reading from the letter to the Hebrews 9:11–15

NOW CHRIST HAS COME, as the high priest of all the blessings which were to come. He has passed through the greater, the more perfect tent, which is better than one made by men's hands because it is not of this created order; and he has entered the sanctuary once and for all, taking with him not the blood of goats and bull calves, but his own blood, having won an eternal redemption for us. The blood of goats and bulls and the ashes of a heifer are sprinkled on those who have incurred defilement and they restore the holiness of their outward lives; how much more effectively the blood of Christ, who offered himself as the perfect sacrifice to God through the eternal Spirit, can purify our inner self from dead actions so that we do our service to the living God.

He brings a new covenant, as the mediator, only so that the people who were called to an eternal inheritance may actually receive what was promised: his death took place to cancel the sins that infringed the earlier covenant.

This is the word of the Lord.
Thanks be to God.

PSALM 115

℟ The blessing-cup that we bless is a communion with the blood of Christ.

How can I repay the Lord
  for his goodness to me?
The cup of salvation I will raise:
  I will call on the Lord's name. ℟

O precious in the eyes of the Lord
  is the death of his faithful.
Your servant, Lord, your servant am I;
  you have loosened my bonds. ℟

A thanksgiving sacrifice I make:
  I will call on the Lord's name.
My vows to the Lord I will fulfil
  before all his people. ℟

Alleluia. Caro mea vere est cibus, et sanguis meus vere est potus: qui manducat meam carnem, et bibit meum sanguinem, in me manet, et ego in eo. Alleluia.

My flesh is true food, my blood is true drink; he who eats my flesh and drinks my blood abides in me, and I in him.

Deacon: The Lord be with you.
All: **And also with you.**
Deacon: A reading from the holy Gospel according to John.
All: **Glory to you, Lord.**

A reading from the holy Gospel according to John **12:18–19. 22–24**

IT WAS PREPARATION DAY, and to prevent the bodies remaining on the cross during the sabbath - since that sabbath was a day of special solemnity - the Jews asked Pilate to have the legs broken and the bodies taken away. Consequently the soldiers came and broke the legs of the first man who had been crucified with him and then of the other. When they came to Jesus, they found he was already dead, and so instead of breaking his legs one of the soldiers pierced his side with a lance; and immediately there came out blood and water. This is the evidence of one who saw it - trustworthy evidence, and he knows he speaks the truth - and he gives it so that you may believe as well. Because all this happened to fulfil the words of scripture:

Not one bone of his will be broken;

and again, in another place scripture says:

They will look on the one whom they have pierced.

Deacon: **This is the Gospel of the Lord.**
All: **Praise to you, Lord Jesus Christ.**

Homily

The Profession of Faith

POPE
Cre-do in u-num De-um,
CANTOR
Pa-trem om-ni-po-tén-tem, fac-tó-rem cae-li et ter-rae,
vi-si-bí-li-um ó-mni-um et in-vi-si-bí-li-um.

vi - si - bí - li - um ó - mni - um et in - vi - si - bí - li - um.
ALL
Et in u - num Dó - mi - num Je - sum Chri - stum, Fí - li - um
CANTOR
De - i u - ni - gé - ni - tum. Et ex Pa - tre na - tum
ALL
an - te ó - mni - a saé - cu - la. De - um de De - o
lu - men de lú - mi - ne, De - um ve - rum de De - o ve - ro.
CANTOR
Gé - ni - tum, non fac - tum, con - sub - stan - ti á - lem Pa - tri:
ALL
per quem ó - mni - a fac - ta sunt. Qui prop - ter nos hó - mi - nes,
et prop - ter nos - tram sa - lú - tem des - cén - dit de cae - lis.
CANTOR
Et in - car - ná - tus est de Spí - ri - tu San - cto
ex Ma - ri - a Vir - gi - ne: Et ho - mo fac - tus est.
ALL
Cru - ci - fí - xus ét - i - am pro no - bis
sub Pón - ti - o Pi - la - to pas - sus, et se - púl - tus est.

Et re-sur-re-xit tér-ti-a di-e, se-cún-dum Scri-ptú-ras.
ALL
Et as-cén-dit in cae-lum se-det ad déx-te-ram Pa-tris.
CANTOR
Et í - te - rum ven - tú - rus est cum gló - ri - a,
ju-di-cá-re vi-vos et mór-tu-os : cu-jus re-gni non e-rit fi-nis.
ALL
Et in Spí-ri-tum San-ctum Dó-mi-num et vi-vi-fi-cán-tem :
qui ex Pa - tre Fi - li - ó - que pro - cé - dit.
CANTOR
Qui cum Pa-tre et Fí-li-o si-mul a-do-rá-tur
et con-glo-ri-fi-cá-tur qui lo-cú-tus est per Pro-phé-tas.
ALL
Et u-nam san-ctam ca-thó-li-cam et a-po-stó-li-cam
Ec-clé-si-am.
CANTOR
Con-fí-te-or u-num ba-ptís-ma
in re-mi-si-ó-nem pec-ca-tó-rum.
ALL
Et ex-spéc-to re-sur-re-cti-ó-nem mor-tu-ó-rum.

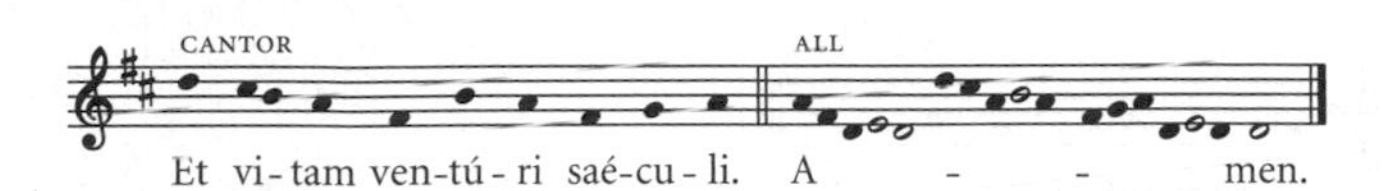

CANTOR
ALL
Et vi-tam ven-tú-ri saé-cu-li. A - - men.

Prayer of the Faithful

Lord, hear us.
Lord, graciously hear us.

• Liturgy of the Eucharist •

OFFERTORY MOTET — Anton Bruckner (1824-1896)

Christus factus est pro nobis oboediens usque ad mortem, mortem autem crucis. Propter quod et Deus exaltavit illum, et dedit illi nomen, quod est super omne nomen.

Christ became obedient for us unto death, even the death of the cross. But God raised him high, and gave him the name which is above all other names.

✠ Pope: Pray, brethren, that our sacrifice may be acceptable to God, the almighty Father.
All: May the Lord accept the sacrifice at your hands for the praise and glory of his name, for our good, and the good of all his Church.

Prayer over the offerings

✠ Pope: Lord,
by offering these gifts in the eucharist
may we come to Jesus, the mediator of the new covenant,
find salvation in the sprinkling of his blood
and draw closer to the kingdom
where he is Lord for ever and ever.
All: Amen.

Preface

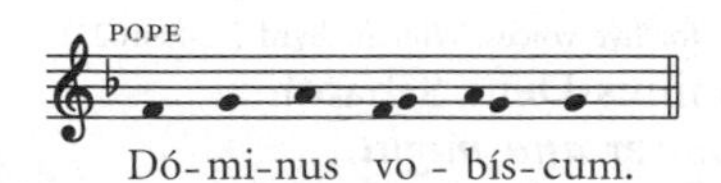

ALL
Et cum spí-ri-tu tu-o.
POPE
Sur-sum cor-da.
ALL
Ha-bé-mus ad Dó-mi-num.
POPE
Grá-ti-as a-gá-mus Dó-mi-no De-o nos-tro.
ALL
Di-gnum et iu-stum est.

Father, all-powerful and ever-living God, we do well always and everywhere to give you thanks.The suffering and death of your Son brought life to the whole world, moving our hearts to praise your glory. The power of the cross reveals your judgement on this world and the kingship of Christ crucified.

We praise you, Lord, with all the angels and saints in their song of joy:

Vere dignum et iustum est, æquum et salutare, nos tibi semper et ubique gratias agere: Domine, sancte Pater, omnipotens æterne Deus: Quia per Filii tui salutiferam passionem sensum confitendæ tuæ maiestatis totus mundus accepit, dum ineffabili crucis potentia iudicium mundi et potestas emical Crucifixi.

Unde et nos, Domine, cum Angelis et Sanctis universis, tibi confitemur, in exsultatione dicentes:

Sanctus

Mass for five voices, William Byrd (1540-1623).

Sanctus, Sanctus, Sanctus Dominus Deus Sabaoth…
Holy, holy, holy Lord, God of power and might…

Eucharistic Prayer I

Te ígitur, clementíssime Pater, per Iesum Christum, Fílium tuum, Dóminum nostrum, súpplices rogámus ac pétimus, uti accépta hábeaset benedícas ✠ hæc dona, hæc múnera,hæc sancta sacrifícia illibáta,in primis, quæ tibi offérimus pro Ecclésia tua sancta cathólica: quam pacificáre, custodíre, adunáre et régere dignéris toto orbe terrárum: me indígno fámulo tuo quem Ecclésiæ tuæ præesse voluísti, et fratre meo Vincentio, Episcopo huius Ecclésiæ, et ómnibus orthodóxis atque cathólicæ et apostólicæ fídei cultóribus.

We come to you, Father, with praise and thanksgiving, through Jesus Christ your Son. Through him we ask you to accept and bless ✠ these gifts we offer you in sacrifice. We offer them for your holy catholic Church, watch over it, Lord, and guide it; grant it peace and unity throughout the world. We offer them for me, your unworthy servant whom you have placed over your Church, for my brother, Vincent, Bishop of this Church, and for all who hold and teach the catholic faith that comes to us from the apostles.

Meménto, Dómine, famulórum famularúmque tuá-rum et ómnium circumstántium, quorum tibi fides cógnita est et nota devótio, pro quibus tibi offérimus: vel qui tibi ófferunt hoc sacrifícium laudis, pro se suísque ómnibus: pro redemptióne animárum suárum, pro spe salútis et incolumitátis suæ: tibíque reddunt vota sua ætérno Deo, vivo et vero.

Remember, Lord, your people especially those for whom we now pray. Remember all of us gathered here before you. You know how firmly we believe in you and dedicate ourselves to you. We offer you this sacrifice of praise for ourselves and those who are dear to us. We pray to you, our living and true God, for our well-being and redemption.

Communicántes, et memóriam venerántes, in primis gloriósæ semper Vírginis Maríæ, Genetrícis Dei et Dómini

In union with the whole Church we honour Mary, the ever-virgin mother of Jesus Christ our Lord and God.

We honour Joseph, her husband, the apostles and martyrs Peter and Paul, Andrew, [James, John, Thomas, James, Philip, Bartholomew, Matthew, Simon and Jude; we honour Linus, Cletus, Clement, Sixtus, Cornelius, Cyprian, Lawrence, Chrysogonus, John and Paul, Cosmas and Damian] and all the saints. May their merits and prayers gain us your constant help and protection. [Through Christ our Lord. Amen.]

nostri Iesu Christi: sed et beáti Ioseph, eiúsdem Vírginis Sponsi, et beatórum Apostolórum ac Mártyrum tuórum, Petri et Pauli, Andréæ, (Iacóbi, Ioánnis, Thomæ, Iacóbi, Philíppi, Bartholomæi, Matthæi, Simónis et Thaddæi: Lini, Cleti, Cleméntis, Xysti, Cornélii, Cypriáni, Lauréntii, Chrysógoni, Ioánnis et Pauli, Cosmæ et Damiáni) et ómnium Sanctórum tuórum; quorum méritis precibúsque concédas, ut in ómnibus protectiónis tuæ muniámur auxílio. (Per Christum Dóminum nostrum. Amen.)

Father, accept this offering from your whole family. Grant us your peace in this life, save us from final damnation, and count us among those you have chosen. [Through Christ our Lord. Amen.]

Hanc ígitur oblatiónem servitútis nostræ, sed et cunctæ famíliæ tuæ, quæsumus, Dómine, ut placátus accípias: diésque nostros in tua pace dispónas, atque ab ætérna damnatióne nos éripi et in electórum tuórum iúbeas grege numerári. (Per Christum Dóminum nostrum. Amen.)

Bless and approve our offering; make it acceptable to you, an offering in spirit and in truth. Let it become for us the body and blood of Jesus Christ, your only Son, our Lord.

Quam oblatiónem tu, Deus, in ómnibus, quæsumus, benedíctam, adscríptam, ratam, rationábilem, acceptabilémque fácere dignéris: ut nobis Corpus et Sanguis fiat dilectíssimi Fílii tui, Dómini nostri Iesu Christi.

Qui, prídie quam paterétur, accépit panem in sanctas ac venerábiles manus suas, et elevátis óculis in cælum ad te Deum Patrem suum omnipoténtem, tibi grátias agens benedíxit, fregit, dedítque discípulis suis, dicens: ACCÍPITE ET MANDUCÁTE EX HOC OMNES: HOC EST ENIM CORPUS MEUM, QUOD PRO VOBIS TRADÉTUR .

The day before he suffered he took break in his sacred hands and looking up to heaven, to you, his almighty Father, he gave you thanks and praise. He broke the bread, gave it to his disciples, and said: TAKE THIS, ALL OF YOU, AND EAT IT: THIS IS MY BODY WHICH WILL BE GIVEN UP FOR YOU.

Símili modo, postquam cenátum est, accípiens et hunc præclárum cálicem in sanctas ac venerábiles manus suas, item tibi grátias agens benedíxit, dedítque discípulis suis, dicens: ACCÍPITE ET BÍBITE EX EO OMNES: HIC EST ENIM CALIX SÁNGUINIS MEI NOVI ET ÆTÉRNI TESTAMÉNTI, QUI PRO VOBIS ET PRO MULTIS EFFUNDÉTUR IN REMISSIÓNEM PECCATÓRUM. HOC FÁCITE IN MEAM COMMEMORATIÓNEM.

When supper was ended, he took the cup. Again he gave you thanks and praise, gave the cup to his disciples, and said: TAKE THIS, ALL OF YOU, AND DRINK FROM IT: THIS IS THE CUP OF MY BLOOD, THE BLOOD OF THE NEW AND EVERLASTING COVENANT. IT WILL BE SHED FOR YOU AND FOR ALL SO THAT SINS MAY BE FORGIVEN. DO THIS IN MEMORY OF ME.

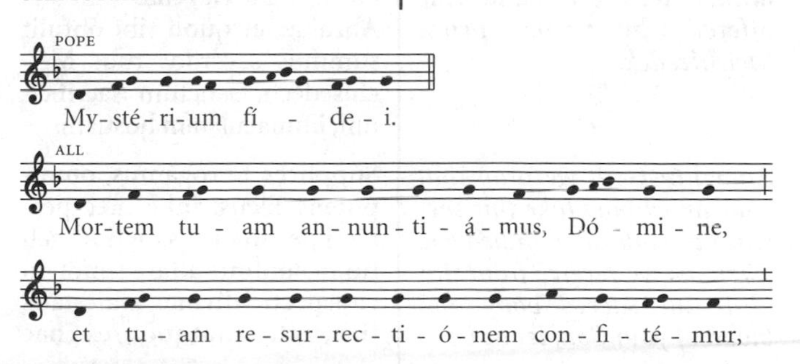
POPE
My- sté - ri- um fí - de - i.
ALL
Mor-tem tu - am an - nun - ti - á - mus, Dó - mi - ne,
et tu - am re - sur - rec - ti - ó - nem con - fi - té - mur,

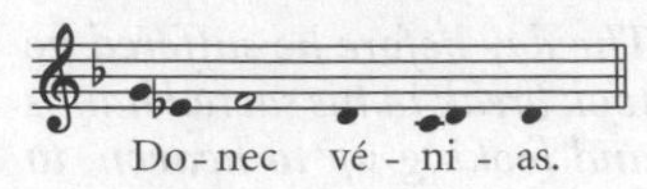

✠ **Pope:** *Let us proclaim the mystery of faith.*
All: *Dying you destroyed our death, rising you restored our life. Lord Jesus, come in glory.*

Father, we celebrate the memory of Christ, your Son. We, your people and your ministers, recall his passion, his resurrection from the dead, and his ascension into glory; and from the many gifts you have given us we offer to you, God of glory and majesty, this holy and perfect sacrifice: the bread of life and the cup of eternal salvation.

Unde et mémores, Dómine, nos servi tui, sed et plebs tua sancta, eiúsdem Christi, Fílii tui, Dómini nostri, tam beátæ passiónis, necnon et ab ínferis resurrectiónis, sed et in cælos gloriósæ ascensiónis: offérimus præcláræ maiestáti tuæ de tuis donis ac datis hóstiam puram, hóstiam sanctam, hóstiam immaculátam, Panem sanctum vitæ ætérnæ et Cálicem salútis perpétuæ.

Look with favour on these offerings and accept them as once you accepted the gifts of your servant Abel, the sacrifice of Abraham, our father in faith, and the bread and wine offered by your priest Melchizedek.

Supra quæ propítio ac seréno vultu respícere dignéris: et accépta habére, sícuti accépta habére dignátus es múnera púeri tui iusti Abel, et sacrifícium Patriárchæ nostri Abrahæ, et quod tibi óbtulit summus sacérdos tuus Melchísedech, sanctum sacrifícium, immaculátam hóstiam.

Almighty God, we pray that your angel may take this sacrifice to your altar in heaven. Then, as we receive from this altar the sacred body and blood of your Son, let us be

Súpplices te rogámus, omnípotens Deus: iube hæc perférri per manus sancti Angeli tui in sublíme altáre tuum, in conspéctu divínæ maiestátis tuæ; ut, quotquot ex hac altáris participatióne sacrosánctum Fílii tui Corpus et Sánguinem sumpsérimus, omni benedictióne cælésti et grátia repleámur. (Per Christum Dóminum nostrum. Amen.)

filled with every grace and blessing. [Through Christ our Lord. Amen.]

Meménto étiam, Dómine, famulórum famularúmque tuárum qui nos præcessérunt cum signo fídei, et dórmiunt in somno pacis. Ipsis, Dómine, et ómnibus in Christo quiescéntibus, locum refrigérii, lucis et pacis, ut indúlgeas, deprecámur. (Per Christum Dóminum nostrum. Amen.)

Remember, Lord, those who have died and have gone before us marked with the sign of faith, especially those for whom we now pray, May these, and all who sleep in Christ, find in your presence light, happiness, and peace. [Through Christ our Lord. Amen.]

Nobis quoque peccatóribus fámulis tuis, de multitúdine miseratiónum tuárum sperántibus, partem áliquam et societátem donáre dignéris cum tuis sanctis Apóstolis et Martyribus: cum Ioánne, Stéphano, Matthía, Bárnaba, (Ignátio, Alexándro, Marcellíno, Petro, Felicitáte, Perpétua, Agatha, Lúcia, Agnéte, Cæcília, Anastásia) et ómnibus Sanctis tuis: intra quorum nos consórtium, non æstimátor mériti, sed véniæ, quæ sumus, largítor admítte. Per Christum Dóminum nostrum.

For ourselves, too, we ask some share in the fellowship of your apostles and martyrs, with John the Baptist, Stephen, Matthias, Barnabas, [Ignatius, Alexander, Marcellinus, Peter, Felicity, Perpetua, Agatha, Lucy, Agnes, Cecilia, Anastasia] and all the saints.

Though we are sinners, we trust in your mercy and love. Do not consider what we truly deserve, but grant us your forgiveness. Through Christ our Lord.

Through him you give us all these gifts. You fill them with life and goodness, you bless them and make them holy.

Per quem hæc ómnia, Dómine, semper bona creas, sanctíficas, vivíficas, benedícis, et præstas nobis.

The Doxology and the Great Amen

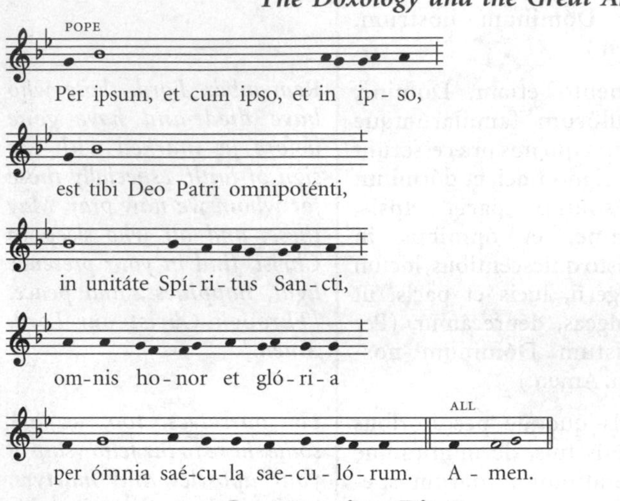
POPE
Per ipsum, et cum ipso, et in ip - so,
est tibi Deo Patri omnipoténti,
in unitáte Spí-ri-tus San-cti,
om-nis ho-nor et gló-ri-a
per ómnia saé-cu-la sae-cu-ló-rum.
ALL
A - men.

• Communion Rite •

✠ **Pope: Praeceptis salutaribus moniti, et divina institutione formati, audemus dicere:**

Let us pray with confidence to the Father in the words our Saviour gave us:

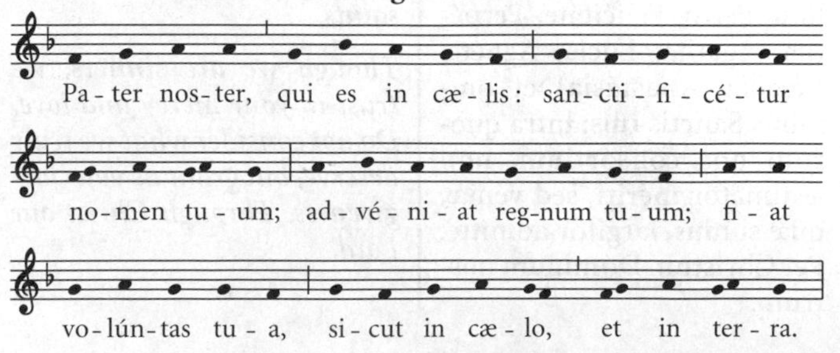
Pa-ter nos-ter, qui es in cæ-lis: san-cti-fi-cé-tur
no-men tu-um; ad-vé-ni-at reg-num tu-um; fi-at
vo-lún-tas tu-a, si-cut in cæ-lo, et in ter-ra.

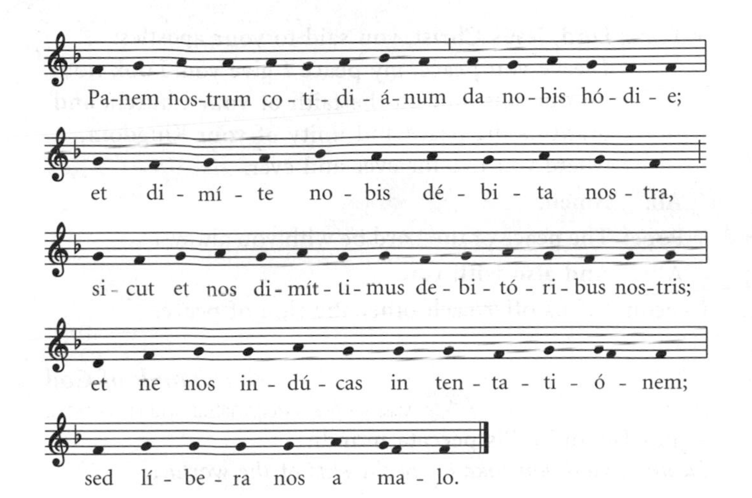
Pa-nem nos-trum co - ti - di - á - num da no - bis hó - di - e;
et di - mí - te no - bis dé - bi - ta nos - tra,
si - cut et nos di - mít - ti - mus de - bi - tó - ri - bus nos-tris;
et ne nos in - dú - cas in ten - ta - ti - ó - nem;
sed lí - be - ra nos a ma - lo.

Our Father, who art in heaven
hallowed be thy name.
Thy kingdom come,
Thy will be done on earth as it is in heaven.
Give us this day our daily bread
and forgive us our trespasses
as we forgive those who trespass against us.
and lead us not into temptation,
but deliver us from evil.

✠ Pope: Deliver us, Lord, from every evil
and grant us peace in our day.
In your mercy, keep us free from sin
and protect us from all anxiety,
as we wait in joyful hope
for the coming of our Saviour, Jesus Christ.

All: **For the kingdom, the power, and the glory are yours, now and for ever. Amen.**

✠ Pope: Lord, Jesus Christ, you said to your apostles: I leave you peace, my peace I give you. Look not on our sins, but on the faith of your Church, and grant us the peace and unity of your Kingdom, where you live for ever and ever.

All: **Amen.**

✠ Pope: The peace of the Lord be with you always.

All: **And also with you.**

Deacon: Let us offer each other the sign of peace.

Lamb of God

Mass for five voices, William Byrd (1540-1623).

Agnus Dei qui tollis peccata mundi…
Lamb of God you take away the sins of the world…

✠ Pope: This is the Lamb of God who takes away the sins of the world. Happy are those who are called to his supper:

All: **Lord, I am not worthy to receive you,
but only say the word and I shall be healed.**

Communion Antiphon

One of the soldiers opened his side with a spear, and at once there came forth blood and water.

Unus militum lancea latus eius aperuit, et continuo exivit sanguis et aqua.

Communion Motet

Hans Leo Hassler (1564-1612)

O sacred banquet in which Christ is consumed; the memory of his passion is contemplated; the mind is filled with grace; and a pledge of future glory is given to us. Alleluia.

O sacrum convivium, in quo Christus sumitur: recolitur memoria passionis eius: mens impletur gratia: et futuræ gloriæ nobis pignus datur. Alleluia.

POST-COMMUNION HYMN

Tune Tynemouth H.F.Hemy (1818-1888)
Words St Alphonsus Liguori (1696-1787) / tr. Edmund Vaughan C.Ss.R. (1827-1908).

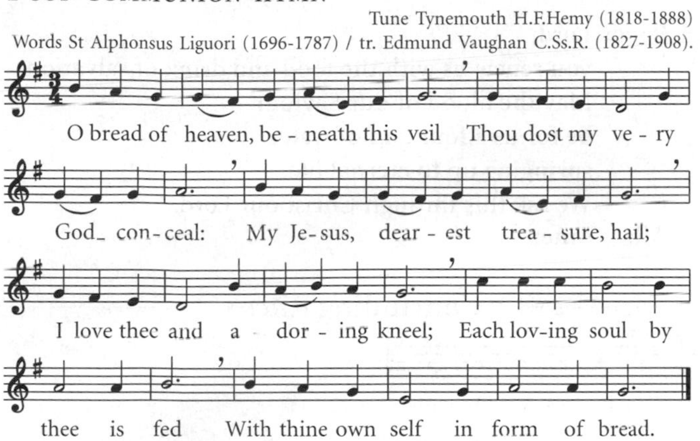
O bread of heaven, be - neath this veil Thou dost my ve - ry
God_ con-ceal: My Je-sus, dear - est trea - sure, hail;
I love thee and a - dor - ing kneel; Each lov-ing soul by
thee is fed With thine own self in form of bread.

2. O Food of life, thou who dost give
The pledge of immortality;
I live, no 'tis not I that live;
God gives me life, God lives in me:
He feeds my soul, he guides my ways,
And every grief with joy repays.

3. O Bond of love, that dost unite
The servant to his living Lord;
Could I dare live, and not requite
Such love - then death were meet reward:
I cannot live unless to prove
Some love for such unmeasured love.

4. Belovèd Lord in heaven above,
There, Jesus, thou awaitest me;
To gaze on thee with changeless love;
Yes, thus, I hope thus shall it be:
For how can he deny me heaven
Who here on earth himself hath given?

Prayer after Communion

✠ **Pope:** **Lord,**
you renew us with the food and drink of salvation.
May the blood of our Saviour
be for us a fountain of water
springing up to eternal life.
We ask this through Christ our Lord.
All: **Amen.**

• Concluding Rites •

POPE
Dó-mi-nus vo-bís-cum.
ALL
Et cum spí-ri-tu tu-o.
POPE
Sit nomen Dómini be-ne-díc-tum.
ALL
Ex hoc nunc et usque in saé-cu-lum.
POPE
Adiutórium nostrum in nómine Dó-mi-ni.
ALL
Qui fecit caelum et ter-ram.
POPE
Benedícat vos om-ni-pó-tens De-us : Pa-ter, et Fí-li-us,
et Spí-ri-tus San-ctus.
ALL
A-men.

DEACON
I - te, mis-sa est.
ALL
De-o grá - ti - as.

Organ voluntary

HYMN DURING PROCESSION TO THE WEST DOOR

Tune Blaenwern William Penfro Rowlands (1860-1937)
Words Charles Wesley (1707-1788

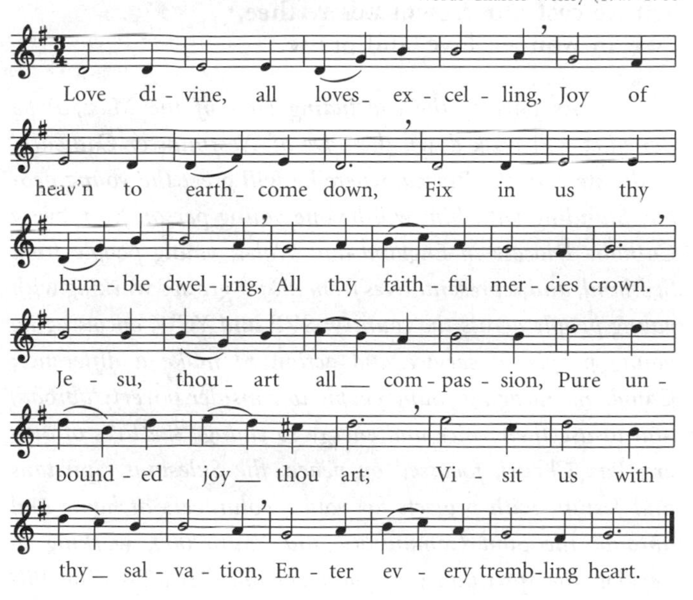
Love di - vine, all loves_ ex - cel - ling, Joy of
heav'n to earth_ come down, Fix in us thy
hum - ble dwel - ling, All thy faith - ful mer - cies crown.
Je - su, thou_ art all__ com - pas - sion, Pure un -
bound - ed joy__ thou art; Vi - sit us with
thy_ sal - va - tion, En - ter ev - ery tremb-ling heart.

2. Come, Almighty to deliver,
Let us all thy grace receive;
Suddenly return, and never,
Never more thy temples leave.
Thee we would be always blessing,

Serve thee as thy hosts above;
Pray, and praise thee, without ceasing,
Glory in thy perfect love.

3. Finish then thy new creation:
Pure and spotless let us be;
Let us see thy great salvation,
Perfectly restored in thee;
Changed from glory into glory
Till in heaven we take our place,
Till we cast our crowns before thee,
Lost in wonder, love, and praise.

As part of the concluding rites of the Mass, Pope Benedict will walk down the nave of Westminster Cathedral to the steps in the Piazza, where he will greet the young people. Standing with him will be one young person from every Catholic Diocese in England and Wales, young people from Scotland, and representatives from major groups working with young people across the country; SVP and YCW, encouraging young people in service and action to make a difference; Cafod, encouraging young people to consider poverty abroad, and to use their voice and energy to change the lives of others; Pax Christi, focussed on peace; the Salesians, Spiritans and Jesuits, with projects for young volunteers at home and abroad; the Sion Community and Youth2000, working to develop the spirituality of young people; HCPT – The Pilgrimage Trust, with its special emphasis on young people with diverse needs; Catholic Scouting, with 30,000 young people involved in Scout groups in all parts of the country.

These groups – offering a tremendous and diverse range of opportunities for young people – are a sign of a

Catholic Church which values young people, supports them, and wants the best for them. All of our youth ministry is modelled on the lived Gospel of Jesus Christ; in practical terms, to find contact details of what is local to you please visit www.cymfed.org – CYMFed is the federation of Dioceses, Movements, Organisations and Religious Congregations working with young people in England and Wales.

During his meeting with young people Pope Benedict will receive and bless a new national symbol for Youth Ministry, It highlights the mysteries of Incarnation and Salvation, together with the commissioning given in the sacraments of initiation and the ministry of the Church to and by young people.

Prayer with the people of Wales

After the meeting with the young people Pope Benedict returns to Westminster Cathedral. The focus of the visit now turns to Wales. The Holy Father is not visiting Wales on this visit but he is now greeted in the name of the Church in Wales and he prays for its people.

The Bishop of Wrexham, the Right Reverend Edwin Regan, greets his Holiness on behalf of the people of Wales.

The Holy Father addresses the people of Wales.

He next blesses a mosaic of St David, Patron of Wales, which is to be installed in Westminster Cathedral, and spends time before the statue of Our Lady of the Taper, brought from Cardigan, the Welsh National Shrine to Our Lady, for this occasion.

The Shrine Prayer to Our Lady of the Taper

My soul glorifies the Lord,

Henceforth all ages will call me Blessed.

The Almighty works marvels for me:

Holy His name.

Behold the handmaid of the Lord.

Be it done unto me according to your word.

Father, Your Son Jesus born of the Virgin Mary by the power of the Holy Spirit is the Light of the world. May the same Spirit lead us to imitate Mary's faith love and humility, that, guided by her example, we may follow the light of her Son on our Journey through life and come at last to see you as you are, and praise you in the everlasting kingdom of heaven.

Amen.

Holy Mary Mother of God,

you offer your Son for our adoration

May we too treasure His word in our hearts

and help bring

His light to the world.

Our Lady of Cardigan — Pray for Wales

Our Lady of Cardigan — Pray for us

"Dear Young Friends"

Reflections on thirty years of affirmation and encouragement by Pope John Paul II and Pope Benedict XVI

Fr Dominic Howarth
Chair, Catholic Youth Ministry Federation

"*Dear young people, in the Church of today you are the hope of tomorrow.*" When Pope John Paul II spoke these words at Ninian Park, Cardiff, on June 2, 1982, he was affirming something that shone through as a defining theme of his Papacy: young people have a vital and essential place at the heart of today's Church as they help shape the Church of the future. Pope Benedict has continued to put young people at the centre of his homilies, messages, and visits abroad. He set the tone in his very first message after his election as Pope and before his inauguration, recognising that young people had been "privileged partners in dialogue" with Pope John Paul II and saying "*With you, dear young people, I will continue to maintain a dialogue, listening to your expectations in an attempt to help you meet ever more profoundly the ever living, ever young, Jesus Christ*" (April 20, 2005). In the Mass where he was inaugurated as Pope, on April 24, 2005, he spoke these memorable words: "*Today, with great strength and great conviction, on the basis of long personal experience of life, I say to you, dear young people: Do not be afraid of Christ! He takes nothing away, and he gives you everything. When we give ourselves to him, we receive a hundredfold in return. Yes, open, open wide the doors to Christ – and you will find true life. Amen."*

Pope John Paul II visited Britain in the early years of his time as Pope – just two years after that visit, in 1984, he entrusted a special Cross to the youth of the world. That Cross has now journeyed many thousands of miles and been venerated by many millions of young people, including here in Britain in January 2004 when it went to every Diocese in the country. The first World Youth Day was held in Rome in 1986, and ever since then it has followed a pattern of a year or two in Rome, with celebrations at diocesan level, then a location elsewhere in the world for an international gathering: Argentina (1987), Spain (1989), Poland (1991), USA (1993), Philippines (1995), France (1997), Italy (2000), Canada (2002), Germany (2005), Australia (2008). During that time there are some remarkable statistics: in 1995 four million people gathered in Manila – the largest single gathering for a common purpose at any time in the history of the world. In 2000 when Rome hosted an international World Youth Day for the Jubilee Year the same became true for Europe: the gathering of 2 million young people at Tor Vergata for the Vigil and Mass with the Pope was the largest gathering for a common purpose at any time in European history.

The World Youth Days are characterised by tremendous energy and joy. For many young people, they have been life changing, opening their eyes to a vision of the praying community of the Church that they did not think was possible. Standing in a field, with young people from virtually every country in the world, stretching in every direction as far as the eye can see, is a moving and dramatic experience. As night falls, a number of the Vigils have been marked by every participant holding a candle, in silent prayer before the Blessed Sacrament; it is breathtaking.

The World Youth Days are most certainly a powerful legacy from Pope John Paul II, embraced by Pope Benedict who will preside at the next International WYD in Madrid in summer 2011, with an estimated 1.5 million young people due to attend. What inspires them to come in such numbers is not rooted simply in the drama and scale of the event, remarkable as it is. The true depth of World Youth Day is in the prayers and witness that is shared by young people and those leading them, and it is in the words spoken to young people. The quotes given here are a very small selection of the profoundly reflective thoughts that Pope John Paul II and Pope Benedict have offered young people.

"*In prayer, united with Jesus – your brother, your friend, your Saviour, your God – you begin to breathe a new atmosphere. You form new goals and new ideals. Yes, in Christ you begin to understand yourself more fully.*" (Ninian Park, Cardiff, 1982.)

"*Dear young people of the century now beginning, in saying 'yes' to Christ, you say 'yes' to all your noblest ideals. I pray that he will reign in your hearts and in all of humanity in the new century and the new millennium. Have no fear of entrusting yourselves to him! He will guide you, he will grant you the strength to follow him every day and in every situation.*

"*Today you have come together to declare that in the new century you will not let yourselves be made into tools of violence and destruction; you will defend peace, paying the price in your person if need be. You will not resign yourselves to a world where other human beings die of hunger, remain illiterate and have no work. You will defend life at every moment of its development; you will strive with all your strength to make this earth ever more livable for all people.*" (World Youth Day, Rome 2000.)

"*Dear young friends, the aged Pope, full of years but still young at heart, answers your youthful desire for happiness with words that are not his own. They are words that rang out two thousand years ago. Words that we have heard again tonight: 'Blessed are they...' The key word in Jesus' teaching is a proclamation of joy: 'Blessed are they…'*

"*People are made for happiness. Rightly, then, you thirst for happiness. Christ has the answer to this desire of yours. But he asks you to trust him. True joy is a victory, something which cannot be obtained without a long and difficult struggle. Christ holds the secret of this victory.*" (World Youth Day, Toronto, 2002.)

"*Dear friends! Sometimes, our initial impression is that having to include time for Mass on a Sunday is rather inconvenient. But if you make the effort, you will realise that this is what gives a proper focus to your free time. Do not be deterred from taking part in Sunday Mass, and help others to discover it too. This is because the Eucharist releases the joy that we need so much, and we must learn to grasp it ever more deeply, we must learn to love it.*

"*I know that you as young people have great aspirations, that you want to pledge yourselves to build a better world. Let others see this, let the world see it, since this is exactly the witness that the world expects from the disciples of Jesus Christ.*" (World Youth Day, Cologne 2005.)

"*Standing before me I see a vibrant image of the universal Church. The variety of nations and cultures from which you hail shows that indeed Christ's Good News is for everyone; it has reached the ends of the earth… This evening I wish also to include those who are not present among us. I am thinking especially of the sick or mentally ill, young people in prison, those struggling on the margins of our societies, and those who for whatever reason feel alienated from the Church. To them I say: Jesus is close to you! Feel his healing embrace, his compassion and mercy.*" (World Youth Day, Sydney 2008.)

In 1995, Pope John Paul II gave this message for the World Day of Prayer for Vocations. He offers a powerful vision of Church:

"*As Jesus with the disciples of Emmaus, so the Church must become today the* ***travelling companion of young people****, who are often marked by confusion, resistance and contradictions, in order to announce to them the ever-astonishing 'news' of the risen Christ.*

"*This is what is needed: a* ***Church for young people****, which will know how to speak to their heart and enkindle, comfort, and inspire enthusiasm in it with the joy of the Gospel and the strength of the Eucharist; a Church which will know how to invite and to welcome the person who seeks a purpose for which to commit his whole existence; a Church which is not afraid to require much, after having given much; which does not fear asking from young people the effort of a noble and authentic adventure, such as that of the following of the Gospel.*"

The Catholic Church in England, Wales and Scotland wholeheartedly embraces the essence of all that Pope Benedict and Pope John Paul II have said to young people. We cherish young people as the present and future of the Church, with a particular and unique place and voice. They are neither children nor yet adults and in that moment in their lives they have something extremely powerful to bring and to receive. In listening and responding to young people, and in passing on the tradition of the faith to them, we aim to "speak to their heart", to accompany them in the "noble and authentic adventure", to see them as a "vibrant image of the universal Church".

What we can offer in Dioceses, retreat houses, parishes, organisations, new Movements and established Religious Congregations is always developing, and stronger in some areas than in others. There is no doubt at all, however, that across England, Wales and Scotland there is tremendous, dedicated youth ministry offering a whole range of possibilities to many thousands of young people. This includes young people helping the poor and most vulnerable, working with the elderly and disabled, receiving fresh insights into prayer and Church teaching, discovering places of contemplation and reflection. It includes eleven retreat houses dedicated entirely to young people, with young adult teams offering vibrant witness. For any young person, Catholic or not, there is a lot to get involved with, there will be something that both suits and deepens the gifts and character of each individual, and everyone is welcome to be involved. Young adults are invited to join groups travelling to World Youth Day in Madrid in 2011, and young people of all ages are encouraged to get involved with many local events and opportunities throughout the year. Every Diocese has a Youth Service, and these and other providers of opportunities for young people are brought together by the Catholic Youth Ministry Federation, CYMFed. Find the local contact details for you by visiting www.cymfed.org.

We are delighted that one young person from virtually every parish in the country – over 2,000 in all – will gather with Pope Benedict XVI in London on Saturday

September 18. We trust his visit will help us in continuing to build a Church which is the "travelling companion" for young people, celebrating the "noble and authentic adventure" of life with Christ.

To finish, these words of blessing for young people were given at the last World Youth Day attended by Pope John Paul II, in Toronto, Canada, in 2002. They continue to resonate:

> "*Jesus Christ, proclaim once more your Beatitudes in the presence of these young people.*
> *Look upon them with love and listen to their young hearts, ready to put their future on the line for you.*
> *You have called them to be the 'salt of the earth and light of the world'.*
> *Continue to teach them the truth and beauty of the vision that you proclaimed on the Mountain.*
> *Make them men and women of the Beatitudes!*
> *Let the light of your wisdom shine upon them,*
> *so that in word and deed they may spread in the world the light and salt of the Gospel.*
> *Make their whole life a bright reflection of you,*
> *who are the true light that came into this world*
> *so that whoever believes in you will not die,*
> *but will have eternal life (cf. Jn 3:16)!*"

CHRISTIANITY IN WALES

Bishop Mullins
Emiritus Bishop of Menevia

Following quickly on the Edict of Milan, by which Emperor Constantine extended religious toleration to Christians within the Roman Empire, a synod of the Church met at Arles in 314, at which the four regions of the Province of Britannia were represented. Christianity had come to Britain with the Roman Legions and was already firmly established in the Roman Province. It was centred particularly on the Roman towns and its organisation was modelled on the imperial arrangements.

However when, in 383, Magnus Maximus withdrew the regular defences of the Province in pursuit of his claim to the imperial crown, since the West of Britain lacked large Roman towns a separate provision for the defence of Wales and the West was established. This would determine the subsequent ecclesiastical structures in the cityless parts of Britain, including what is now Wales, but also Ireland. The Church here was organised more around monastic communities than territorial dioceses. In the struggles against invading Germanic tribes, what is now Wales developed a distinct and separate identity as the safeguarders of the Roman inheritance. The characteristics of this self-awareness have been summed up by Sir J.E. Lloyd, the father of modern Welsh historical studies. "During this period the Welsh tribes cast off all traces of heathenism and of political submission ... and became well–organised communities, ruled by powerful monarchs, ministered to by a learned clergy, led to battle by champions whose renown has not yet faded".

In the troubled years that would follow bishops throughout Europe looked to the monastic movement to provide for the needs of the people and to take the Faith outside the towns. Saint Patrick witnesses to the importance of learning, to the study of Scripture and to schools in his homeland. There were many learned clerics who devoted their lives to such study to the detriment of the preaching of the Faith among the people and to the heathens. To Patrick, the new monasticism was a sign of a new vigour in the Church. In the 6th century it would become the driving force for a re–evangelisation of the people of Wales. In Wales this sixth century is remembered as the Age of the Saints of Illtud, Teilo, Padam, of Saint David and their many companions still honoured in the Church calendar for Wales. By the time of the Norman invasion, this older monastic structure had become static and much of church administration was in the hands of laymen, a situation which the Normans found scandalous. In a spirit of renewal and reform, newer Religious Orders came to Wales. The Cistercian Order took root and became a part of the fabric of Welsh life. The orders of Friars and especially the Dominicans and Franciscans brought the reforms of the Fourth Lateran Council, reforms that would have a profound effect on Welsh culture and on the production of manuscript collections of both secular and sacred writings.

The 14th century was a disastrous one for the whole of Europe. In an area that was already poor and thinly populated, the effects of the Black Death were severe. And yet, by the end of the following century, a great renewal of vernacular literature, of the restoration and renewal of churches and the use of these in the religious formation of the people was taking place. Something of what was achieved may be seen in the restoration of Saint Teilo's church as it might have been in 1520 at the Welsh History Museum near Cardiff.

The accepted view among historians is that the Reformation was not welcomed in Wales but that by the end of Elizabeth's reign, Wales had become a Protestant nation. This opinion requires closer examination. Among the Cecil papers at Hatfield is a letter dated 1603 from a judge in the Recusant courts lamenting that Wales is still steeped in superstition and popery. Even in the time of Charles II, Wales is listed as one of the four strongholds of Catholicism.

In 1536, an Act usually known as the Act of Union decreed that Wales should be "incorporated, united and annexed" to the realm of England. This was to have some unforeseen effects. In 1579, Owen Lewis would write to Cardinal Sirleto appealing for funds to print religious works in Welsh. The Welsh exiles on the continent were very clear that Wales needed different treatment from England if the Faith was to survive in Wales. Because of the political assumptions of the age, such an approach met with little understanding in Rome or elsewhere.

Only Charles Borromeo in Milan responded positively to such appeals.

Catholicism did survive strongly in the Monmouthshire area, due in large measure to the influence of the Somerset family of Raglan Castle. Edward Somerset, Fourth Earl of Worcester (1553-1628) was a proud Welshman who used the Welsh language and saw it as a key to the pastoral work of his age. Described as a stiff papist who was also a loyal subject, he settled Catholic families from Glamorganshire and from different areas of England on his lands. He helped establish the College of St Francis on the Monmouth/Hereford border and was sufficiently confident in 1615 to register the lease in the name of the Jesuit superior. His influence explains why the English county of Herefordshire still today comes within the ecclesiastical Province of Cardiff. Until 1679, the College was the spearhead of the Jesuit mission in Wales. The College survived only in name following the persecution occasioned by the Popish Plot.

In 1767, Charles Walmesley sent a report on the Western District to Propaganda. The statistics given for Herefordshire are of 190 Catholics served by seven missionaries. The whole of Wales is said to have 750 Catholics and nine missionaries. In the information sent to Rome prior to the establishment of the Welsh District in 1840, the area had a total of 17 priests and 6,519 Catholics. The following decade saw a further big increase in numbers due to the Irish Famine and subsequent migration.

In the restoration of the Hierarchy in 1850, Herefordshire and the southern counties of Wales were formed into the Diocese of Newport and Menevia; the six counties of North Wales formed part of the Diocese of Shrewsbury.

On becoming Archbishop of Westminster in 1892, Cardinal Vaughan of the recusant family of Courtfield returned to the position of the Elizabethan exiles. He insisted that the religious needs of Wales were distinct from those of England and therefore required to be treated separately. In 1895, the three counties of Glamorgan, Monmouth and Hereford became the Diocese of Newport; the remaining counties became the Vicariate of Wales. In 1898, this became the Diocese of Menevia. The Cardinal did not live to see the erection of the Province of Cardiff in 1916 and the establishment of a Welsh Hierarchy. In 1987 a further reorganisation saw the creation of a third diocese. Menevia was restored to what was very nearly its medieval territory and the Diocese of Wrexham was formed.

Since 1850, there have been notable converts to Catholicism in every generation. The most influential of these in the twentieth century was Saunders Lewis. Scholar, poet, playwright and political thinker, he was described by a contemporary as "the most learned one among us". Descended from a long line of Nonconformist leaders, Mr Lewis had to contend all his life with the suspicion which his Catholic convictions aroused in Wales.

The Gospel and Life

Archbishop Bernard Longley

During his time in the United Kingdom the Holy Father will visit a Catholic home for elderly people. St Peter's at Vauxhall in London is one of a number of residences founded and run by the Little Sisters of the Poor. Their work continues to be inspired by the vision of their foundress, Saint Jeanne Jugan, who was aware of the need to recognise the intrinsic dignity and value of the lives of elderly people. She reflected the Church's concern that every individual human life is of inestimable value because each person is brought into being, valued and loved by God. This evaluation is not based on how useful or productive a person's life may or may not be. Everybody's life is uniquely precious and deserves to be cherished.

This particular visit by Pope Benedict serves to remind us of the Church's teaching on the dignity of human life and its inherent value from the moment of conception to the point of natural death. When a society loses sight of the objective value of life at its beginning and its end it becomes less clear about how to value and esteem all that constitutes the experience of life in between. The Gospel of Life underscores the abiding value of human lives at every moment along life's way, for these lives are destined to find their fulfilment in the new and eternal life of the Kingdom of God.

As a practical and evangelical way of promoting and spreading this teaching, Pope John Paul II called on Bishops' Conferences around the world to establish a Day for Life in his 1995 encyclical letter *Evangelium Vitae*. He wrote:

> "*The celebration of this Day should be planned and carried out with the active participation of all sectors of the local Church. Its primary purpose should be to foster in individual consciences, in families, in the Church and in civil society a recognition of the meaning and value of human life at every stage and in every condition. Particular attention should be drawn to the seriousness of abortion and euthanasia, without neglecting other aspects of life which from time to time deserve to be given careful consideration, as occasion and circumstances demand.*" (§ 85)

Responding to this, Catholic parishes in Scotland, England and Wales have observed a dedicated Day for Life each year. The reason for doing this is clear: the gift of life is to be treasured and the Church wishes to encourage a deeper awareness of the riches of her teaching on life. This teaching offers a wonderful and positive vision of life and its purpose, and it encourages us to recognise and celebrate the gift of life.

The Day for Life is first and foremost a celebration which highlights some particular aspect of the Gospel of Life through prayer and practical support for those who work to maintain the dignity of life. In recent years the Day for Life has focused on the meaning and value of life in the womb, helping women face the demands of an unexpected or unwanted pregnancy; valuing and supporting family life; living life to the full with disability; understanding and supporting people with mental illness; presenting Church teaching about suicide and assisted dying, and cherishing the end of life. In each case a clear explanation of each issue and related Church teaching is accompanied by suggestions about how individuals and parishes may become better informed or more actively engaged (see www.dayforlife.org).

An annual Day for Life collection in England and Wales has enabled the Church to help local and national initiatives supporting the Gospel of Life. Day for Life funds have also enabled the Church to support ethical stem-cell research, the Care-not-Killing campaign and the work of the Linacre Centre. In this way prayer and celebration have been linked with education and outreach.

The Day for Life offers an opportunity for us all to reaffirm our commitment to the God-given dignity, beauty and holiness of life and to find creative and fruitful ways of expressing that commitment. It also becomes a day for individuals, families and communities to seek out those people who share with us the basic values guiding our attitude to life – a day when we can promote together the real choice of choosing life more effectively.

In his visit to St Peter's Residence in Vauxhall we are grateful for the Holy Father's witness to the God-given intrinsic value of every person's life from its beginning to its cherished ending.

VIGIL OF PRAYER including the Rite of Eucharistic Exposition and Benediction

Hyde Park, London

• Gathering •

As people make themselves comfortable in Hyde Park, a variety of groups welcome them, showing a rich diversity of styles and traditions which are all part of the Catholic community in England and Wales. The distinctive feature of many of these groups is that they work hard to include those who may otherwise not find a place and a voice for such a performance.

The groups presenting dance, mime and movement this afternoon include:

RISEtheatre! Rise seek to equip young people and those working with them to use their creativity to its full potential, and offer training and workshops all over the country.
www.risetheatre.co.uk

Larondina Dance Group, London based and offering dance opportunities to show the artistic talent of those with special needs. The dance company's structured syllabus helps to improve their posture, coordination, concentration and communication – all to create that most vital of qualities: a heads-up-confidence. www.asneeds.org.uk/larondina

More Than Dance, based in the North East of England, introduces young people to dance, covering the area of faith, personal development and well being. Today they will offer dynamic, strong and prayer filled reflective movement. www.morethandance.co.uk

Zywiec Folk Song and Dance Group are named after a town in the mountainous region in the highlands of southern Poland. Their signature dances are the lively and loud dances of the highlanders of the Zywiec mountains. The group is based in West London. www.zywiec.co.uk

Doherty Academy (Coventry) and Brooks Academy (London) are two well established groups of Irish dancers, following a long tradition of Irish Dance. See www.irish-dancer.co.uk for these and other Irish Dance groups.

Romani Rad, dancers from the Roma tradition, blending colourful costumes and folk music with roots from many centuries ago. Information from the Roma support group, London.

We are very grateful to all the performance groups, and apologise to those whose details arrived too late for inclusion in this booklet. Full details of all the performance groups are on the website for the Papal Visit, along with powerful and moving testimonies given by some of the individuals who are performing this afternoon.

At the conclusion of these pieces there is a procession of banners carried by representatives from the parishes of Scotland, England and Wales. Diocesan groups will be met by their Bishop or his delegate, and each Diocesan group includes twenty young people from the Diocese as well as representatives from HCPT – The Pilgrimage Trust – and from Catholic Scouting. Concluding the procession, representatives from major national Catholic organisations will bring their banners.

This procession witnesses to the presence of the Catholic Church in every part of England and Wales and of Scotland, and of the range and diversity of the many, many groups within the Catholic Church – groups for the service of others, for prayer and evangelisation, for the care of the ill and elderly, with and for the young, for the care of the poor and vulnerable both at home and across the world.

• Entrance Procession •

SAVE US LORD OUR GOD

Save us, Lord our God.
Gather us from the nations,

that we may proclaim your holy name.
We may proclaim your holy name,
and glory in your praise,
and glory in your praise,
and glory in your praise for evermore!

Sing a new song, sing a new song to God.
Sing to the Lord, sing to the Lord all the earth.
Sing to the Lord and bless God's name.
Save us Lord our God…

Tell the nations of God's help day by day.
Tell all the world, tell all the world of God's glory.
Tell all the world the wonders of God.
Save us Lord our God…

I extol you, my God:
Glory and praise for evermore!
Always blessing your name:
Glory and praise for evermore!
Every day I will bless you,
Glory and praise for evermore!
Always praising your name,
Glory and praise for evermore!

Save us Lord our God…

Save us Lord our God for ever, for ever and evermore!

The compères introduce the theme of the Vigil and explain the composition of the Entrance Procession.

CHRIST BE OUR LIGHT

1. Longing for light, we wait in darkness.
Longing for truth, we turn to you.
Make us your own, your holy people,
light for the world to see. ℟

℟ Christ, be our light! Shine in our hearts.
Shine through the darkness.
Christ, be our light!
Shine in your church gathered today.

2. Longing for peace, our world is troubled.
Longing for hope, many despair.
Your word alone has power to save us.
Make us your living voice. ℟

3. Longing for food, many are hungry.
Longing for water, many still thirst.
Make us your bread, broken for others,
shared until all are fed. ℟

4. Longing for shelter, many are homeless.
Longing for warmth, many are cold.
Make us your building, sheltering others,
walls made of living stone. ℟

5. Many the gifts, many the people,
many the hearts that yearn to belong.
Let us be servants to one another,
making your kingdom come. ℟

Fire!

The fire has been lit today
The fire is the work of Jesus
The fire has been lit today
We'll sing Alleluia
The fire is lit.

Even Europeans are being saved
Even Kiga is being saved
Even Chotera is being saved
The people of every tribe will be saved.

Moto!

Moto, I mewaka leo
Moto, ni kasi ya Jesu
Moto, I mewaka leo
Tuimbe Alleluia
Moto mewaka

Hata wa zungu waokoke,
Hata wa Kiga waokoke,
Hata Chotera waokoke,
Watu wok wata okoka.

Hata wa Teso waokoke	*Even Teso is being saved*
Hata Lubara waokoke	*Even Lubara is being saved*
Hata wa Chaga waokoke	*Even Chaga is being saved*
Hata Uganda waokoke	*Even Uganda is being saved*
Hata mbinguni tutaenda	*We'll even go to heaven!*
Hata Jesu tutamonen	*We'll even see Jesus!*
Moto was Jesu nirrewaka	*I have lit the fire of Jesus*
Moto Moto Moto Moto	*Fire, fire, fire, fire!*

I WILL BLESS THE LORD AT ALL TIMES

I will bless the Lord at all times,
his praise always on my lips;
In the Lord my soul shall make its boast;
the humble shall hear and be glad.
Glorify the Lord with me, together let us praise his name.
I sought the Lord, he answered me; from all my terrors he set me free -
he set me free.
From my terrors, he set me free

Taste and see that the Lord is good.
He is happy who takes refuge in him.
Taste and see that the Lord is good.
He is happy who takes refuge in him. (x2)

Look towards him and be radiant; let your faces not be abashed.
This poor man called; the Lord rescued him from distress.
He turns His eyes to the just and turns His ears to their appeal.

They call and the Lord hears and rescues them in all their distress,
All their distress;
rescues them in all their distress

The Lord is close to the broken-hearted;
Those whose spirit is crushed he will save.
The Lord is close to the broken-hearted;
Those whose spirit is crushed he will save. (x2)

LET THE GLORY OF THE LORD

Let the glory of the Lord, let it rise among us.
Let the glory of the Lord, let it rise among us.
Let the glory of the King rise among us, let it rise.

Oh, let it rise, Oh, let it rise!

Let the power of the Lord…
Let the Spirit of the Lord…
Let the joy of the Lord…
Let the dance of the Lord…
Let the shout of the Lord…

OUT OF DARKNESS

℟ *Out of darkness God has called us,*
claimed by Christ as God's own people.
Holy nation, royal priesthood,
walking in God's marv'lous light.

Let us take the words you give,
strong and faithful words to live.
Words that in our hearts are sown;
words that bind us as your own. ℟

Let us take the Christ you give.
Broken Body, Christ we live.

Christ the risen from the tomb;
Christ who calls us as your own. ℟

Let us take the love you give,
that the way of love we live.
Love to bring your people home;
love to make us all your own. ℟

ALLELUIA

℟ Alleluia a a , alleluia a a.
Ngo, ngo , ghamte Chabe
Njob ta kwi swe ghamte lense.

1. Bi lonsi fa ghamte, fa
ghamte num len Chabe
2. Bon sion, bi nju ki?
Bi lonsi ghamte Chabe.

Coda 1: Israel tsiante
Resp. Israel tsiante, tsiante
num si o a be napte o
(bis) ℟

Coda 2: Bin bu be niang a,
bin bu niang a fen ba fen
Bin bu niang a a.

1. Le ma njuga yogbe ndane
2. Ben Christo tum nda fa ℟

Alleluia. All the people, stand up and glorify the Lord. Children of God, are you listening? Raise your voices and glorify the Lord.

Israel, rejoice in the Lord your creator. Play and dance for the King of Kings.

Traditionnal song from Bangangte
West Cameroon

Sung by the Coventry Catholic Choral Group, the 3CG. (www.3CG.org.uk)

ONE BREAD, ONE BODY, ONE LORD OF ALL

One bread, one body, one Lord of all,
one cup of blessing which we bless.
And we, though many, throughout the earth,
we are one body in this one Lord.

Gentile or Jew, servant or free,
woman or man, no more.

Many the gifts, many the works,
one in the Lord of all.

Grain for the fields,
scattered and grown, gathered to one, for all.

YES I BELIEVE THAT GOD LOVES ME

1. When I behold thy glory share,
the stars unfold the splendid sky,
all nature bows creation shouts,
then I believe that God is real. ℟

℟ *Yes I believe that God loves me,*
His hand I feel, His ways I see,
from moving tides, cross space so wide,
for I believe that God is real.
Yes I believe that God loves me,
His hand I feel, His ways I see,
from moving tides, cross space so wide,
for I believe that God is real.

2. I see His face in every storm,
a fleeting glance on wings of morn,
His wonders ever to perform,
for I believe that God is real. ℟

3. The little drops of dew that fall,
the birds that sing God's creatures call,
from ocean wide he is by my side,
and I believe that God is real. ℟

4. The morning sun night's shade enfolds,
a million tongues could not recall,
his mighty power but speak thy word,
and I believe that God is real.

WE ARE MARCHING IN THE LIGHT OF GOD
Traditional South African.

We are marching in the light of God,
we are marching in the light of God,
we are marching in the light of God.
We are marching in the light of,
the light of God.
We are marching, marching,
we are marching, marching,
we are marching in the light of,
the light of God.
We are marching, marching,
we are marching, marching,
we are marching in the light of God.

SHINE, JESUS, SHINE
Graham Kendrick © 1987 Make Way Music.

Lord, the light of Your love is shining
in the midst of the darkness, shining;
Jesus, Light of the World, shine upon us,
set us free by the truth You now bring us,
shine on me, shine on me.

Shine, Jesus, shine,
fill this land with the Father's glory;
blaze, Spirit, blaze,
set our hearts on fire
Flow, river, flow
flood the nations with grace and mercy
send forth Your word, Lord,
and let there be light.

Lord, I come to Your awesome presence
from the shadows into Your radiance;
by the blood I may enter Your brightness,
search me, try me, consume all my darkness.
Shine on me, shine on me.

As we gaze on Your kingly brightness
so our faces display Your likeness
Ever changing from glory to glory
mirrored here may our lives tell Your story.
Shine on me, shine on me.

SURREXIT CHRISTUS, ALLELUIA

Surrexit Christus, alleluia (Christ is risen, alleluia)

• The Heart of the Church •

There follows a presentation on the heart of the Church. The story of the Catholic Church in Britain today is told as "A Heart that Sees", "A Heart that Serves", "A Heart that Seeks Justice" and "A Heart that Understands". We invite you to enter into our meditation and reflection on Cardinal Newman's motto, "Heart speaks unto heart".

We thank CAFOD (www.CAFOD.org.uk) for sponsoring this presentation and producing it in collaboration with the Catholic Enquiry Office (www.Life4seekers.co.uk). For more information about the organisations and Charities shown in the presentation, please refer to the papal visit website, www.thepapalvisit.org.uk

• The Arrival of Pope Benedict •

The screens in the park will show highlights of the papal visit from the last two days. This will be followed by live coverage of Pope Benedict's approach to Hyde Park, accompanied by music from *The Priests.*

Laudamus Te from Vivaldi's *Gloria*

Lift Thine Eyes: Mendelssohn

King of Kings

Pieces from Handel's *Messiah*: *Glory to God; And the Glory of the Lord; Rejoice greatly; Since by man came death; Hallelujah Chorus*

• Heart Speaks unto Heart •

CHRIST BE BESIDE ME

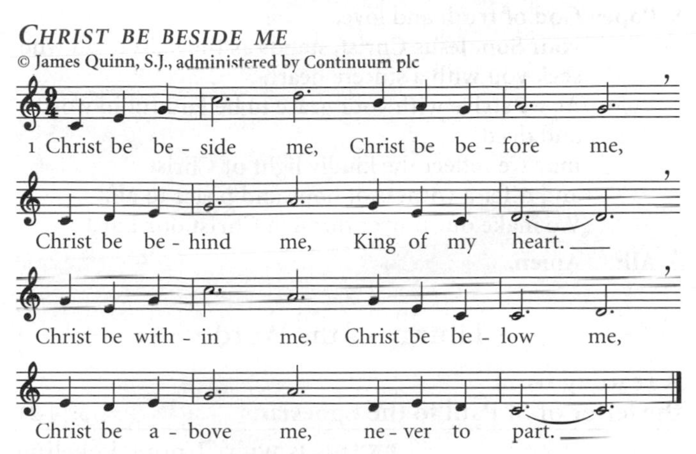

1 Christ be be - side me, Christ be be - fore me,
Christ be be - hind me, King of my heart.
Christ be with - in me, Christ be be - low me,
Christ be a - bove me, ne - ver to part.

2. Christ on my right hand, Christ on my left hand,
Christ all around me, shield in the strife.
Christ in my sleeping, Christ in my sitting,
Christ in my rising, light of my life.

3. Christ be in all hearts thinking about me,
Christ be in all tongues telling of me.
Christ be the vision in eyes that see me,
In ears that hear me, Christ ever be.

Welcome

The Archbishop of Southwark, the Most Revd Peter Smith, welcomes the Holy Father to the Vigil.

Greeting

✠ **Pope:** In the name of the Father, and of the Son, and of the Holy Spirit.

All: **Amen.**

✠ **Pope:** Peace be with you.

All: **And also with you.**

Opening Prayer

✠ Pope: God of truth and love,
your Son, Jesus Christ, stands as the light to all who seek you with a sincere heart.
As we strive with your grace to be faithful in word and deed,
may we reflect the kindly light of Christ
and offer a witness of hope and peace to all.
We make our prayer through Christ our Lord.

All: Amen.

• Liturgy of the Word •

A reading from the letter of St Paul to the Ephesians 3:14-21

THIS IS WHAT I pray, kneeling before the Father, from whom every family, whether spiritual or natural, takes its name:

Out of his infinite glory, may he give you the power through his Spirit for your hidden self to grow strong, so that Christ may live in your hearts through faith, and then, planted in love and built on love, you will with all the saints have the strength to grasp the breadth and the length, the height and the depth; until, knowing the love of Christ, which is beyond all knowledge, you are filled with the utter fullness of God.

Glory be to him whose power, working in us, can do infinitely more than we can ask or imagine; glory be to him from generation to generation in the Church and in Christ Jesus for ever and ever. Amen.

This is the word of the Lord.
Thanks be to God.

PSALM 119

Your word is a lamp to my feet and a light for my path.

They are happy whose life is blameless,
who follow God's law!
They are happy who do his will,
seeking him with all their hearts. ℟

I have sought you with all my heart:
let me not stray from your commands.
I treasure your promise in my heart
lest I sin against you. ℟

I call with all my heart; answer me, O Lord,
and I will obey your decrees.
I call out to you: save me
and I will keep your commands. ℟

Gospel Acclamation

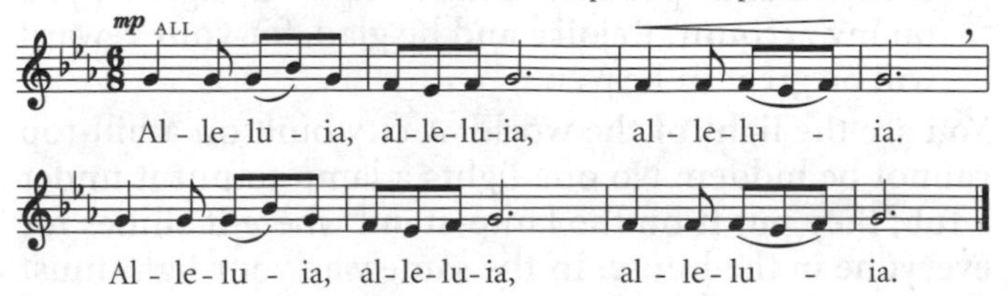

Alleluia. I am the light of the world says the Lord. All who follow me will have the light of life. Alleluia.

Deacon: **The Lord be with you.**
All: **And also with you.**

A reading from
the holy Gospel according to Matthew 5:1-22, 14-15

SEEING THE CROWDS, Jesus went up the hill. There he sat down and was joined by his disciples. Then he began to speak. This is what he taught them:

"Blessed are the poor in spirit; theirs is the kingdom of heaven.

Blessed are the gentle: they shall have the earth for their inheritance.

Blessed are those who mourn: they shall be comforted.

Blessed are those who hunger and thirst for what is right: they shall be satisfied. Blessed are the merciful: they shall have mercy shown them.

Blessed are the pure in heart: they shall see God.

Blessed are the peacemakers: they shall be called sons of God.

Blessed are those who are persecuted in the cause of right: theirs is the kingdom of heaven.

Blessed are you when people abuse you and persecute you and speak all kinds of calumny against you on my account. Rejoice and be glad, for your reward will be great in heaven.

You are the light of the world. A city built on a hill-top cannot be hidden. No one lights a lamp to put it under a tub; they put it on the lamp-stand where it shines for everyone in the house. In the same way your light must shine in the sight of men, so that, seeing your good works, they may give the praise to your Father in heaven."

Deacon: This is the Gospel of the Lord.
All: Praise to you, Lord Jesus Christ.

Homily

After the homily, the Holy Father lights the Paschal Candle; the light is taken to the candles borne by parish representatives as the Blessed Sacrament procession begins.

Lord Jesus Christ, your light shines within us

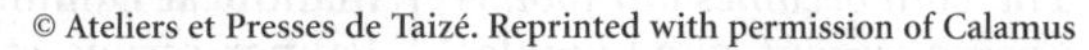

Lord Je - sus Christ, your light shines with-in us.
Let not my doubts and my dark-ness speak to me.
Lord Je - sus Christ, your light shines with-in us.
Let my heart al - ways wel - come your love.

Exposition of the Blessed Sacrament

While the Blessed Sacrament is brought in procession to the altar, all sing: "Adoramus Te Domine":

(hum)
A-do-ra-mus te, Do-mi - ne.

Adoramus te, Domine. *We adore you, Lord.*

Adoration

A period of silence for adoration of the Blessed Sacrament follows.

PANIS ANGELICUS

Bread of Angels,	Panis angelicus
made the bread of men;	fit panis hominum;
The Bread of heaven	Dat panis caelicus
puts an end to all symbols:	figuris terminum:
A thing wonderful!	O res mirabilis!
The Lord becomes our food:	manducat Dominum
poor, a servant, and humble.	Pauper, servus, et humilis.
We beseech Thee,	Te trina Deitas
Godhead One in Three	unaque poscimus:
That Thou wilt visit us,	Sic nos tu visita,
as we worship Thee,	sicut te colimus;
lead us through Thy ways,	Per tuas semitas
We who wish to reach the light	duc nos quo tendimus,
in which Thou dwellest.	Ad lucem quam inhabitas.
	Amen.

LITANY OF THE SACRED HEART

Lord, have mercy **Lord, have mercy**
Christ, have mercy **Christ, have mercy**
Lord, have mercy **Lord, have mercy**

God our Father in heaven **have mercy on us**
God the Son, Redeemer of the world
God the Holy Spirit
Holy Trinity, one God

Heart of Jesus, Son of the eternal Father
Heart of Jesus, formed by the Holy Spirit in the womb of the Virgin Mother
Heart of Jesus, one with the eternal Word
Heart of Jesus, infinite in majesty
Heart of Jesus, holy temple of God
Heart of Jesus, tabernacle of the Most High
Heart of Jesus, house of God and gate of heaven

Heart of Jesus, aflame with love for us
Heart of Jesus, source of justice and love

Heart of Jesus, full of goodness and love
Heart of Jesus, well-spring of all virtue
Heart of Jesus, patient and full of mercy
Heart of Jesus, generous to all who turn to you
Heart of Jesus, fountain of life and holiness

Heart of Jesus, source of healing
Heart of Jesus, sharer in our sorrow
Heart of Jesus, safe-guarder of the vulnerable
Heart of Jesus, friend of the betrayed
Heart of Jesus, companion of the ignored
Heart of Jesus, face of the misjudged
Heart of Jesus, wounded by our failings
Heart of Jesus, bearer of our sufferings
Heart of Jesus, acquainted with grief

Heart of Jesus, atonement for our sins
Heart of Jesus, overwhelmed with insults
Heart of Jesus, broken for our sins
Heart of Jesus, obedient even to death
Heart of Jesus, pierced by a lance
Heart of Jesus, source of all consolation
Heart of Jesus, our life and resurrection
Heart of Jesus, our peace and reconciliation
Heart of Jesus, victim for our sins
Heart of Jesus, salvation of all who trust in you
Heart of Jesus, hope of all who die in you
Heart of Jesus, delight of all the saints

Lamb of God, you take away the sins of the world
Lamb of God, you take away the sins of the world
Lamb of God, you take away the sins of the world

✠ Pope: Jesus, gentle and humble of heart.

All: **Touch our hearts and make them like your own.**

✠ Pope: Let us pray
Father, we rejoice in the gifts of love we have received from the heart of Jesus your Son. Open our hearts to

share his life and continue to bless us with his love. We ask this through the same Christ our Lord. Amen.

"BE STILL AND KNOW THAT I AM GOD"

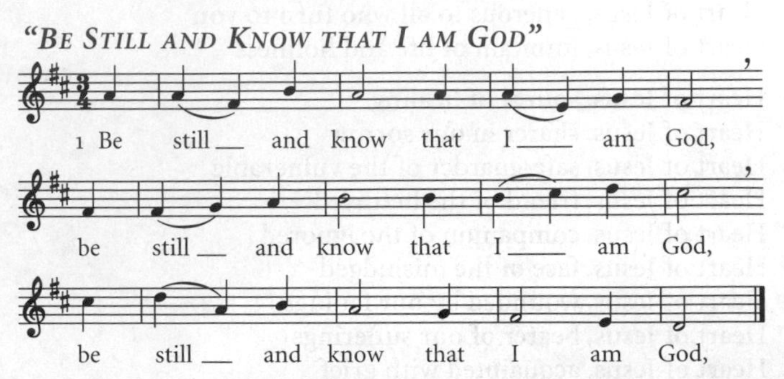
1 Be still and know that I am God,
be still and know that I am God,
be still and know that I am God,

I am the Lord that healeth thee,
I am the Lord that healeth thee,
I am the Lord that healeth thee.

In thee, O Lord, I put my trust,
In thee, O Lord, I put my trust,
In thee, O Lord, I put my trust.

CARDINAL NEWMAN'S PRAYER: RADIATING CHRIST

Dear Jesus,
help me to spread Thy fragrance everywhere I go.
Flood my soul with Thy spirit and life.
Penetrate and possess my whole being so utterly
that all my life may only be a radiance of Thine.
Shine through me,
and be so in me that every soul I come in contact with
may feel Thy presence in my soul.
Let them look up and see no longer me
but only Jesus!
Stay with me,

and then I shall begin to shine
as Thou shinest,
so to shine as to be a light to others;
the light, O Jesus, will be all from Thee;
none of it will be mine;
it will be Thou shining on others through me.
Let me thus praise Thee in the way Thou dost love best
by shining on those around me.
Let me preach Thee without preaching,
not by words but by my example,
by the catching force of the sympathetic influence
of what I do,
the evident fullness of the love my heart bears to Thee.
Amen.

LEAD KINDLY LIGHT

J.H.Newman (1801-1890). Melody C.H. Purday (1799-1885).

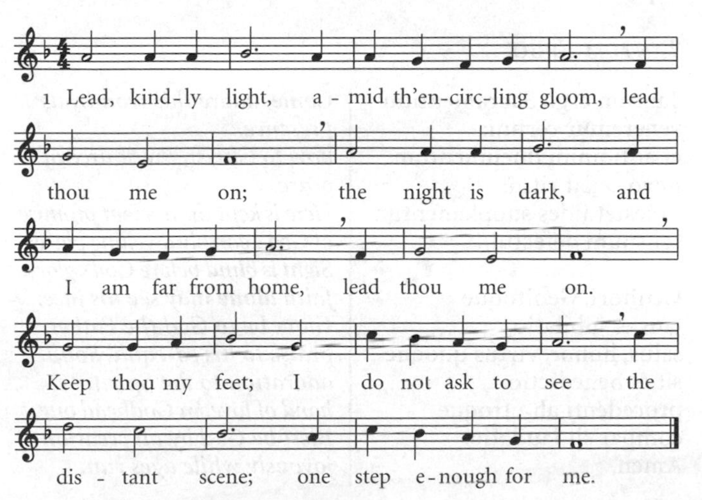
1 Lead, kind-ly light, a - mid th'en-circ-ling gloom, lead
thou me on; the night is dark, and
I am far from home, lead thou me on.
Keep thou my feet; I do not ask to see the
dis - tant scene; one step e-nough for me.

2. I was not ever thus, nor prayed that
Thou shouldst lead me on;
I loved to choose and see my path;
but now lead Thou me on!
I loved the garish day, and, spite of fears,
pride ruled my will. Remember not past years!

3. So long Thy power hath blest me,
sure it still will lead me on.
O'er moor and fen, o'er crag and torrent,
till the night is gone,
and with the morn those angel faces smile,
which I have loved long since, and lost awhile!

4. Meantime, along the narrow rugged path,
thyself hast trod,
lead, Saviour, lead me home in childlike faith,
home to my God.
To rest forever after earthly strife
in the calm light of everlasting life.

TANTUM ERGO

Tantum ergo Sacramentum veneremur cernui: et antiquum documentum novo cedat ritui: praestet fides supplementum sensuum defectui. Genitori, Genitoque laus et jubilatio, salus, honor, virtus quoque sit et benedictio: procedenti ab utroque compar sit laudatio. Amen.	*Come, adore this wondrous presence,* *bow to Christ, the source of grace.* *Here is kept the ancient promise* *of God's earthly dwelling place.* *Sight is blind before God's glory,* *faith alone may see his face.* *Glory be to God the Father,* *praise to his co-equal Son,* *adoration to the Spirit,* *bond of love, in Godhead one.* *Blest be God by all creation* *joyously while ages run.*

Prayer

✠ **Pope: Lord our God,**
in this great sacrament we come into the presence of Jesus Christ, your Son born of the Virgin Mary and crucified for our salvation. May we who declare our faith in this fountain of love and mercy drink from it the water of everlasting life. We ask this through Christ our Lord.

All: Amen.

Benediction

Reposition of the Blessed Sacrament

Recessional

TELL OUT, MY SOUL

1 Tell out, my soul, the great-ness of the Lord! Un-
num-bered bless-ings give my spi - rit voice; ten-der to
me the pro-mise of his word; in God my
Sa-viour shall my heart re - joice.

2. Tell out, my soul, the greatness of his name!
Make known his might, the deeds his arm has done;
his mercy sure, from age to age the same;
his holy name - the Lord, the Mighty One.

3. Tell out, my soul, the greatness of his might!
Powers and dominions lay their glory by.

Proud hearts and stubborn wills are put to flight,
the hungry fed, the humble lifted high.

4.Tell out, my soul, the glories of his word!
Firm is his promise, and his mercy sure.
Tell out, my soul, the greatness of the Lord
to children's children and forever more!

THE LORD BLESS YOU AND KEEP YOU

The Lord bless you and keep you:
The Lord make His face to shine upon you,
to shine upon you and be gracious,
and be gracious unto you.

The Lord bless you and keep you:
The Lord make His face to shine upon you,
to shine upon you and be gracious,
and be gracious unto you

The Lord lift up the light of his countenance upon you.
The Lord lift up the light of his countenance upon you,
and give you peace, and give you peace,
and give you peace, and give you peace.

Amen.

• Recessional programme •

BUT THANKS BE TO GOD

G.F. Handel

If God be for us, who can be against us? Who shall lay anything to the charge of God's elect? It is God that justifieth, who is he that condemneth? It is Christ that died, yea rather, that is risen again, who is at the right hand of God, who makes intercession for us.

(Romans 8:31,33-34)

WORTHY IS THE LAMB

G.F. Handel

Worthy is the Lamb that was slain, and hath redeemed us to God by his blood, to receive power, and riches, and wisdom, and strength, and honour, and glory, and blessing. Blessing and honour, glory and power, be unto Him that sitteth upon the throne, and unto the Lamb, for ever and ever. (Revelation 5:12-14)

The organisers wish to thank Vanpoulles for their partnership in this evening's Vigil. They have donated 3,000 candles, one to be taken from the Vigil to every parish. www.vanpoulles.co.uk

The New English Orchestra established in 1976 is a freelance orchestra comprising professional instrumentalists from all over the British Isles, together with NEO Singers and Dancers.

They perform throughout the UK and in many parts of Europe, aiming to shed a specifically Christian light on a broad range of music. During the past 12 months, the NEO has made a specialism of events called 'Recreatio'. These are 40 minute sequences of Bible readings and spiritual music. All members of the NEO are Christians drawn from different ecumenical traditions.

Musical Director: Mr Nigel Swinford

TYBURN

Tyburn field, near the present Marble Arch, was a place of public execution from 1196 to 1783. Amongst the many thousands who died there were 105 people who have been officially recognised as martyrs for the Catholic faith. English law made it an act of treason to refuse to assent to the royal supremacy over the Church claimed by Henry VIII, or to be (or to harbour) a Catholic priest. The standard penalty for all those convicted of treason at the time was execution by being hanged, drawn and quartered. The first martyrs at Tyburn were Saint John Houghton and his companions, executed on May 4, 1535. The last martyr executed at Tyburn was Saint Oliver Plunkett on July 11, 1681. Religious persecution was not uniquely practised against Catholics, of course: at other times Protestant believers faced similar fates.

In 1571, under Queen Elizabeth I, a novel form of gallows was erected at Tyburn, the "Tyburn Tree". This "Tree" was formed from a horizontal wooden triangle supported by three legs. It was introduced better to permit the execution of several people at once.

The Catholic martyrs brought a new spirit into the barbarities and butchery of Tyburn: a spirit of spiritual joy, spontaneous humour and, in imitation of Christ, a wholehearted forgiveness of those who had brought them to their place of execution.

This spirit flowed over into the crowds around the Tyburn Gallows. When Blessed Thomas Maxfield was dragged to Tyburn in 1616, the Gallows had been adorned with garlands of fragrant flowers while the ground around it was strewn with sweet-smelling herbs and branches of laurel and bay.

Blessed Philip Powel announced from the Tyburn Tree: "This is the happiest day and the greatest joy that ever befell me, for I am brought hither for no other cause or reason than that I am a Roman Catholic priest and a monk of the Order of Saint Benedict" (1646).

Saint Edmund Campion, Jesuit priest, prayed on the scaffold for those responsible for his death: "I recommend your case and mine to Almighty God, the Searcher of hearts, to the end that we may at last be friends in heaven, when all injuries shall be forgotten" (1581).

Edward Morgan, priest, was reproved by a minister on the scaffold for being so cheerful. The martyr replied: "Why should anyone be offended at my going to heaven cheerfully? For God loves a cheerful giver" (1642).

Thus the holy martyrs transformed Tyburn's Deadly Nevergreen Tree into the Tree of Life and the Gate of Heaven, which it remains to this very day.

In the early 19th century all the place names associated with Tyburn field were changed to Oxford Street, Park Lane etc: the little stream Ty was built over and Tyburn, with its unsavoury reputation, was forgotten, except by a small number of Catholics who kept alive the memory of the martyrs and hoped that one day a fitting shrine would be erected to commemorate their sacrifices.

In 1901 the law on associations was passed in France ordering the dissolution of every religious community not authorised by the government. One such order was the Benedictine Adorers of the Sacred Heart of Jesus of Montmartre, and its members left France to make a new home in England. In 1903 they made that home in Tyburn Convent, Hyde Park Place, where they have remained for over 100 years.

The ancient gallows, where so many saints and sinners died is now commemorated in a modern replica of the "Tree" which stands over the altar at the Convent. There, night and day, before the Blessed Sacrament, the Living Bread that is Christ present for us, the sisters pray for the needs of all humankind and especially for the people of Britain: ever mindful of the Catholic Martyrs who suffered and died on the scaffold of Tyburn Tree.

The Adorers of the Sacred Heart, Tyburn Convent

Sunday, September 19

The final day of the Papal visit

England

On the final day of his visit to the United Kingdom, Pope Benedict visits the English Midlands, and during the celebration of Mass beatifies Cardinal John Henry Newman. This is the first ever Beatification to take place in this country; and Cardinal Newman is the first English "confessor of the faith" to be beatified in over 600 years. Following the Mass the Holy Father travels to Oscott College to meet with the Bishops of England, Scotland and Wales. After that meeting he goes to Birmingham Airport for the final State occasion of his visit, the State Farewell Ceremony, and then travels back to Rome and the Vatican.

Programme

09.30: Arrival by helicopter in Birmingham and travel by Popemobile to Cofton Park.

10.00: Pope Benedict XVI presides at the Mass of Beatification of John Henry Newman.

- Recitation of the Angelus

13.00: Pope Benedict makes a private visit to the Oratory of St Philip Neri, Birmingham.

13.45: Pope Benedict arrives at Oscott College to have lunch with the Bishops of England, Scotland and Wales.

16.45: Meeting with the Bishops of England, Scotland and Wales in Oscott College Chapel.

17.15: The Holy Father meets with the Seminarians of England, Scotland and Wales in the grounds of Oscott College.

18.15: State Farewell Ceremony at Birmingham Airport.

18.45: Departure for Rome Ciampino Airport.

HEART SPEAKS TO HEART

Ian Ker

John Henry Newman was born on February 21, 1801, the eldest son of a London banker, whose bank closed when Newman was fifteen in the financial collapse after the Napoleonic wars. That same year, 1816, Newman, who had been brought up in a conventional Church of England home, fell under the religious influence of a Calvinist Evangelical schoolmaster. A brilliant student, Newman entered Trinity College, Oxford next year at the early age of sixteen. However, exhausted by overworking he practically failed his final examinations in 1820. Nevertheless, two years later he was elected to a fellowship at Oriel College, then the intellectual centre of Oxford.

The liberal Anglicanism Newman encountered among his colleagues soon began to undermine his Evangelicalism. However, he was ordained a deacon in 1824 and priest in 1825, working as a curate in an Oxford working-class parish before being appointed a tutor at Oriel in 1826. Two years later he began systematically to read the Church Fathers, and, after being deprived of his tutorship by the Provost of Oriel in 1830 owing to a disagreement over the more personal tutorial system he had introduced, he began work on his first book, *The Arians of the Fourth Century* (1833), which reflects his own reaction against the theological liberalism he had encountered at Oriel.

In December 1832 Newman, together with a sympathetic colleague, Richard Hurrell Froude, set sail for the

Mediterranean. He was deeply disconcerted by what he saw of Rome, his imagination having been "stained" by the Evangelical view of the pope as the anti-Christ. While in Sicily, he nearly died of typhoid fever but he was confident that God had "work" for him to do. He reached England in July 1833, five days before John Keble preached the sermon in the University Church protesting against threatened state interference in the Church of England that Newman always regarded as the start of the Oxford or Tractarian Movement.

In September Newman published the first of the *Tracts for the Times*, which aroused furious controversy. Almost as central to a Movement that sought to establish or recover the Catholic heritage of the Church of England were Newman's pastoral sermons in the University Church, of which he had been vicar since 1828, in which he avoided theological issues but concentrated on the call to holiness. In his *Lectures on the Prophetical Office of the Church* (1837) and his *Lectures on Justification* (1838) Newman argued that Anglicanism was Catholic but "reformed", occupying a *via media* or middle way between Protestantism and Roman Catholicism.

In the summer of 1839 Newman suffered his first doubt about this Anglican "middle way" position. While studying the fifth-century Monophysite heresy, he was disconcerted by the fact that at the Council of Chalcedon Pope Saint Leo the Great had upheld the orthodox Catholic faith while the Monophysites had divided into an extreme and more moderate "middle way" party. In the autumn he was again disconcerted by an article on the fourth-century Donatist schism in which Saint

Augustine's maxim that there is no appeal against the judgement of the universal Church was quoted. Nevertheless, Newman's doctrinal objections to the Church of Rome still remained.

In February 1841 in the famous *Tract 90*, Newman argued that the ostensibly Protestant Thirty-Nine Articles could be interpreted in a Catholic sense. Publicly censured by the University authorities as well as by the bishops, Newman withdrew in February 1842 to the village of Littlemore, which was in his parish and where he had had a church built, where he leased a row of cottages and began a religious community with other like-minded Tractarians. A year later he preached the last of his University as opposed to Parish sermons on "The Theory of Developments in Religious Doctrine". At the end of 1844 he began work on his theological classic *An Essay on the Development of Christian Doctrine* (1845), to test his growing conviction that so-called Roman accretions to Christian doctrine were in fact authentic developments. Having preached his last sermon as an Anglican on "The Parting of Friends" in September 1843, after earlier resigning as Vicar of the University Church, Newman was received into the Catholic Church on October 9, 1845 by the Passionist missionary, Blessed Dominic Barberi.

The convert Littlemore community was offered the use of old Oscott College by Bishop Nicholas Wiseman, which Newman renamed Maryvale, and where he stayed till September 1846 when he left for Rome to study for the Catholic priesthood at the College of Propaganda. Ordained priest in May 1847, Newman began an

Oratorian novitiate with other members of the old Littlemore community prior to establishing the Oratory of Saint Philip Neri at Maryvale in February 1848, from where it moved in February 1849 to Alcester Street in the centre of Birmingham, before moving out to the suburb of Edgbaston to a newly-built house and church in February 1852.

In May and June 1852 Newman, having been appointed first president of the new Catholic University of Ireland, delivered five lectures in Dublin on the idea of a university, which would eventually form part of his classic work of that title. In July he delivered at Oscott College his famous sermon "The Second Spring" on the revival of Catholicism in England. The new University finally opened in Dublin in November 1854. But it was beset by difficulties and Newman resigned after four years. The clericalism that had hampered his efforts to involve the laity was denounced in his celebrated article "On Consulting the Faithful in Matters of Doctrine", which was published in 1859, the year when the Oratory School was founded in Edgbaston.

An attack on Newman's integrity in 1863 by the novelist Charles Kingsley led to his writing the *Apologia pro Vita sua* (1864), his classic theological autobiography. A year later he published *The Dream of Gerontius* that would inspire Edward Elgar's oratorio. The following year appeared *A Letter to Pusey*, actually a slim volume in which Newman put forward a balanced and moderate Mariology. As in his later *Letter to the Duke of Norfolk* (1875) on the First Vatican Council's 1870 definition of papal infallibility, Newman took the opportunity to dissociate himself from extreme Ultramontanism or papalism. 1870 saw the publication of his philosophical classic, the *Grammar of Assent*, in which he completed the philosophy of faith that he had begun in his earlier *Oxford University Sermons* (1843).

Newman's election that year to an honorary fellowship of his old Oxford college, Trinity, was followed by his being made a cardinal in 1879, an honour that finally put an end to Ultramontane suspicions of his orthodoxy and loyalty to the Church. On August 11, 1890 he died of pneumonia. The pall on his coffin bore his cardinal's motto *Cor ad cor loquitur*, "Heart speaks to heart". He was buried in the same grave as his old and closest collaborator, Ambrose St John, between the graves of the other two founding fathers of the Birmingham Oratory.

On January 22, 1991, Pope John Paul II declared Newman to be "Venerable". Then on August 15, 2001, an American training for the permanent diaconate was inexplicably cured of a severe spinal disorder that had left him bent double. Jack Sullivan had been praying to Newman ever since watching a television interview with this writer the previous year. On July 3, 2009 Pope Benedict XVI decreed that Newman be beatified, a beatification he himself will perform on September 19, 2010, on his state visit to England.

Educator, writer, philosopher, preacher, Newman is most remembered for his theology, as one of the two or three greatest Anglican theologians, and as one of the greatest Catholic theologians, whose writings anticipated the teachings of the Second Vatican Council.

CELEBRATION OF THE HOLY EUCHARIST AND BEATIFICATION OF THE SERVANT OF GOD, JOHN HENRY NEWMAN

25th Sunday in Ordinary Time

Cofton Park, Birmingham

GATHERING IN PRAYER - HYMN

Music - BLAENWERN - William Rowlands (1860-1937) arr. Alan Smith.

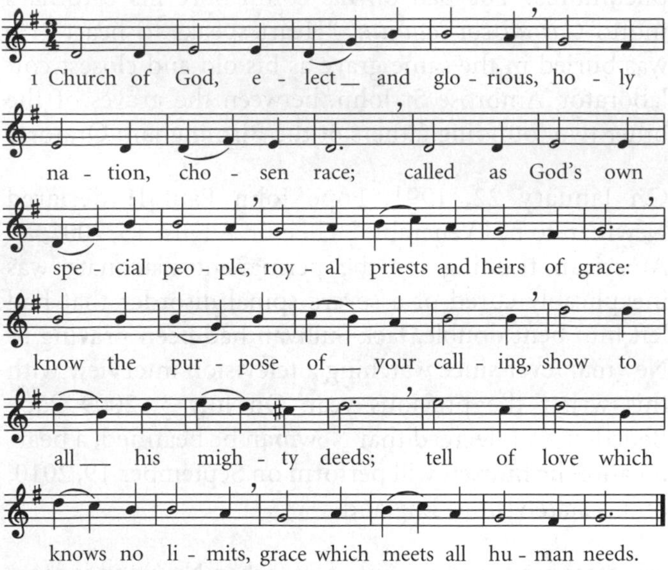

1 Church of God, e - lect and glo - rious, ho - ly
na - tion, cho - sen race; called as God's own
spe - cial peo - ple, roy - al priests and heirs of grace:
know the pur - pose of your call - ing, show to
all his migh - ty deeds; tell of love which
knows no li - mits, grace which meets all hu - man needs.

2. God has called you out of darkness
into his most marvellous light,
brought his truth to life within you,
turned your blindness into sight.

Let your light so shine around you
that God's name is glorified;
and all find fresh hope and purpose
in Christ Jesus crucified.
the Babe of Bethlehem.

3. Once you were an alien people,
strangers to God's heart of love;
but he brought you home in mercy,
citizens of heaven above.
Let his love flow out to others,
let them feel a Father's care;
that they too may know his welcome
and his countless blessings share.

4. Church of God, elect and holy,
be the people he intends;
strong in faith and swift to answer
each command your master sends:
royal priests fulfil your calling
through your sacrifice and prayer;
give your lives in joyful service –
sing his praise, his love declare.

MOTET

From Psalms 95 and 97 - Music - Claudio Monteverdi (1567-1643)

Cantate Domino canticum novum, cantate et benedicite nomini ejus: Quia mirabilia fecit. Cantate et exultate et psallite in cythara et voce psalmi: Quia mirabilia fecit	*Sing to the Lord a new song, sing and give praise to his name: for he has done marvellous deeds. Sing and exult and praise in songs with the harp and the voice: for he has done marvellous deeds.*

HYMN

1 Long-ing for light, we wait in dark-ness. Long-ing for
truth, we turn to you. Make us your own,
your ho-ly peo-ple, light for the world to see.
REFRAIN
Christ, be our light! Shine in our
hearts. Shine through the dark - ness.
Christ, be our light! Shine in your
Church gath-ered to - day.

2. Longing for peace, our world is troubled.
Longing for hope, many despair.
Your word alone has pow'r to save us.
Make us your living voice.

3. Longing for food, many are hungry.
Longing for water, many still thirst.
Make us your bread, broken for others,
shared until all are fed.

4. Longing for shelter, many are homeless.
Longing for warmth, many are cold.
Make us your building, sheltering others,
walls made of living stone.

5. Many the gifts, many the people,
many the hearts that yearn to belong.
Let us be servants to one another,
making your kingdom come.

ENTRANCE PROCESSION

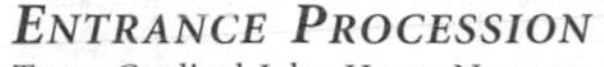

Text - Cardinal John Henry Newman / Music - R.R.Terry arr.Andrew Wright.

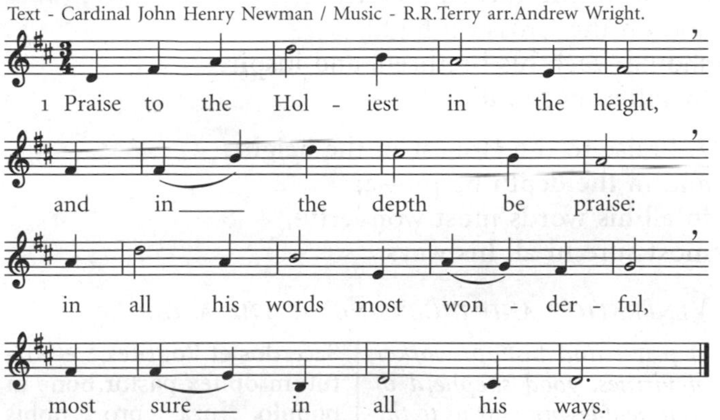
1 Praise to the Hol - iest in the height,
and in ___ the depth be praise:
in all his words most won - der - ful,
most sure ___ in all his ways.

All:
2. O loving wisdom of our God!
When all was sin and shame,
a second Adam to the fight,
and to the rescue came.

Choir only:
3. O wisest love! That flesh and blood
which did in Adam fail,
should strive afresh against the foe,
should strive and should prevail;

All:
4. And that a higher gift than grace
should flesh and blood refine,
God's presence and his very self,
and Essence all divine.

5. O generous love! That he who smote
in man for man the foe,
the double agony in man
for man should undergo.

6. And in the garden secretly
and on the Cross on high,
should teach his brethren, and inspire
to suffer and to die.

7. Praise to the Holiest in the height,
and in the depth be praise,
in all his words most wonderful,
most sure in all his ways.

VENERATION AND INCENSING OF THE ALTAR

O priest and bishop, worker of virtues, good shepherd of your people, pray for us to the Lord. Alleluia.	Sacerdos et Pontifex * et virtutum opifex pastor bone in populo, ora pro nobis Dominum. Alleluia.
Come, ring out our joy to the Lord; hail the rock who saves us. Let us come before him, giving thanks, with songs let us hail the Lord. Glory be…	Venite, exsultemus Domino; jubilemus Deo salutari nostro; præoccupemus faciem ejus in confessione, et in psalmis jubilemus ei: Gloria Patri…

The Archbishop of Birmingham, the Most Reverend Bernard Longley, welcomes his Holiness to Birmingham and to this celebration of the Holy Eucharist.

Introductory Dialogue

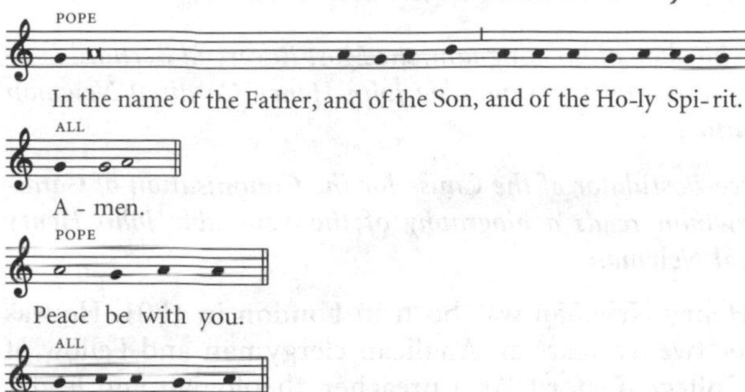

POPE
In the name of the Father, and of the Son, and of the Ho-ly Spi-rit.
ALL
A - men.
POPE
Peace be with you.
ALL
And al-so with you.

The Penitential Act

✠ **Pope: My brothers and sisters, to prepare ourselves to celebrate the sacred mysteries, let us call to mind our sins.**

All: I confess to almighty God, and to you my brothers and sisters, that I have sinned through my own fault, in my thoughts and in my words, in what I have done and in what I have failed to do; and I ask the Blessed Mary, ever virgin, all the angels and saints, and you, my brothers and sisters, to pray for me to the Lord, our God.

✠ **Pope: May almighty God have mercy on us, forgive us our sins, and bring us to everlasting life. Amen.**

Kyrie (Orbis factor)

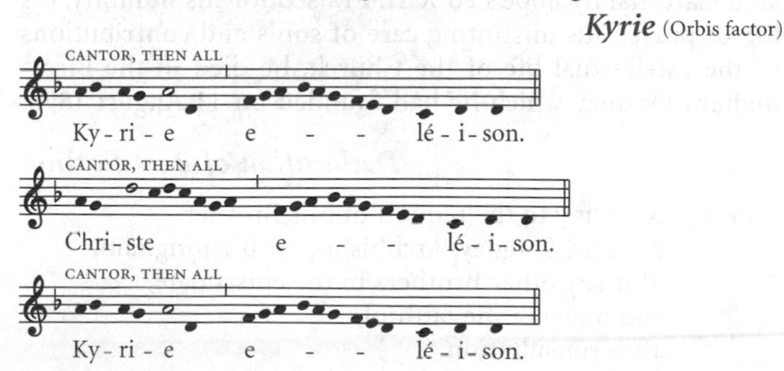

CANTOR, THEN ALL
Ky-ri-e e - - lé-i-son.
CANTOR, THEN ALL
Chri-ste e - - lé-i-son.
CANTOR, THEN ALL
Ky-ri-e e - - lé-i-son.

• The Rite of Beatification •

The Archbishop of Birmingham, the Most Reverend Bernard Longley requests that the Venerable John Henry Cardinal Newman be beatified

The Vice-Postulator of the Cause for the Canonisation of Cardinal Newman reads a biography of the Venerable John Henry Cardinal Newman

John Henry Newman was born in London in 1801. He was for over twenty years an Anglican clergyman and Fellow of Oriel College, Oxford. As a preacher, theologian and leader of the Oxford Movement, he was a prominent figure in the Church of England. His studies of the early Church drew him progressively towards full communion with the Catholic Church. With his companions he withdrew to a life of study and prayer at Littlemore outside Oxford where in 1845 Blessed Dominic Barberi, a Passionist priest, received him into the Catholic Church.

In 1847 he was himself ordained priest in Rome and, encouraged by Blessed Pope Pius IX, went on to found the Oratory of St Philip Neri in England. He was a prolific and influential writer on a variety of subjects, including the development of Christian doctrine, faith and reason, the true nature of conscience, and university education. In 1879 he was created Cardinal by Pope Leo XIII. Praised for his humility, his life of prayer, his unstinting care of souls and contributions to the intellectual life of the Church, he died in the Birmingham Oratory which he had founded on 11 August 1890.

Declaration of Beatification

✠ **Pope:** Acceding to the request of our Brother
Bernard Longley, Archbishop of Birmingham,
of many other Brothers in the episcopate,
and many of the faithful,
after consultation

with the Congregation for the Causes of Saints,
by our apostolic authority
we declare that the venerable Servant of God
John Henry, Cardinal, Newman,
priest of the Congregation of the Oratory,
shall henceforth be invoked as Blessed
and that his feast shall be celebrated
every year of the ninth of October,
in the places and according to the norms
established by Church law.

In the name of the Father, and of the Son,
and of the Holy Spirit.

All: **Amen.**

The portrait of the new Blessed is unveiled and his relics are placed beside the altar.

Acclamation at the Beatification

Text - Cardinal John Henry Newman / Music - R.R.Terry arr.Andrew Wright.

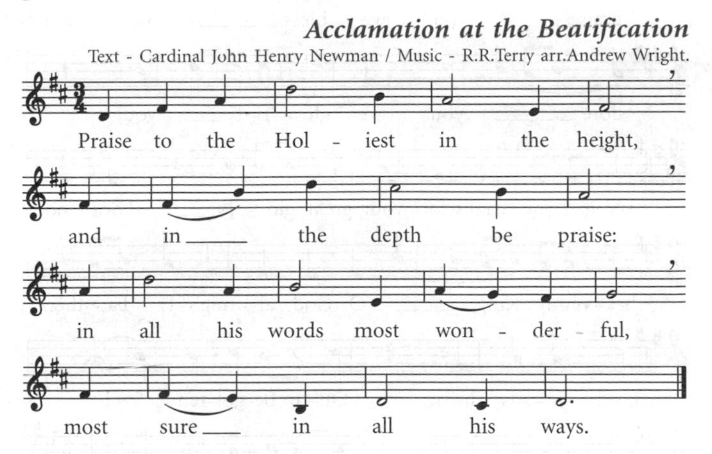
Praise to the Hol - iest in the height,
and in ___ the depth be praise:
in all his words most won - der - ful,
most sure ___ in all his ways.

The Archbishop of Birmingham thanks the Holy Father:

Most Holy Father, I, the Ordinary of Birmingham, give heartfelt thanks to your Holiness for having today proclaimed Blessed the Venerable Servant of God John Henry Newman.

The Archbishop and the Postulator of the cause of Blessed John Henry Newman receive the kiss of peace from the Holy Father.

Procession of reliquary including members of the Newman family and the Oratorians, to greet the Holy Father

Gloria

CANTOR
Glo-ry to God in the high-est,
ALL
and on earth peace to peo-ple of good will. We
praise you, we bless you, we a-
dore you, we glo-ri-fy you,
We give you thanks for your great glo-ry, Lord God,
hea-ven-ly King, O God, al-migh-ty Fa-ther.
Lord Je-sus Christ, On-ly Be-got-ten Son,
Lord God, Lamb of God, Son of the Fa-ther, you
take a-way the sins of the world, have mer-cy on

us; you take a-way the sins of the world, re -
ceive our _ prayer; you are seat-ed at the right _
hand ___ of the Fa-ther, have mer - cy on us.
For you a-lone are the Ho-ly One, you a-lone are the Lord,
you a-lone are the Most _ High, Je-sus Christ, _ with the
Ho - ly Spi - rit, ___ in the glo - ry of God the Fa - ther. _
___ A - - men. ___________

Collect

✠ **Pope:** **O God,**
who bestowed on the priest
Blessed John Henry Newman
the grace to follow your kindly light
and find peace in your Church;
graciously grant that,
through his intercession and example,
we may be led out of shadows and images
into the fullness of your truth.
Through our Lord Jesus Christ your Son,
who lives and reigns with you in the unity of the
Holy Spirit, one God for ever and ever.

All: **Amen.**

• Liturgy of the Word •

A reading from the Prophet Amos **8:4–7**

LISTEN TO THIS you who trample on the needy, and try to suppress the poor people of the country, you who say: 'When will New Moon be over, so that we can sell our corn, and sabbath, so that we can market our wheat? Then by lowering the bushel, raising the shekel, by swindling and tampering with the scales, we can buy up the poor for money, and the needy for a pair of sandals, and get a price for a pair of sandals, and get a price even for the sweepings of the wheat.' The Lord swears by the pride of Jacob, 'Never will I forget a single thing you have done.'

This is the word of the Lord.
Thanks be to God.

• PSALM 115 •

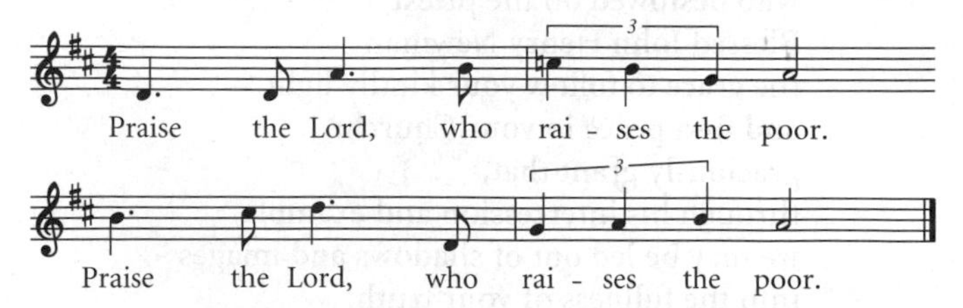

Praise the Lord, who rai - ses the poor.
Praise the Lord, who rai - ses the poor.

Praise, O servants of the Lord,
praise the name of the Lord!
May the name of the Lord be blessed
both now and for evermore! ℟

High above all nations is the Lord,
  above the heavens his glory.
Who is like the Lord, our God,
  who has risen on high to his throne
yet stoops from the heights to look down,
  to look down upon heaven and earth? ℟

From the dust he lifts up the lowly,
  from the dungheap he raises the poor
to set them in the company of princes,
  yes, with the princes of his people. ℟

A reading from
the First letter of St Paul to Timothy 2:1–8

MY ADVICE IS THAT, first of all, there should be prayers offered for everyone – petitions, intercessions and thanksgiving – and especially for kings and others in authority, so that we may be able to live religious and reverent lives in peace and quiet. To do this is right, and will please God our saviour: he wants everyone to be saved and reach full knowledge of the truth. For there is only one God, and there is only one mediator between God and mankind, himself a man, Christ Jesus, who sacrificed himself as a ransom for them all. He is the evidence of this, sent at the appointed time, and I have been named a herald and apostle of it and – I am telling the truth and no lie – a teacher of the faith and the truth to the pagans. In every place, then, I want the men to lift their hands up reverently in prayer, with no anger or argument.

This is the word of the Lord.
Thanks be to God.

Gospel Acclamation

Music: Salisbury Alleluia © 1988, 1992, Christopher Walker, published by OCP publications. Reprinted with permission of Calamus

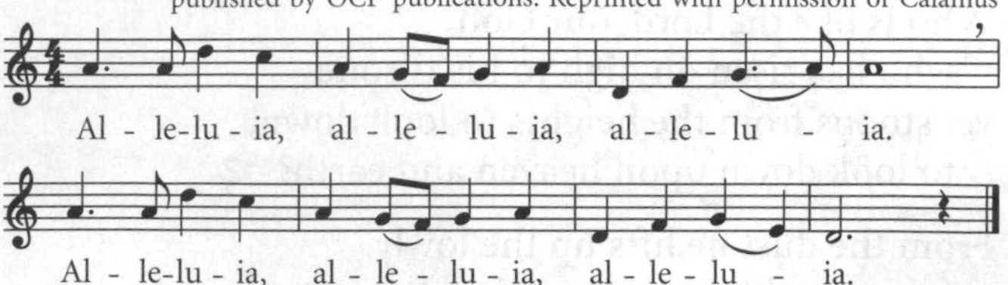
Al - le-lu - ia, al - le - lu - ia, al - le - lu - ia.
Al - le-lu - ia, al - le - lu - ia, al - le - lu - ia.

Your words are Spirit, your words are life. Lord Jesus Christ, only you have the words, the words of eternal life.

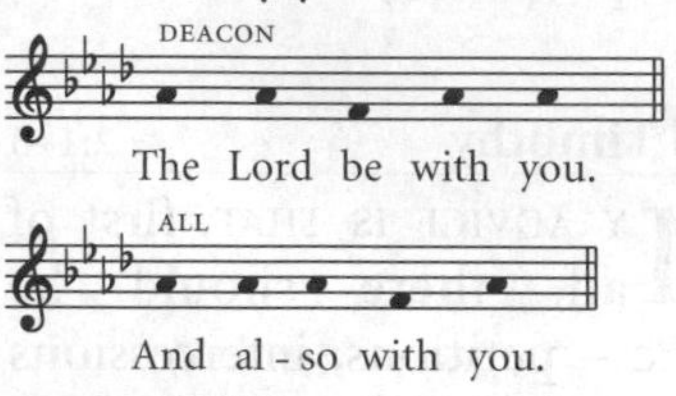
DEACON
The Lord be with you.
ALL
And al - so with you.

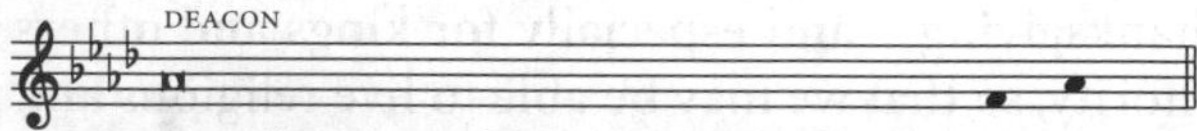
DEACON
A reading from the holy Gospel according to Luke.

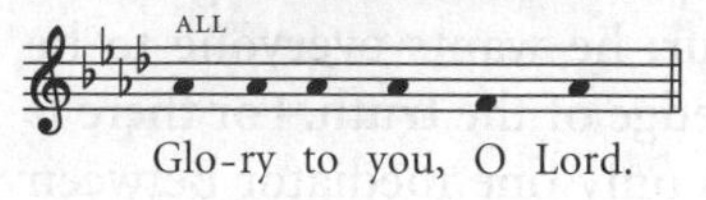
ALL
Glo-ry to you, O Lord.

A reading from the Gospel according to St Luke **16:1–13**

JESUS SAID TO his disciples: 'There was a rich man and he had a steward who was denounced to him for being wasteful with his property. He called for the man and said, "What is this I hear about you? Draw me up an account of your stewardship because you are not to be my steward any longer." Then the steward said to himself, "Now that my master is taking the stewardship from me, what am I to do? Dig? I am not strong enough. Go

begging? I should be too ashamed. Ah, I know what I will do to make sure that when I am dismissed from office there will be some to welcome me into their homes."

'Then he called his master's debtors one by one. To the first he said, "How much do you owe my master?" "One hundred measures of oil," was the reply. The steward said, "Here, take your bond; sit down straight away and write fifty." To another he said, "And you, sir, how much do you owe?" "One hundred measures of wheat," was the reply. The steward said, "Here, take your bond and write eighty."

'The master praised the dishonest steward for his astuteness. For the children of this world are more astute in dealing with their own kind than are the children of light.

'And so I tell you this: use money, tainted as it is, to win you friends, and thus make sure that when it fails you, they will welcome you into the tents of eternity. The man who can be trusted in little things can be trusted in great; the man who is dishonest in little things will be dishonest in great. If then you cannot be trusted with money, that tainted thing, who will trust you with genuine riches? And if you cannot be trusted with what is not yours, who will give you what is your very own?

'No servant can be the slave of two masters: he will either hate the first and love the second, or treat the first with respect and the second with scorn. You cannot be the slave both of God and of money.'

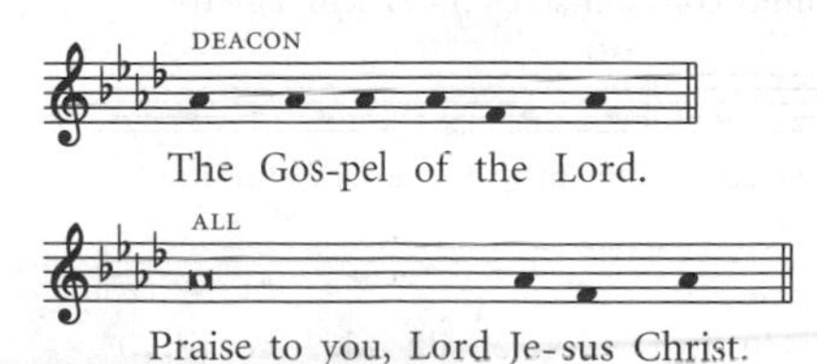

DEACON
The Gos-pel of the Lord.
ALL
Praise to you, Lord Je-sus Christ.

The Alleluia is reprised while the Gospel Book is reverenced by the Holy Father.

Homily

The Profession of Faith

POPE
Cre-do in u-num De-um,
CANTOR
Pa-trem om-ni-po-tén-tem, fac-tó-rem cae-li et ter-rae,
vi-si-bí-li-um ó-mni-um et in-vi-si-bí-li-um.
ALL
Et in u-num Dó-mi-num Je-sum Chri-stum, Fí-li-um
De-i u-ni-gé-ni-tum.
CANTOR
Et ex Pa-tre na-tum
an-te ó-mni-a saé-cu-la.
ALL
De-um de De-o
lu-men de lú-mi-ne, De-um ve-rum de De-o ve-ro.
CANTOR
Gé-ni-tum, non fac-tum, con-sub-stan-ti-á-lem Pa-tri:
per quem ó-mni-a fac-ta sunt.
ALL
Qui prop-ter nos hó-mi-nes,
et prop-ter nos-tram sa-lú-tem des-cén-dit de cae-lis.

CANTOR
Et in-car-ná-tus est de Spí-ri-tu San-cto
ex Ma-ri-a Vir-gi-ne: Et ho-mo fac-tus est.
ALL
Cru-ci-fí-xus ét-i-am pro no-bis
sub Pón-ti-o Pi-la-to pas-sus, et se-púl-tus est.
CANTOR
Et re-sur-re-xit tér-ti-a di-e, se-cún-dum Scri-ptú-ras.
ALL
Et as-cén-dit in cae-lum se-det ad déx-te-ram Pa-tris.
CANTOR
Et í-te-rum ven-tú-rus est cum gló-ri-a,
ju-di-cá-re vi-vos et mór-tu-os: cu-jus re-gni non e-rit fi-nis.
ALL
Et in Spí-ri-tum San-ctum Dó-mi-num et vi-vi-fi-cán-tem:
qui ex Pa-tre Fi-li-ó-que pro-cé-dit.
CANTOR
Qui cum Pa-tre et Fí-li-o si-mul a-do-rá-tur
et con-glo-ri-fi-cá-tur qui lo-cú tus est per Pro-phé-tas.

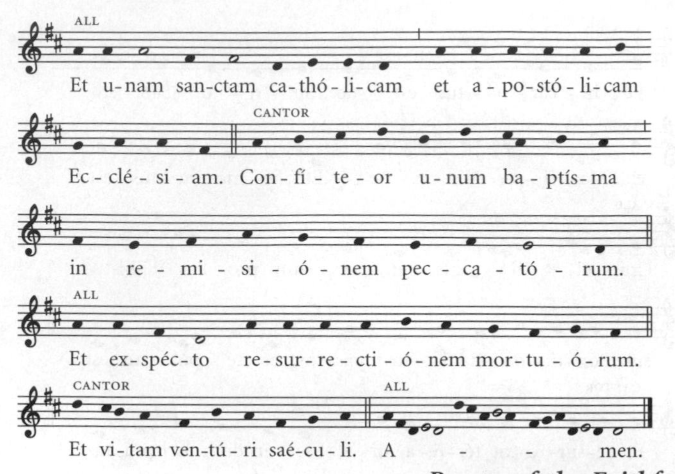

Prayer of the Faithful

The Church in the United Kingdom draws its members from many cultures and nations. Today the Prayer of the Faithful is offered in six languages commonly spoken in the United Kingdom: German, Welsh; Irish; French; Vietnamese, and Punjabi.

✠ Pope: Let us present our needs to the Lord, trusting in His abundant love and mercy:

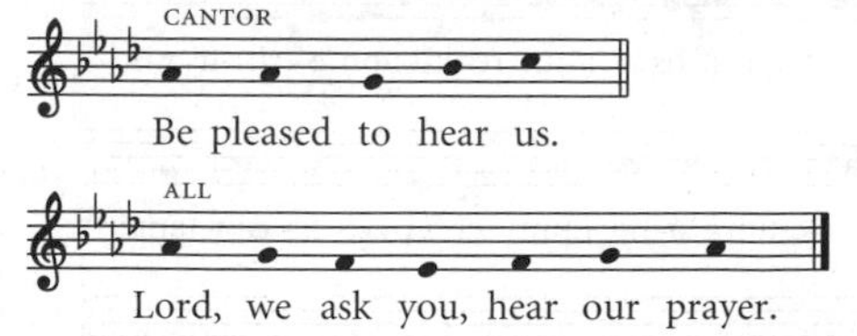

CANTOR
Be pleased to hear us.
ALL
Lord, we ask you, hear our prayer.

1. Let us pray for our Holy Father, Pope Benedict. May the Lord's grace protect and guide him as he serves the Church as Vicar of Christ and successor of St Peter.

2. Let us pray for our nation: for Queen Elizabeth, for those who govern, and for all who hold responsibility in public life; that they may serve the common good and recognise the dignity of every person.

3. Let us pray for all members of the Church. May all respond generously to their vocation to be salt for the earth and light for the world, witnessing to God's presence especially in consecrated service and family life.

4. Let us pray for the unity of the Church. May the example of Blessed John Henry Newman inspire all Christians to seek after closer unity in Christ.

5. Let us pray for the gifts of wisdom and truth for theologians, artists and educators. In their response to the beauty of God may they help others to a deeper appreciation of the Gospel message.

6. On this Home Mission Sunday let us pray that our mission may be inspired by Blessed John Henry Newman. As we celebrate the recognition of holiness of one of our countrymen, may we seek the holiness that presents itself to us in everyday living.

✠ **Pope:** Almighty God and Father,
we entrust ourselves to your care.
In your mercy hear the prayers we bring to you
and answer our petitions according to your will,
through Christ our Lord. Amen.

• Liturgy of the Eucharist •

OFFERTORY SONG

Text - Cardinal John Henry Newman / Music - Stuttgart arr. Peter Jones.

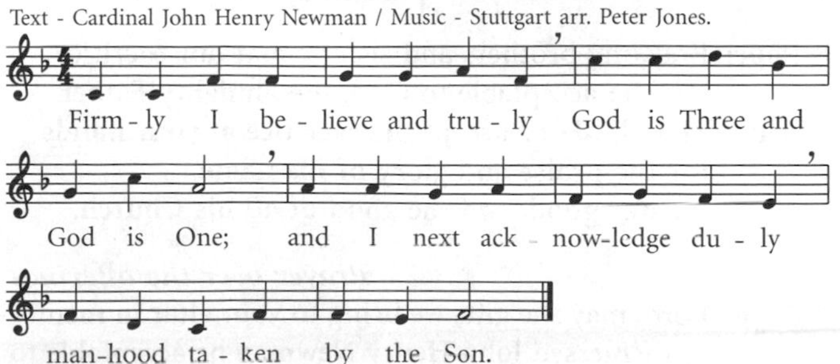
Firm - ly I be - lieve and tru - ly God is Three and
God is One; and I next ack - now-ledge du - ly
man-hood ta - ken by the Son.

2. And I trust and hope most fully
in that manhood crucified;
and each thought and deed unruly
do to death, as he has died.

3. Simply to his grace and wholly
light and life and strength belong;
and I love supremely, solely,
him the holy, him the strong.

4. And I hold in veneration,
for the love of him alone,
Holy Church, as his creation,
and her teachings, as his own.

5. Adoration aye be given,
with and through the angelic host,
to the God of earth and heaven,
Father, Son and Holy Ghost.

MOTET AT THE INCENSING OF THE ALTAR AND GIFTS
Music: C. V. Stanford (1852-1924).

Psalm 118 v.1	Psalm 118 v.1
They are happy whose life is blameless, who follow God's law!	Beati quorum via integra est: qui ambulant in lege Domini.

✠ Pope: Pray, my brothers and sisters, that our sacrifice may be acceptable to God, the almighty Father.

All: **May the Lord accept the sacrifice at your hands for the praise and glory of his name, for our good, and the good of all his Church.**

Prayer over the offerings

✠ Pope: Lord, may the gifts we bring to your altar in memory of Blessed John Henry Newman be acceptable to you. Free us from the things that keep us from you and teach us to seek you as our only good. We ask this through Christ our Lord.

All: **Amen.**

Preface

POPE
Dó-mi-nus vo - bís-cum.
ALL
Et cum spí-ri-tu tu - o.
POPE
Sur - sum cor - da.
ALL
Ha-bé - mus ad Dó-mi-num.
POPE
Grá-ti - as a-gá - mus Dó-mi-no De-o nos-tro.
ALL
Di - gnum et iu - stum est.

Vere dignum et iustum est, æquum et salutáre, nos tibi semper et ubíque grátias ágere: Dómine, sancte Pater, omnípotens ætérnae Deus: per Christum Dóminum nostrum.

Qui in Sanctórum concílio celebráris, et eórum coronándo mérita tua dona corónas.

Father, all-powerful and ever-living God, we do well always and everywhere to give you thanks.

You are glorified in your saints, for their glory is the crowning of your gifts. In their lives on earth, you give us an example. In our communion with them, you give us their friendship.

In their prayer for the Church, you give us strength and protection. This great company of witnesses spurs us on to victory, to share their prize of everlasting glory, through Jesus Christ our Lord.

With angels and archangels and the whole company of saints we sing our unending hymn of praise:

Qui nobis eórum conversatióne largíris exémplum, et communióne consórtium, et intercessióne subsídium; ut, tantis téstibus confirmáti, ad propósitum certámen currámus invícti et immarcescíbilem cum eis corónam glóriæ consequámur, per Christum Dóminum nostrum.

Et ídeo cum Angelis et Archángelis, cumque multíplici congregatióne Sanctórum, hymnum laudis tibi cánimus, sine fine dicéntes:

Sanctus

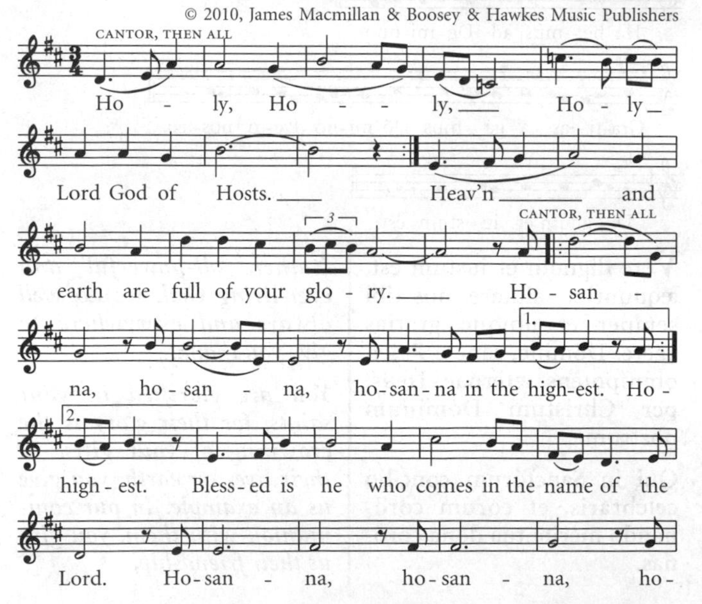

CANTOR, THEN ALL
Ho - ly, Ho - - ly, Ho - ly
Lord God of Hosts. Heav'n and
CANTOR, THEN ALL
earth are full of your glo - ry. Ho - san -
na, ho - san - na, ho - san - na in the high - est. Ho -
1.
2.
high - est. Bless - ed is he who comes in the name of the
Lord. Ho - san - na, ho - san - na, ho -

CANTOR, THEN ALL
san - na, ho - san - na, ho - san -
na, ho - san - na in the high - est, ho - high - est.
1.
2.

Eucharistic Prayer III

Vere Sanctus es, Dómine, et mérito te laudat omnis a te cóndita creatúra, quia per Fílium tuum, Dóminum nostrum Iesum Christum, Spíritus Sancti operánte virtúte, vivíficas et sanctíficas univérsa, et pópulum tibi congregáre non désinis, ut a solis ortu usque ad occásum oblátio munda offerátur nómini tuo.

Súpplices ergo te, Dómine, deprecámur, ut hæc múnera, quæ tibi sacránda detúlimus, eódem Spíritu sanctificáre dignéris, ut Corpus et ✠ Sanguis fiant Fílii tui Dómini nostri Iesu Christi, cuius mandáto hæc mystéria celebrámus.

Ipse enim in qua nocte tradebátur accépit panem et tibi grátias agens benedíxit, fregit, dedítque discípulis suis, dicens: ACCÍPITE ET MANDUCÁTE EX HOC OMNES: HOC EST ENIM CORPUS MEUM, QUOD PRO VOBIS TRADÉTUR.

Father, you are holy indeed, and all creation rightly gives you praise. All life, all holiness comes from you through your Son, Jesus Christ our Lord, by the working of the Holy Spirit.

From age to age you gather a people to yourself, so that from east to west a perfect offering may be made to the glory of your name.

And so, Father, we bring you these gifts. We ask you to make them holy by the power of your Spirit, that they may become the body ✠ and blood of your Son, our Lord Jesus Christ, at whose command we celebrate this eucharist.

On the night he was betrayed, he took bread and gave you thanks and praise. He broke the bread, gave it to his disciples and said: TAKE THIS, ALL OF YOU, AND EAT IT: THIS IS MY BODY WHICH WILL BE GIVEN UP FOR YOU.

When supper was ended, he took the cup. Again he gave you thanks and praise, gave the cup to his disciples and said: TAKE THIS, ALL OF YOU AND DRINK FROM IT: THIS IS THE CUP OF MY BLOOD, THE BLOOD OF THE NEW AND EVERLASTING COVENANT. IT WILL BE SHED FOR YOU AND FOR ALL SO THAT SINS MAY BE FORGIVEN. DO THIS IN MEMORY OF ME.

The Mystery of Faith.

Símili modo, postquam cenátum est, accípiens cálicem, et tibi grátias agens benedíxit, dedítque discípulis suis, dicens: ACCÍPITE ET BÍBITE EX EO OMNES: HIC EST ENIM CALIX SÁNGUINIS MEI NOVI ET ÆTÉRNI TESTAMÉNTI, QUI PRO VOBIS ET PRO MULTIS EFFUNDÉTUR IN REMISSIÓNEM PECCATÓRUM. HOC FÁCITE IN MEAM COMMEMORATIÓNEM.

Mysterium fidei.

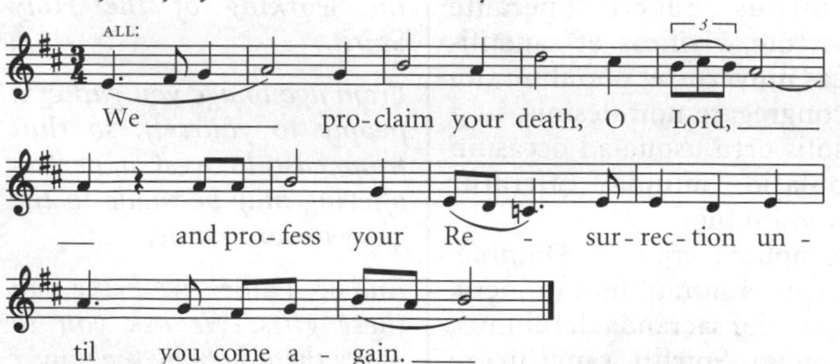
ALL:
We pro-claim your death, O Lord,
and pro-fess your Re - sur-rec-tion un -
til you come a - gain.

Father, calling to mind the death your Son endured for our salvation, his glorious resurrection and ascension into heaven, and ready to greet him when he comes again, we offer you in thanksgiving this holy and living sacrifice.

Look with favour on your Church's offering, and see the Victim whose death has reconciled us to yourself. Grant

Mémores ígitur, Dómine, eiúsdem Fílii tui salutíferæ passiónis necnon mirábilis resurrectiónis et ascensiónis in cælum, sed et præstolántes álterum eius advéntum, offérimus tibi, grátias referéntes, hoc sacrifícium vivum et sanctum.

Réspice, quæ sumus, in oblatiónem Ecclésiæ tuæ et, agnóscens Hóstiam, cuius voluísti immolatióne placári, concéde, ut qui Córpore et Sánguine Fílii tui refícimur, Spíritu eius Sancto repléti, unum corpus et unus spíritus inveniámur in Christo.

that we, who are nourished by his body and blood, may be filled with his Holy Spirit, and become one body, one spirit in Christ.

Ipse nos tibi perfíciat munus ætérnum, ut cum eléctis tuis hereditátem cónsequi valeámus, in primis cum beatíssima Vírgine, Dei Genetríce, María, cum beátis Apóstolis tuis et gloriósis Martyribus cum Beato Ioanne Henrico et ómnibus Sanctis, quorum intercessióne perpétuo apud te confídimus adiuvári.

May he make us an everlasting gift to you and enable us to share in the inheritance of your saints, with Mary, the virgin Mother of God; with the apostles, the martyrs, Blessed John and all your saints, on whose constant intercession we rely for help.

Hæc Hóstia nostræ reconciliatiónis profíciat, quæsumus, Dómine, ad totíus mundi pacem atque salútem. Ecclésiam tuam, peregrinántem in terra, in fide et caritáte firmáre dignéris cum fámulo tuo Papa nostro Benedicto et Epíscopo nostro Bernado, cum episcopáli órdine et univérso clero et omni pópulo acquisitiónis tuæ.

Lord, may this sacrifice, which has made our peace with you, advance the peace and salvation of all the world. Strengthen in faith and love your pilgrim Church on earth; your servant, Pope Benedict, our bishop Bernard, and all the bishops, with the clergy and the entire people your Son has gained for you.

Votis huius famíliæ, quam tibi astáre voluísti, adésto propítius. Omnes fílios tuos ubíque dispérsos tibi, clemens Pater, miserátus coniúnge.

Father, hear the prayers of the family you have gathered here before you. In mercy and love unite all your children wherever they may be.

Fratres nostros defúnctos et omnes qui, tibi placéntes, ex

Welcome into your kingdom our departed brothers and

sisters, and all who have left this world in your friendship. We hope to enjoy for ever the vision of your glory, through Christ our Lord, from whom all good things come.

hoc sæculo transiérunt, in regnum tuum benígnus admítte, ubi fore sperámus, ut simul glória tua perénniter satiémur, iungit manus per Christum Dóminum nostrum, per quem mundo bona cuncta largíris.

The Doxology and Great Amen

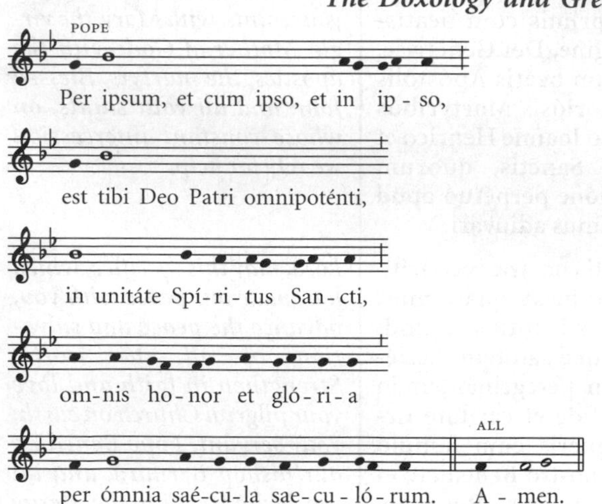
POPE
Per ipsum, et cum ipso, et in ip - so,
est tibi Deo Patri omnipoténti,
in unitáte Spí-ri-tus San-cti,
om-nis ho-nor et gló-ri-a
per ómnia saé-cu-la sae-cu-ló-rum.
ALL
A - men.

• Communion Rite •

✠ Pope: Let us pray with confidence to the Father in the words our Saviour gave us:

Our Father, who art in heaven,
hallowed be thy name.
Thy kingdom come,
Thy will be done on earth as it is in heaven.
Give us this day our daily bread
and forgive us our trespasses

as we forgive those who trespass against us.
and lead us not into temptation,
but deliver us from evil.

✠ **Pope:** Deliver us, Lord, from every evil
and grant us peace in our day.
In your mercy, keep us free from sin
and protect us from all anxiety,
as we wait in joyful hope
for the coming of our Saviour, Jesus Christ.

All: **For the kingdom, the power, and the glory are yours, now and for ever. Amen.**

✠ **Pope:** Lord, Jesus Christ, you said to your apostles: I leave you peace, my peace I give you. Look not on our sins, but on the faith of your Church, and grant us the peace and unity of your kingdom, where you live for ever and ever.

All: **Amen.**

✠ **Pope:** The peace of the Lord be with you always.

All: **And also with you.**

Deacon: Let us offer each other the sign of peace.

Lamb of God

ALL
Lamb of God, you take a - way the sins of the
CANTOR
ALL
world, have mer - cy on us, have mer - cy on us.
3
ALL
Lamb of God, you take a - way the
CANTOR
sins of the world, have mer - cy on us,

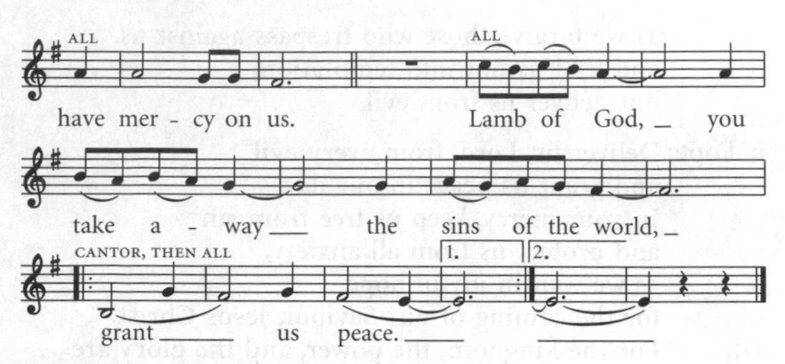
ALL
have mer - cy on us.
ALL
Lamb of God, you
take a - way the sins of the world,
CANTOR, THEN ALL
1.
2.
grant us peace.

✠ **Pope:** **This is the Lamb of God who takes away the sins of the world. Happy are those who are called to his supper:**

All: **Lord, I am not worthy to receive you, but only say the word and I shall be healed.**

SONGS DURING THE DISTRIBUTION OF HOLY COMMUNION

Verses 1 and 3 by John Keble (1792-1866), verses 2 and 4 from W. J. Hall's Psalms and Hymns (1836) Melody - Franconia - J B König (1738).

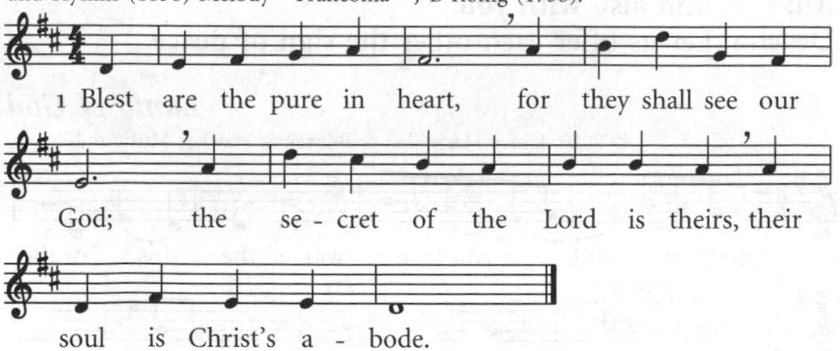
1 Blest are the pure in heart, for they shall see our
God; the se - cret of the Lord is theirs, their
soul is Christ's a - bode.

2. The Lord who left the heavens
our life and peace to bring,
to dwell in lowliness with men,
their pattern and their king.

3. Still to the lowly soul
he doth himself impart

and for his dwelling and his throne
chooseth the pure in heart.

4. Lord, we thy presence seek;
may ours this blessing be:
give us a pure and lowly heart,
a temple meet for thee.

COMMUNION MOTET

Magnificat antiphon 2nd Vespers, All Saints Music - William Byrd (1539-1623).

O quam gloriosum est regnum, in quo cum Christo gaudent omnes sancti, amicti stolis albis sequuntur Agnum quocunque ierit, laudantes Deum et dicentes: Benedictio et claritas ct sapientia et gratiarum actio, honor, virtus et fortitudo Deo nostro in saecula saeculorum. Amen.

O how glorious is the kingdom wherein all the Saints rejoice with Christ; arrayed in white robes they follow the Lamb wherever he goes, praising God and saying: Blessing and glory and wisdom and thanksgiving, honour and power and strength, to our God, for ever and ever. Amen. (Revelation 7:12)

HYMN

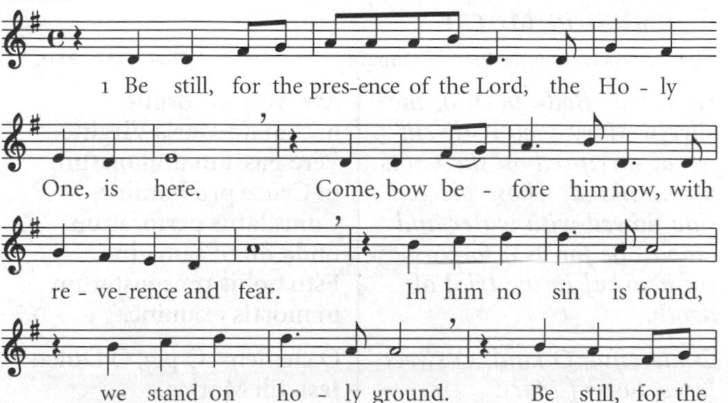

1 Be still, for the pres-ence of the Lord, the Ho - ly
One, is here. Come, bow be - fore him now, with
re - ve-rence and fear. In him no sin is found,
we stand on ho - ly ground. Be still, for the

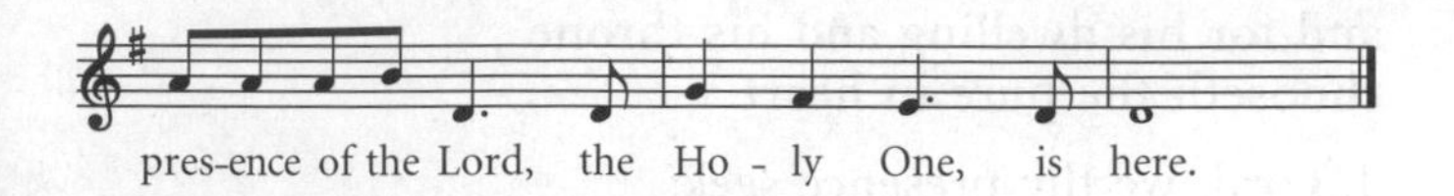

pres-ence of the Lord, the Ho - ly One, is here.

2. Be still, for the glory of the Lord
is shining all around;
He burns with holy fire,
with splendour He is crowned.
How awesome is the sight,
our radiant King of light!
Be still, for the glory of the Lord
is shining all around.

3. Be still, for the power of the Lord
is moving in this place,
He comes to cleanse and heal,
to minister His grace.
No work too hard for Him,
in faith receive from Him;
Be still, for the power of the Lord
is moving in this place.

COMMUNION MOTET

Medieval Sequence for the Feast of Corpus Christi. / Music: E. Elgar (1857-1934).

Hail, true Body, born of the Virgin Mary, who truly suffered, sacrificed on the Cross for mankind, whose pierced side flowed with water and blood: be for us a foretaste [of heaven] in the trial of death.	**Ave, verum corpus natum de Maria Virgine, Vere passum immolatum in Cruce pro homine, Cujus latus perforatum unda fluxit sanguine, Esto nobis praegustatum in mortis examine.**
O merciful, O kind, O sweet Jesus, Son of Mary.	**O clemens, O pie, O Dulcis Jesu fili Mariae.**

TAIZÉ CHANT

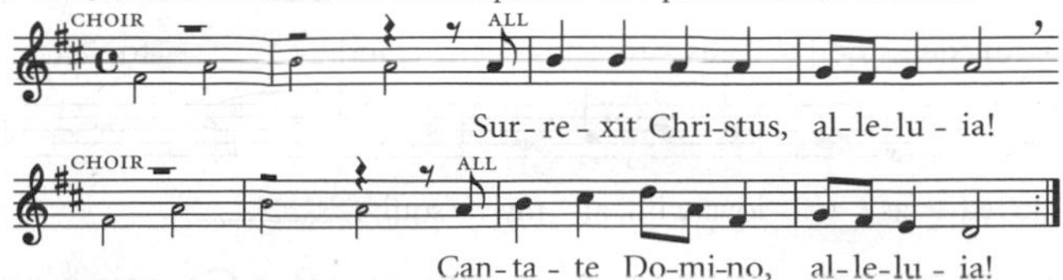

CHOIR
ALL
Sur-re-xit Chri-stus, al-le-lu-ia!
CHOIR
ALL
Can-ta-te Do-mi-no, al-le-lu-ia!

Christ is risen, alleluia! Sing to the Lord, alleluia!

HYMN

1 Make me a chan-nel of your peace. Where
2 Make me a chan-nel of your peace. Where
4 Make me a chan-nel of your peace. It
there is ha-tred let me bring your love; where
there's des-pair in life let me bring hope; where
is in par-don-ing that we are par-doned, in
there is in-ju-ry, your par-don, Lord; and
there is dark-ness, on-ly light; and
giv-ing to all men that we re-ceive; and in
to verse 2
to verse 3
where there's doubt, true faith in you.
where there's sad-ness, ev-er joy.
dy-ing that we're born to e-ter-nal life.
3 Oh, Mas-ter, grant that I may ne-ver seek so
much to be con-soled as to con-sole; to be

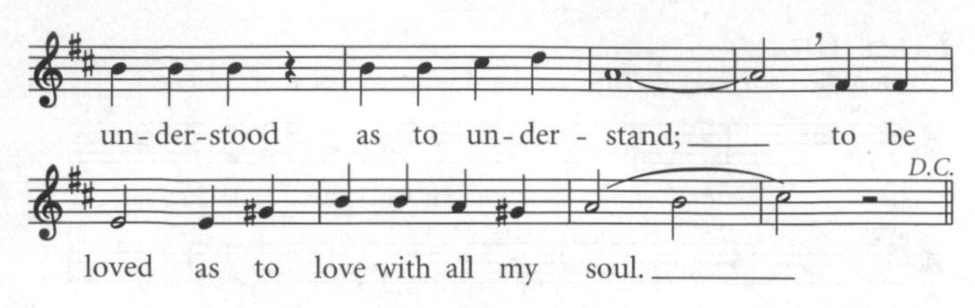
un-der-stood as to un-der - stand; to be
D.C.
loved as to love with all my soul.

Prayer after Communion

✠ **Pope:** **Lord,**
By the power of this sacrament and the example of Blessed John Henry Newman,
Guide us always in your love.
May the good work you have begun in us reach perfection in the day of Christ Jesus,
Who is Lord for ever and ever.

All: **Amen.**

• Concluding Rites •

The Holy Father delivers his weekly Angelus address.

The Angelus

V. The angel of the Lord declared unto Mary.
R. And she conceived of the Holy Spirit.

Hail Mary, full of grace; the Lord is with Thee: blessed art thou among women, and blessed is the fruit of thy womb, Jesus. Holy Mary, Mother of God, prayer for us sinners, now and at the hour of our death.*

V. Behold the handmaid of the Lord,
R. Be it done to me according to Thy word.

V. Angelus Domini nuntiavit Mariae.
R. Et concepit de Spiritu Sancto.

Ave Maria, gratia plena; Dominus tecum: benedicta tu in mulieribus, et benedictus fructus ventris tui Iesus. Sancta Maria, Mater Dei ora pro nobis peccatoribus, nunc et in hora mortis nostrae. Amen.

V. Ecce ancilla Domini,
R. Fiat mihi secundum verbum tuum.

Ave Maria, gratia plena...

Hail Mary, full of grace...

V. Et Verbum caro factum est,
R. Et habitavit in nobis.

V. And the Word was made flesh,
R. And dwelt among us.

Ave Maria, gratia plena...

Hail Mary, full of grace...

V. Ora pro nobis, sancta Dei Genetrix,
R. Ut digni effi ciamur promissionibus Christi.

V. Pray for us, O holy Mother of God,
R. That we may be made worthy of the promises of Christ.

Oremus. Gratiam tuam, quaesumus, Domine, mentibus nostris infunde; ut qui, Angelo nuntiante, Christi Filii tui incarnationem cognovimus, per passionem eius et crucem ad resurrectionis gloriam perducamur.

Let us pray: Pour forth, we beseech Thee, O Lord, Thy grace into our hearts, that we to whom the Incarnation of Christ Thy Son was made known by the message of an angel, may by His Passion and Cross be brought to the glory of His Resurrection.

Per eumdem Christum Dominum nostrum. Amen.

Through the same Christ Our Lord. Amen.

Final Blessing

POPE
Dó-mi-nus vo-bís-cum.
ALL
Et cum spí-ri-tu tu-o.
POPE
Sit nomen Dómini be-ne-díc-tum.
ALL
Ex hoc nunc et usque in saé-cu-lum.

POPE
Adiutórium nostrum in nómine Dó-mi-ni.
ALL
Qui fecit caelum et ter-ram.
POPE
Benedícat vos om-ni-pó-tens De-us: Pa-ter, et Fí-li-us,
ALL
et Spí-ri-tus San-ctus. A-men.
DEACON
I-te, mis-sa est.
ALL
De-o grá-ti-as.

CONCLUDING HYMN

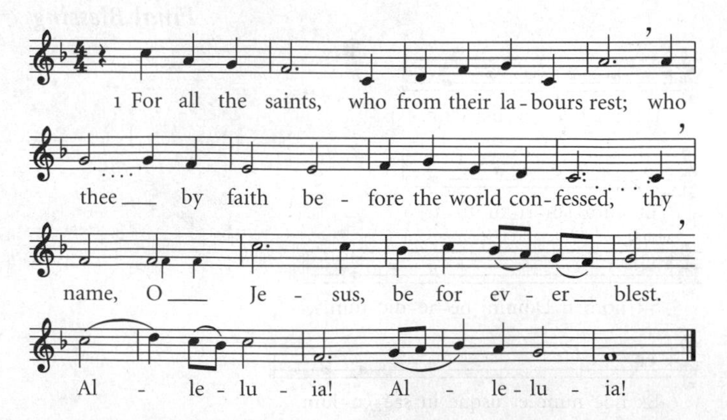
1 For all the saints, who from their la-bours rest; who
thee by faith be-fore the world con-fessed, thy
name, O Je-sus, be for ev-er blest.
Al-le-lu-ia! Al-le-lu-ia!

2. Thou wast their rock, their fortress,
and their might;
thou, Lord, their captain in the well–fought fight;
thou in the darkness drear their one true light.

3. O may thy soldiers, faithful, true and bold,
fight as the saints who nobly fought of old,
and win, with them, the victor's crown of gold.

4. O blest communion! Fellowship divine!
We feebly struggle, they in glory shine;
yet all are one in thee, for all are thine.

5. And when the strife is fierce, the warfare long,
steals on the ear the distant triumph–song,
and hearts are brave again, and arms are strong.

6. The golden evening brightens in the west;
soon, soon to faithful warriors cometh rest:
sweet is the calm of paradise the blest.

7. But lo! There breaks a yet more glorious day;
the saints triumphant rise in bright array:
the king of glory passes on his way.

8. From earth's wide bounds,
from ocean's farthest coast,
through gates of pearl streams in the countless host,
singing to Father, Son and Holy Ghost.

Text: William Walsham How (1823-1897) - Music: R Vaughan Williams (1872-1958).

CHORAL ENDING

Music: Te Deum in C - Franz Joseph Haydn (1732-1809).
For English text see endpapers.

MARY IN THE LIFE OF THE CHURCH

Bishop Malcolm McMahon OP

Mary is the first of the believers of the new covenant. Just as the divine voice put Abraham at the head of a new and countless people, God's people of the covenant, so that he is the father of believers in the Old Testament, so Mary is the beginning of the fulfilment of the promise made to Abraham and the beginning of actual salvation for all who follow. Throughout the biblical message, the gospel of the incarnation is at the same time fulfilment and new promise. The God of the bible is always a God who speaks and acts, and Mary is now involved for good in God's saving action. In other words Mary is involved with us. Mary who was the lowliest, from "the poor of the Lord", who was from that group who wanted nothing for themselves yet relied on God for everything, was chosen to fulfil God's promise made to Abraham. Her "lowliness" has nothing to do with material need but everything to do with humility. It relativises human ability and produces a strong sense of dependence on human beings and being open to God's grace. Mary's role in the salvation of mankind is characterised by these two things: dependence on others and openness to God's grace. That is why we pray, **Mary, full of Grace.**

God himself became completely human specifically to give us a picture of humanity that is sound and whole.

Christ is the representative of the whole of redeemed humanity; he is the new person. **Mary is the first to be redeemed**, the first believer and the radically redeemed person in whom everything is done through the fullness of grace. So praise to Mary is always praise to the re-creative power of God's love and God's spirit. Only through God's grace is Mary what she is, the radically and completely redeemed human person – but we too are in that process. Redemption is happening in us, in the same way (by God's grace). But can we put aside our own concerns, become dependent on others and leave ourselves open to God? Yes, is the answer, but it will take us a lifetime, that's all.

Being human in Christ is an on-going process where possibilities and questions which make us who we are are fulfilled by the grace of redemption given as sheer and utter gift. But it is only in giving ourselves, to and for others, that we can be sufficiently open and vulnerable to receive the gift of God. Can you see yourself in this action of giving and receiving which makes you who you are? Are you the sort who will open up yourself to other people and the grace of God? It is terribly risky, of course, but then it was for Mary too. It is the only way of being fully human, so that you can take your place in Christ.

What happens if you stay closed down to grace and people? At best you dry up and remain unfulfilled, at worst you end up being part of that machine of war and destruction that dominates our planet. It is no coincidence that the doctrine of **Mary's Assumption into Heaven** was defined by Pope Pius XII in 1950, just a few years after humanity's worst war ever. Millions upon millions of people had died, on the Eastern and Western Fronts, in the gas chambers, and as a result of nuclear explosions. The body count was enormous. We know that this is no way forward for humanity and the cry which is contained in that doctrine that Mary was assumed body and soul into heaven, is that bodies do matter. You matter. The whole of you matters. Dying well is obviously important, vital even. But so is living well. Your redemption in Jesus Christ is about the whole you, not just a part of you, your soul. Mary, the first believer of the new covenant, was redeemed body and soul by sheer gift. We too can hope for that. We too can hope for complete fulfilment in Christ. We too can receive that gift, but first we have to give.

And what we give is life. Mary gave life to Jesus. We say: **Mary, Mother of God**. The God who gave his Son to be our saviour. She enfleshed him. Unlike giving life in our worldly way, Mary did it as a virgin. Is this how God intervenes in our world – in a strange paradoxical, revolutionary way? I think so. What makes it possible for this to happen in Mary is her virginity. It is the potentiality that is implied in Mary's virginity that we should try to grasp. We tend to see virginity in terms of purity – but let's now look at it in terms of power. Not the power to tempt and beguile, but the power to create. A power which is within each of us. A power which begins not with goods, success, wealth and material things, but starts with emptiness. The power of being detached is based in the freedom that goes with it. This freedom if used wisely enables us to reach out to others and to be dependent on God. It cnables us to take Christ within us to fill the empty space in our life. What other answer is there? Within each of us is an empty space. We should not fill this with imaginary things, but with Christ. Mary's empty womb, so empty and so powerful, is filled with that which is the only thing that can satisfy us. Christ himself. Because it is only in Christ that we can have hope, otherwise we would remain empty and the paradise we chase is but a dream. Within each of us there is that empty womb, not just a space waiting to be filled, but a source of great power, the re-creative power of our saviour. We can receive that gift of God's life within us. It can fill up that space, transform us.

Pray for us, O holy Mother of God. That we may be made worthy of the promises of Christ.

Catholic Bishops' Conferences

The 1983 *Code of Canon Law*, drawing on *Christus Dominus*, the Decree on the Pastoral Office of Bishops in the Church promulgated by the Second Vatican Council, defines Bishops' Conferences in this way: "The Bishops' Conference, a permanent institution, is the assembly of the bishops of a country or a particular territory, exercising together certain pastoral offices for Christ's faithful of their territory. By forms and means of the apostolate suited to the circumstances of the time and place, it is to promote, in accordance with the law, that greater good which the Church offers to humankind." (Can. 447; cf. *Christus Dominus* 38).

Both the Bishops' Conference of Scotland and that of England and Wales meet regularly during the year. To ensure that the Conferences, as permanent institutions, continue to operate between plenary sessions, they also each have a Standing Committee; and permanent Departments or Commissions and Committees. They are also served by their own General Secretariats.

General Secretariats

Each General Secretariat has overall responsibility for recording, communicating and carrying out the policies and decisions of their respective Conference. Working closely with Departments and Commissions, the General Secretariat assists the Conference in the preparation of policies by arranging for the provision of expert advice.

The General Secretariats have continuing tasks of liaison with the Apostolic Nuncio, the Apostolic See, government departments and other national bodies. They are responsible for encouraging and coordinating cooperation between their two Conferences and fostering relations between Bishops' Conferences of other nations.

Meeting with Pope Benedict XVI

The two Bishops' Conferences will meet with His Holiness Pope Benedict XVI during his State Visit to the United Kingdom in September at Oscott College in Birmingham. It was here that Cardinal John Henry Newman preached his sermon, known subsequently as 'The Second Spring', on the occasion of the first meeting of the Catholic Hierarchy in England and Wales since its restoration in 1850. The re-establishment of the hierarchy of the Catholic Church in Scotland followed in 1878. The meeting will recall these historic events and be a renewal of the vital bonds of communion between the Catholic Bishops in these lands and the Holy Father. It will be an encouragement for the two Bishops' Conferences to continue their work of promoting that "greater good which the Church offers to humankind" in union with the Successor of Saint Peter.

Bishops' Conference of Scotland

President: His Eminence Keith Patrick Cardinal O'Brien,
Archbishop of St Andrews and Edinburgh
Vice-President: Most Rev Mario Conti,
Archbishop of Glasgow
General Secretary: Fr Paul Conroy

Bishops' Conference of England and Wales

President: Most Rev Vincent Nichols,
Archbishop of Westminster
Vice-President: Most Rev Peter Smith,
Archbishop of Southwark
General Secretary: Fr Marcus Stock

VOCATION

Fr Stephen Wang

Do I have a vocation? – God calls all the souls he has created to love him with their whole being, here and hereafter, which means that he calls all of them to holiness, to perfection, to a close following of him and obedience to his will. But he does not ask all souls to show their love by the same works, to climb to heaven by the same ladder, to achieve goodness in the same way. What sort of work, then, must I do? Which is *my* road to heaven? In what kind of life am I *to sanctify myself*?" (*Blessed Charles de Foucauld.*)

Created to share God's love – The fundamental vocation of every human being is to love. This is not obvious to everyone today. Many believe that human life is just an accident, a chance product of evolution, a meaningless event in a vast mechanical universe. It is certainly true that our lives have been shaped by many different forces, but there is a much deeper truth that we can discover through faith: *Every single human being has been created by God out of love* so that we could know his love, and share that love with others, and delight in that love forever in the glory of heaven. So whatever you feel about your own worth – *never doubt that your life has a meaning*. God loves you and cares for you. You are precious to him and he has a purpose for your life, even if that does not seem very clear to you.

What is a vocation? – The word "vocation" comes from the Latin word that means "calling". For the Christian, a vocation is not just something that God calls us to do, it is also the person God calls us to be. When Jesus called his first disciples by the Lake of Galilee it wasn't just so that they could help him in his work, it was so that their lives could be transformed through his friendship and love. We have been called to follow Christ, the Son of God, the eternal Word of the Father, who came to save us and to lead us back to heaven with him. He has sent his Holy Spirit so that we can share in his divine life even now, and express that life by trying to love him and to love our neighbour. The Christian vocation is a call to share in the life of the Most Holy Trinity.

Vocation as a call to holiness – One way of expressing this is to say that the fundamental human vocation is the call to holiness, the call to be a saint. The saints are not just heroic people who live in history books; they are ordinary Christians who have tried to live their faith without holding anything back – to love God with their whole hearts, to love those around them without counting the cost, to work at what is worthwhile with dedication and purpose, to be people of joy and kindness and prayerfulness. *All of us are called to be saints* – however weak or sinful we feel. This is not so much a command as a promise that God makes: he promises us, by giving us his Holy Spirit, that he will help us to find our true happiness in following him, and that he will give us whatever we need for the journey.

You already have a vocation – This vocation to holiness is already a part of your life, given to you at your baptism, and it is so important to remember that. Whatever situation you are in now, however unsatisfactory it seems, you already have a vocation. You might be working, studying, travelling, unemployed, or caring for someone at home; you might be very content, or utterly miserable; full of hope, or close to despair. Whatever your situation, you can trust that God is with you, and that he calls you to be holy in this very situation. Things may well change – and perhaps they need to; but at this moment you must have the confidence to believe that *even now there is a meaning and a purpose to your life*; and that you can begin to fulfil that by everyday acts of love and kindness and patience.

Living well in the present – This call to live well in the present is the *Little Way* recommended by St Thérèse of Lisieux – the importance of simply doing your duty, saying your prayers, loving your neighbour, bearing your sufferings; and doing all this with a generous and loving heart. It is not very dramatic, but it is the secret of holiness, and it reminds us that *your first and fundamental vocation is not something to be discovered in the future – it is living the Christian life in the here and now.* Perhaps this is all God wants of you for the moment. You must avoid the temptation of thinking that your Christian life can only properly begin in the future, when everything is crystal clear. And if you do not discover a more concrete vocation, or if you are to die young, then you should not feel that you have wasted your life, or that your life is unfinished or unfulfilled.

Vocation as a call to a concrete 'state of life' – Christ has always called some people to follow him in concrete ways, by giving them a more specific vocation. In previous generations, the word 'vocation' would only have been used to describe the lives of priests and religious – because these people had in some sense been called 'away' from an ordinary life to a life of celibacy and service in the Church. But today the word 'vocation' is rightly used also of marriage, permanent diaconate, consecrated life, and some forms of single life – because each of these is a wholehearted commitment that we make in response to an invitation from the Lord. These concrete vocations are also known as 'states of life', because we make a lifelong commitment to living our Christian faith in a particular context. *This lifelong commitment becomes the place in which we live out our fundamental vocation to holiness.* God calls us all to be saints; and sometimes he calls us to be saints in a particular way – as husbands or wives, as priests or deacons or consecrated persons.

Vocation as a call to be the unique person you are made to be – There is yet another level to "vocation". Each saint is unique, and you are called to be holy not just in a general way, but in the particular way that God has made you to be. *God created you as a unique individual, and calls you by a name that no-one else has been* *given. You reflect Christ's love and show something of his face in a way that no-one else can. This is your 'personal' vocation – the call to be the person you are meant to be.* The more you discover who you are, and the more you discover what lies deepest in your heart, the more you will be able to discern what God's will is for you and what direction he wants you to take in life. Your lifelong vocational commitments and the particular path of holiness that you are called to follow will inevitably grow out of the person God created you to be.

> "Love makes us seek what is good; love makes us better persons. It is love that prompts men and women to marry and form a family, to have children. It is love that prompts others to embrace the religious life or become priests. Love makes you reach out to others in need, whoever they are, wherever they are. Every genuine human love is a reflection of the Love that is God himself."
>
> *Pope John Paul II*

This article has been extracted from* How to Discover your Vocation *by Fr Stephen Wang, published by CTS Publications.

PRAYER IN THANKSGIVING
for the visit of Pope Benedict

A suitable service of thanksgiving might take the form of Evening Prayer as given in the Divine Office of the Church, or of the Worship of the Eucharist outside of Mass (for example Exposition). The Church's ritual books provide guidance on how to prepare and adapt these liturgies for particular occasions.

The form of worship that follows offers another alternative, and might be considered more appropriate for an Ecumenical worship service.

OPENING SONG

Choose a song that picks up the focus of the liturgy, and is suitable as an opening song. Choose a song that is familiar to those likely to be present or which can be taught to them before the service begins.

Some suggestions are:

In the Lord I'll be ever thankful (308 CHE; 868 LHO&N; 944 LAUD)

This day God gives me (729 CHE; 680 LHO&N; 673 LAUD)

Though the mountains may fall (739 CHE; 688 LHO&N; 785 LAUD)

We walk by faith (789 CHE; 284 LAUD)

Blest be the Lord (91 CHE; 954 LAUD)

Be thou my vision (74 CHE; 168 LHO&N; 970 LAUD)

Key: CHE: Celebration Hymnal for Everyone; LHO&N: Liturgical Hymns Old and New; Laud: Laudate

Greeting

Leader: In the name of the Father, and the Son, and the Holy Spirit.
All: **Amen.**
Leader: The grace and peace of God our Father and the Lord Jesus Christ be with you.
All: **And also with you.**

Welcome and introduction

Opening Prayer

God our Father, shepherd and guide,
look with love on Pope Benedict your servant,
the pastor of your Church.
May his word and example inspire and guide the Church,
and may he, and all those entrusted to his care,
come to the joy of everlasting life.
Grant this through our Lord Jesus Christ, your Son,
who lives and reigns with you and the Holy Spirit,
one God, for ever and ever.

All: **Amen.**

• Liturgy of the Word •

Either

A reading from
the first letter of St Paul to the Corinthians 1:3–9

I NEVER STOP THANKING God for all the graces you have received through Jesus Christ. I thank him that you have been enriched in so many ways, especially in your teachers and preachers; the witness to Christ has indeed been strong among you so that you will not be without any of the gifts of the Spirit while you are waiting for our Lord Jesus Christ to be revealed; and he will keep you steady and without blame until the last day, the day of our Lord Jesus Christ, because God by calling you has joined you to his Son, Jesus Christ; and God is faithful.

This is the Word of the Lord.
Thanks be to God.

or

A reading from
the letter of Saint Paul to the Colossians 3:12–17

YOU ARE GOD'S CHOSEN race, his saints; he loves you, and you should be clothed in sincere compassion, in kindness and humility, gentleness and patience. Bear with one another; forgive each other as soon as a quarrel begins. The Lord has forgiven you; now you must do the same. Over all these clothes, to keep them together and complete them, put on love. And may the peace of Christ reign in your hearts, because it is for this that you were called together as parts of one body. Always be thankful.

Let the message of Christ, in all its richness, find a home with you. Teach each other, and advise each other, in all wisdom. With gratitude in your hearts sing psalms and hymns and inspired songs to God; and never say or do anything except in the name of the Lord Jesus, giving thanks to God the Father through him.

This is the Word of the Lord.
Thanks be to God.

PSALM 144

**℟ I will bless your name for ever,
O Lord.**

I will bless you day after day
and praise your name for ever.
The Lord is great, highly to be praised,
his greatness cannot be measured. ℟

Age to age shall proclaim your works,
shall declare your might deeds,
shall speak of your splendour and glory,
tell the tale of your wonderful works. ℟

They will speak of your terrible deeds,
recount you greatness and might.
They will recall your abundant goodness;
age to age shall ring out your justice. ℟
The Lord is kind and full of compassion,
slow to anger, abounding in love.
How good is the Lord to all,
compassionate to all his creatures. ℟

All your creatures shall thank you, O Lord,
and your friends shall repeat their blessing.
They shall speak of the glory of your reign
and declare your might, O God. ℟

Alleluia. You are Peter, and on this rock I will build my church. And the gates of the underworld can never hold out against it. **Alleluia.**

Either

A reading from
the holy Gospel according to Luke 17:11–19

ON THE WAY to Jerusalem Jesus travelled along the border between Samaria and Galilee. As he entered one of the villages, ten lepers came to meet him. They stood some way off and called to him, "Jesus! Master! Take pity on us." When he saw them he said, "Go and show yourselves to the priests." Now as they were going away they were cleansed. Finding himself cured, one of them turned back praising God at the top of his voice and threw himself at the feet of Jesus and thanked him. The man was a Samaritan. This made Jesus say, "Were not all ten made clean? The other nine, where are they? It seems that no one has come back to give praise to God, except this foreigner." And he said to the man, "Stand up and go on your way. Your faith has saved you."

This is the Gospel of the Lord.
Praise to you, Lord Jesus Christ.

or

A reading from
the holy Gospel according to John 15:9–17

JESUS SAID TO his disciples:
"As the Father has loved me,
so have I loved you.
Remain in my love.
If you keep my commandments
you will remain in my love,
just as I have kept my Father's commandments
and remain in his love.

I have told you this
so that my own joy may be in you
and your joy be complete.
This is my commandment:
love one another,
as I have loved you.
A man can have no greater love
than to lay down his life for his friends.
You are my friends,
if you do what I command you.
I shall not call you servants any more,
because a servant does not know
his master's business;
I call you friends,
because I have made known to you
everything I have learnt from my Father.
You did not choose me,
no, I chose you;
and I commissioned you
to go out and to bear fruit,
fruit that will last;
and then the Father will give you
anything you ask him in my name.
What I command you
is to love one another."

This is the Gospel of the Lord.
Praise to you, Lord Jesus Christ.

Homily or reflection

(With a smaller group it might be easier to invite people to share with their neighbour memories or insights from the Papal Visit. Encourage participants to consider what difference the visit has

made to them, and how it might encourage them to live out their Christian vocation.)

General Intercessions

The following simple biddings might be used as they are, with each one being followed by a time of silent prayer for the intention. It is usual to end the prayer for each bidding with a responsory such as "Lord in your mercy: hear our prayer". Alternatively they might be elaborated.

Let us pray for Pope Benedict

Let us pray for the Church in the United Kingdom

Let us pray for all the peoples and institutions of our nation

Let us pray for our local community

Let us pray for our own needs

Concluding Prayer

Almighty and eternal God,
in Christ your Son
you have shown your glory to the world.
Guide the work of your Church:
help it to proclaim your name,
to persevere in faith
and to bring your salvation to people everywhere.
We ask this through Christ, our Lord

All: Amen.

CONCLUDING SONG

Lead kindly light (348 CHE 415 LHO&N; 961 LAUD)

If you would follow me (299 CHE; 743 LAUD)

I will be with you (289 CHE; 379 LHO&N; 866 LAUD)

Key: CHE: Celebration Hymnal for Everyone; LHO&N: Liturgical Hymns Old and New; Laud: Laudate

And now…

The visit of Pope Benedict XVI to the United Kingdom to beatify the Venerable John Henry Newman was a remarkable occasion. At a time when Christianity itself seems to many to be dying out in our country, the interest of so many Catholics and others in the visit of Saint Peter's successor – the first ever State visit to this country, an event unthinkable since the Reformation – signified a new moment in the life of the Church and kindled the hope of a new springtime of faith. But how the visit will be interpreted and what fruits it will bear in years to come depends now on us. Graces have been poured out in response to the prayers of so many people, not least of the Pope himself. If we allow those graces to fall on stony ground, it will be to our everlasting shame. We must become fertile ground for the Word of God to bear fruit in us.

The only way to prepare ourselves to bear "fruit that will last", fruit in the form of love towards God and neighbour, is through prayer. MAGNIFICAT *is designed to help you to pray, day by day, and to continue to persevere in prayer long after the Papal Visit itself. The texts and prayers of the Mass, the prayers and meditations for Morning and Evening, provide continuing food for the soul.* MAGNIFICAT *can help you to become part of the great revival of faith in our time, builders of a new Second Spring.*

Magnificat

From September 20th to 30th

MONDAY, SEPTEMBER 20
Saint Andrew Kim Taegon, Saint Paul Chong Hasang, and their companions

Prayer for the Morning

Jesus Christ is the glory of the martyrs:
come, let us adore him!

Glory be to the Father, and to the Son, and to the Holy Spirit, as it was in the beginning, is now and ever shall be, world without end. Amen. Alleluia!

Hymn

Metre: LM
This hymn can be sung to the tune used for ***When I Behold the Wondrous Cross***

In robes washed white, with palms held high,
The martyr host goes marching by;
They climb the hill to Sion's gate
Wherein the choirs of glory wait.

No moon by night, no sun by day
Can harm them on their royal way;
No prowling beast, no hunter's snare
Can hinder them who travel there.

The Lamb, their Shepherd, leads them in,
Who would not yield to death or sin;
He bids them rest in fields of peace,
In rock-born waters find surcease.

May we who walk the pathways beat
By those no terror could defeat
Join in their psalms of victory
Before the holy One in Three.

CANTICLE **Wisdom 3: 1-6**

He holds in his power the soul of every living thing,/ and the breath of each man's body. (cf. Jb 12: 10)

The martyrs bear witness to the heart of Christ's sacrifice: they surrender their lives into God's hands to do with as he will. To them, the present cost of their offering counts as nothing in comparison with life with the Lord who awaits them.

But the souls of the virtuous are in the hands of God,
no torment shall ever touch them.

In the eyes of the unwise, they did appear to die,
their going looked like a disaster,
their leaving us, like annihilation;
But they are in peace.

If they experienced punishment as men see it,
their hope was rich with immortality;
slight was their affliction, great will their blessings be.
God has put them to the test
and proved them worthy to be with him;

he has tested them like gold in a furnace,
and accepted them as a holocaust.

Glory be to the Father…

Word of God **2 Corinthians 4: 16-18**

THAT IS WHY THERE IS no weakening on our part, and instead, though this outer man of ours may be falling into decay, the inner man is renewed day by day. Yes, the troubles which are soon over, though they weigh little, train us for the carrying of a weight of eternal glory which is out of all proportion to them. And so we have no eyes for things that are visible, but only for things

that are invisible; for visible things last only for a time, and the invisible things are eternal.

The kingdom, the power, and the glory are yours!

CANTICLE OF ZECHARIAH (Text, back cover B)

The crucible for silver, a furnace for gold,/ but the LORD for the testing of hearts! (Pr 17: 3)

INTERCESSIONS

The martyrs bear witness to the cost and the reward of living according to the Gospel. Through their intercession, let us pray:

℟ Make your people steadfast in faith, O Lord.

For the Church throughout the world:
– that we may live the Gospel faith for which the martyrs died. ℟

For those who suffer persecution for the Gospel's sake:
– that they may find strength in the example of the martyrs. ℟

For the Christians of Korea, and the Korean churches in this country:
– that their lives may be a light to their neighbours. ℟

Personal intentions

Our Father…

O God of all glory, the genuineness of the martyrs' faith, more precious than gold that is perishable even though tested by fire, serves the praise, glory, and honour of Jesus Christ. Through their intercession, grant to all your Church the fortitude of faith, the joy of love, and the determination born of hope through the same Christ our Lord. Amen.

MASS

Monday of the Twenty-Fifth Week in Ordinary Time

SAINTS ANDREW KIM TAEGON, PAUL CHONG HASANG, AND COMPANIONS *Memorial*

● *During the persecutions of 1839, 1846, 1866, and 1867, one hundred and three Christians in Korea gave their lives as martyrs. Among them were Father Andrew Kim Taegon, first Korean priest and pastor, and the lay apostle, Paul Chong Hasang. The martyrs included bishops and priests, but for the most part, they were members of the laity. They consecrated the rich beginnings of the Church in Korea with their blood. "I urge you to remain steadfast in faith, so that at last we will all reach heaven and there rejoice together." – Saint Andrew Kim Taegon, Final Exhortation* ●

ENTRANCE ANTIPHON

Let us all rejoice in the Lord, and keep a festival in honour of Andrew and Paul and their companions. Let us join with the angels in joyful praise to the Son of God.

OPENING PRAYER

O God,
you have created all nations
and you are their salvation.
In the land of Korea your call to Catholic faith
formed a people of adoption,
whose growth you nurtured
by the blood of Andrew, Paul, and their companions.
Through their martyrdom and their intercession
grant us strength
that we too may remain faithful to your commandments
even until death.

We ask this through our Lord Jesus Christ, your Son,
who lives and reigns with you and the Holy Spirit,
one God, for ever and ever.

● *The wilful wrong-doer is abhorrent to the LORD.* ●

A reading from the Book of Proverbs 3: 27-34

MY SON, DO NOT REFUSE a kindness to anyone who begs it,/ if it is in your power to perform it./ Do not say to your neighbour, "Go away! Come another time!/ I will give it you tomorrow", if you can do it now.

Do not plot harm against your neighbour/ as he lives unsuspecting next door./ Do not pick a groundless quarrel with a man/ who has done you no harm.

Do not emulate the man of violence,/ never model your conduct on his;/ for the wilful wrong-doer is abhorrent to the LORD,/ who confides only in honest men.

The LORD's curse lies on the house of the wicked,/ but he blesses the home of the virtuous./ He mocks those who mock,/ but accords his favour to the humble.
This is the word of the Lord.

• PSALM 14 •

℟ (1) **The just will live in the presence of the Lord.**

He who walks without fault;
he who acts with justice
and speaks the truth from his heart. ℟

He who does no wrong to his brother,
who casts no slur on his neighbour,
who holds the godless in disdain,
but honours those who fear the LORD. ℟

He who keeps his pledge, come what may;
who takes no interest on a loan
and accepts no bribes against the innocent.
Such a man will stand firm for ever. ℟

Alleluia, alleluia! Your light must shine in the sight of men,/ so that, seeing your good works,/ they may give the praise to your Father in heaven. Alleluia!

● *A lamp is placed on a lamp-stand so that people may see the light when they come in.* ●

A reading from
the holy Gospel according to Luke 8: 16-18

JESUS SAID TO HIS DISCIPLES: "No one lights a lamp to cover it with a bowl or to put it under a bed. No, he puts it on a lamp-stand so that people may see the light when they come in. For nothing is hidden but it will be made clear, nothing secret but it will be known and brought to light. So take care how you hear; for anyone who has will be given more; from anyone who has not, even what he thinks he has will be taken away."
This is the Gospel of the Lord.

PRAYER OVER THE GIFTS

All-powerful God,
in your goodness accept these gifts we offer
and through the intercession of your holy martyrs
grant that our own lives will become a sacrifice
acceptable to you
for the salvation of all the world.
We ask this in the name of Jesus the Lord.

COMMUNION ANTIPHON
If anyone declares himself for me in the presence of men, I will declare myself for him in the presence of my Father in heaven.(Mt 10: 32)

PRAYER AFTER COMMUNION
Lord,
we have been nourished in this celebration of your holy martyrs
with the food that gave them strength.
Grant that we too will remain loyal to Christ
and labour in your Church for the salvation of all.
We ask this in the name of Jesus the Lord.

MEDITATION OF THE DAY

How Our Light Shines

Martyrdom means bearing witness to God. Every soul that seeks in pureness of heart to know God and obeys the commandments of God is a martyr, bearing witness by life or by words.

In fact even if it is not a matter of shedding blood, the soul is pouring out its faith because it is by faith that the soul will be separated from the body before a person dies.

That is why, in the Gospel, the Lord praises the person "who has left house or brothers or sisters or mother or father or children or lands for my sake and for the Gospel." That person is blessed because he too is going to meet martyrdom simply by living in a way that is different from the crowd, because he is following the rule of the Gospel for love of his Lord.

The truly righteous are set apart from the world because they produce the fruits of grace in their actions. They do this because they have been able to become a friend of God and to obtain a place at the right hand of the Father, as the apostles have done.

SAINT CLEMENT OF ALEXANDRIA

Saint Clement of Alexandria († 215) was a renowned theologian and teacher of the faith.

Prayer for the Evening

In God let our hearts rejoice;
he is our help and our shield.

Glory be to the Father, and to the Son, and to the Holy Spirit, as it was in the beginning, is now and ever shall be, world without end. Amen. Alleluia!

HYMN Metre: LM

This hymn can be sung to the tune used for *Jesu, Dulcis Memoria*

Around the throne a glorious band,
The saints in countless numbers stand,
Of ev'ry tongue, redeemed to God,
Arrayed in garments washed in blood.

Through tribulation great they came;
They bore the cross, despised the shame;
From all their labours now they rest
In God's eternal glory blest.

PSALM 32 8-9, 12-13, 18-22

My portion is the LORD, says my soul,/ and so I will hope in him. (Lm 3: 24)

The martyrs' portion is the Lord. For them, that is reward enough. Is it reward enough for us in bearing with love the small burdens of the day?

Let all the earth fear the Lord,
all who live in the world revere him.
He spoke; and it came to be.
He commanded; it sprang into being.

They are happy, whose God is the Lord,
the people he has chosen as his own.
From the heavens the Lord looks forth,
he sees all the children of men.

The Lord looks on those who revere him,
on those who hope in his love,
to rescue their souls from death,
to keep them alive in famine.

Our soul is waiting for the Lord.
The Lord is our help and our shield.
In him do our hearts find joy.
We trust in his holy name.

May your love be upon us, O Lord,
as we place all our hope in you.

Glory to the Father…

Word of God Philippians 3: 8-9a, 9c-11

NOT ONLY THAT, BUT I believe nothing can happen that will outweigh the supreme advantage of knowing Christ Jesus my Lord. For him I have accepted the loss of everything, and I look on everything as so much rubbish if only I can have Christ and be given a place in him. I want only the perfection that comes through faith in Christ, and is from God and based on faith. All I want is to know Christ and the power of his resurrection and to share his sufferings by reproducing the pattern of his death. That is the way I can hope to take my place in the resurrection of the dead.

Bear the hardships for the sake of the Good News,
relying on the power of God.
(2 Tm 1: 8)

CANTICLE OF MARY **(Text, back cover A)**

Life to me, of course, is Christ, but then death would bring me something more. (Ph 1: 21)

INTERCESSIONS

Strengthened by the faith of the martyrs, let us pray:

℟ Hear us, O Lord.

You delivered the disciples imprisoned for preaching without fear in your name:
– deliver all those imprisoned in infidelity by fear of displeasing others. ℟

You kept your martyrs steadfast in the face of every threat:
– make steadfast those tempted to compromise their discipleship for fear of consequences. ℟

You raised to life the martyrs who chose death rather than faithlessness:
– raise all those who have died. ℟

Personal intentions

Our Father…

May the God of peace be with you all! Amen. (cf. Rm 15: 33)

MARIAN ANTIPHON **(Text, page 23)**

SAINTS
OF TODAY AND YESTERDAY

Trust in the Lord!

SAINT AGATHA YI KAN-NAN
Widow and Martyr (1813-1846)

At the age of twenty, Agatha Yi Kan-nan, the daughter of a pagan Korean family, lost her husband only two years after her wedding. Soon afterward, the young widow learned of the Catholic faith. Refusing to remarry, she asked her mother to find for her a Catholic to instruct her in the faith. Having arranged for a Catholic relative to teach her daughter, Agatha's mother decided to become a Catholic also, as did Agatha's brother. Agatha's father, however, angered by the conversion of his family, punished Agatha by ordering her to live with her deceased husband's family. These relatives, touched by Agatha's gentle disposition, came to admire her to the point that one sister-in-law also became a Catholic. Agatha ultimately bought a home of her own. She was known to be deeply devout, mortifying herself with frequent fasting. Her fellow Catholics revered her for her exceptional chastity, deeming her "as clear as a mirror and as pure as snow." On July 10, 1846, Agatha was arrested for her faith by agents of Korea's pagan regime. After being repeatedly tortured, the thirty-three-year-old widow was put to death on September 20, 1846.

Help me, O Lord, for I am resolved to amend my life.

Saint Alphonsus Liguori

[TUESDAY, SEPTEMBER 21
Saint Matthew]

Prayer for the Morning

The word goes out to all the earth:
let us give thanks and praise!
Glory be to the Father, and to the Son, and to the Holy Spirit, as it was in the beginning, is now and ever shall be, world without end. Amen. Alleluia!

HYMN Metre: CMD
This hymn can be sung to the tune used for ***I Heard the Voice of Jesus Say***

The tax collector left his tolls
To count a different coin
As wealth his gospel word extols
Though folly would rejoin
That passing treasure gives delight
Enough to fill our days.
Saint Matthew, walking in the light,
Saw riches in God's praise.

The tax collector left the gold
Of Rome for gold from Christ
Who offered words both new and old
That haunted and enticed
A man of worldly means to give
All that he had to write
Those words for all who yet would live
To ponder day and night.

The tax collector left to us
The story he had learned
That we might rise from ash and dust
To treasure what he earned:

A life beyond what gold can buy,
A pearl that has no price,
A wealth that folly passes by,
The love of Jesus Christ.

Psalm 18 2-7

Go, therefore, make disciples of all the nations; baptise them in the name of the Father and of the Son and of the Holy Spirit.(Mt 28: 19)

We who take access to words for granted should pause to be grateful to those who preserved the Gospel words so carefully and spread them to the utmost bounds of the world without benefit of the printing press or instantaneous media.

The heavens proclaim the glory of God
and the firmament shows forth the work of his hands.
Day unto day takes up the story
and night unto night makes known the message.

No speech, no word, no voice is heard
yet their span extends through all the earth,
their words to the utmost bounds of the world.

There he has placed a tent for the sun;
it comes forth like a bridegroom coming from his tent,
rejoices like a champion to run its course.

At the end of the sky is the rising of the sun;
to the furthest end of the sky is its course.
There is nothing concealed from its burning heat.

Glory be to the Father…

Word of God 1 Thessalonians 2: 13

Another reason why we constantly thank God for you is that as soon as you heard the message that we brought you as God's message, you accepted it for what it really is, God's message and not some human thinking; and it is still a living power among you who believe it.

Repent and believe the Good News. (Mk 1: 15)

CANTICLE OF ZECHARIAH (Text, back cover B)
For this is what I received from the Lord, and in turn passed on to you (1 Co 11: 23)

INTERCESSIONS

In gratitude for the Gospel given to us through the faithful ministry of the evangelists and their hearers, let us pray:

℟ Plant in every place the seed of your Gospel.

For the literate and those who have easy access to many media:
– grant us the reverence of former ages for the sacredness of your word. ℟

For the illiterate:
– send preachers and teachers to open for them the riches of your word. ℟

For those who live in places where your word is banned:
– bless the efforts of societies and individuals who seek ways to carry the good news to them. ℟

Personal intentions

Our Father…

Lord Jesus Christ, you changed Matthew's life by the good news which you entrusted to him. May we receive the Gospel with reverence, live it in faith, and hand it on in love. Grant this our prayer, who live and reign with God the Father and the Holy Spirit, one God for ever and ever. Amen.

MASS

Feast of Saint Matthew

Saint Matthew is a familiar figure among the apostles. His Gospel, with its constant references to the messianic prophecies, throws most light on the continuity between the two covenants. Moreover, his vocation is one of the most popular episodes in the life of Jesus, because of the personality of the one called "the tax collector" and the revelation of redeeming love that concludes and crowns the story. Mark and Luke call Matthew by his Jewish name of Levi, and Mark says he was "the son of Alphaeus" (Mk 2: 14). He may have been the brother of another apostle, James, who is also called "the son of Alphaeus" (Mk 3: 18), which would explain how he already had some contacts with Jesus' followers. Because of his profession, Jews of strict observance would have nothing to do with him, for he fell under a religious ban. Jesus' call (Opening Prayer) was therefore all the more remarkable, as was Matthew's generous response. He stood up at once, "leaving everything" (Lk 5: 28). Then came the feast of friendship, at which the publican turned disciple invited to his table, with Jesus, both old and new friends. And the Lord said, "I did not come to call the virtuous, but sinners" (Communion Antiphon, Prayer after Communion).

ENTRANCE ANTIPHON

Go and preach to all nations: baptise them and teach them to observe all that I have commanded you, says the Lord. (Mt 28: 19-20)

GLORIA ——— page 450

OPENING PRAYER

God of mercy,
you chose a tax collector, Saint Matthew,
to share the dignity of the apostles.
By his example and prayers
help us to follow Christ
and remain faithful in your service.
We ask this through our Lord Jesus Christ, your Son,

who lives and reigns with you and the Holy Spirit,
one God, for ever and ever.

● *To some, his gift was that they should be apostles; to some evangelists.* ●

A reading from
the Letter of Saint Paul to the Ephesians 4: 1-7, 11-13

I, THE PRISONER IN THE LORD, implore you to lead a life worthy of your vocation. Bear with one another charitably, in complete selflessness, gentleness and patience. Do all you can to preserve the unity of the Spirit by the peace that binds you together. There is one Body, one Spirit, just as you were all called into one and the same hope when you were called. There is one Lord, one faith, one baptism, and one God who is Father of all, over all, through all and within all.

Each one of us, however, has been given his own share of grace, given as Christ allotted it.

To some, his gift was that they should be apostles; to some, prophets; to some, evangelists; to some, pastors and teachers; so that the saints together make a unity in the work of service, building up the body of Christ. In this way we are all to come to unity in our faith and in our knowledge of the Son of God, until we become the perfect Man, fully mature with the fullness of Christ himself.

This is the word of the Lord.

PSALM 18

℟ (5) **The heavens proclaim the glory of God.**

The heavens proclaim the glory of God;
and the firmament shows forth the work of his hands.

Day unto day takes up the story
  and night unto night makes known the message. ℟

No speech, no word, no voice is heard
yet their span extends through all the earth,
  their words to the utmost bounds of the world. ℟

Alleluia, alleluia! We praise you, O God,/ we acknowledge you to be the Lord./ The glorious company of the apostles praise you. Alleluia!

● *Follow me. And he got up and followed him.* ●

A reading from
the holy Gospel according to Matthew 9: 9-13

As Jesus was walking on he saw a man named Matthew sitting at the customs post. He said to him, "Follow me." And he got up and followed him. While he was at table in his house, many tax collectors and sinners came and sat with Jesus and his disciples. The Pharisees saw this and said to his disciples, "Why does your teacher eat with tax collectors and sinners?" He heard this and said, "Those who are well do not need a physician, but the sick do. Go and learn the meaning of the words, *I desire mercy, not sacrifice.* I did not come to call the righteous but sinners."
This is the Gospel of the Lord.

PRAYER OVER THE GIFTS

Lord,
accept the prayers and gifts we present
on this feast of Saint Matthew.
Continue to guide us in your love
as you nourished the faith of your Church
by the preaching of the apostles.
We ask this in the name of Jesus the Lord.

PREFACE OF THE APOSTLES I

Father, all-powerful and ever-living God,
we do well always and everywhere to give you thanks.

You are the eternal Shepherd
who never leaves his flock untended.
Through the apostles
you watch over us and protect us always.
You made them shepherds of the flock
to share in the work of your Son,
and from their place in heaven they guide us still.

And so, with all the choirs of angels in heaven
we proclaim your glory
and join in their unending hymn of praise: Holy…

Or:

PREFACE OF THE APOSTLES II

Father, all-powerful and ever-living God,
we do well always and everywhere to give you thanks.

You founded your Church on the apostles
to stand firm for ever
as the sign on earth of your infinite holiness
and as the living Gospel for all men to hear.

With steadfast love
we sing your unending praise:
we join with the hosts of heaven
in their triumphant song: Holy…

COMMUNION ANTIPHON

I did not come to call the virtuous, but sinners, says the Lord.
(Mt 9: 13)

PRAYER AFTER COMMUNION

Father,
in this Eucharist we have shared the joy of salvation
which Saint Matthew knew when he welcomed your Son.
May this food renew us in Christ,
who came to call not the just
but sinners to salvation in his kingdom
where he is Lord for ever and ever.

MEDITATION OF THE DAY

Prologos

LORD, a dream of Thee lies on my soul, but
I cannot reach Thee for all my gates are barred!
I am besieged as by armies, I am locked
in my everlasting solitude.
My hands are broken and my head is bruised in
trying to escape, all the images of my spirit
have become shadows.
For no ray falls from Thee into the depth of my
loneliness, it is lighted only by the moonbeams
of my soul.
How did you come in to me, O voice of my God?
Is it only the cry of wild birds over the waters?
I have carried you to all the mountains of hope,
but they too are but my own hilltops.
I have gone down to the waters of despair,
but they are not deeper than my own heart.
My love is like a stairway in the soul – but ever and
forever I am only in myself.
I can find no rest in my many chambers,
the stillest of them is like a single cry.
The last of them is yet but an antechamber,
the holiest of them is like an awaiting,
the darkest of all yet like a song of day!

GERTRUDE VON LE FORT

Gertrude von Le Fort († 1971) was born in Germany. She was a convert to Catholicism and the author of novels and poems.

Prayer for the Evening

The word of the LORD is faithful/ and all his works to be trusted: let us give him thanks and praise!
(cf. Ps 32: 4)

Glory be to the Father, and to the Son, and to the Holy Spirit, as it was in the beginning, is now and ever shall be, world without end. Amen. Alleluia!

HYMN **Metre: LM**

This hymn can be sung to the tune used for *When I Behold the Wondrous Cross*

To Mercy's table are we called,
By Mercy are we bidden eat
The bread of life that Mercy breaks
Upon the cross, true Mercy's seat.

The tax collector feeds on wealth
That cost the poor their board and bread.
The tax collector seems to thrive,
But deep within, the heart is dead.

The Word of life bids Matthew rise
And feast upon a different fare
Where Christ hoards nothing but the good
Of starving sinners nourished there.

The sinner lives, the dead arise,
The poor are fed by Mercy's hand
On bread and wine which taste of love
That flows from heaven's promised land.

PSALM 18 **8-11, 15**

You have the message of eternal life. (Jn 6: 68)

In response to Jesus' call, Matthew left his tax collector's table for the table to which Jesus called sinners. He exchanged the gold of this

world for the gold of God's word. May we learn from him to lay up treasures in heaven by storing in our hearts the treasures of the Gospel.

The law of the Lord is perfect,
it revives the soul.
The rule of the Lord is to be trusted,
it gives wisdom to the simple.

The precepts of the Lord are right,
they gladden the heart.
The command of the Lord is clear,
it gives light to the eyes.

The fear of the Lord is holy,
abiding for ever.
The decrees of the Lord are truth
and all of them just.

They are more to be desired than gold,
than the purest of gold,
and sweeter are they than honey,
than honey from the comb.

May the spoken words of my mouth,
the thoughts of my heart,
win favour in your sight, O Lord,
my rescuer, my rock!

Glory be to the Father…

Word of God Sirach 24: 18-19, 21

APPROACH ME, you who desire me,/ and take your fill of my fruits,/ for memories of me are sweeter than honey,/ inheriting me is sweeter than the honeycomb./ Whoever listens to me will never have to blush,/ whoever acts as I dictate will never sin.

Taste and see how sweet the Lord is! (cf. Ps 33: 9)

CANTICLE OF MARY (Text, back cover A)

But Israel I would feed with finest wheat,/ and fill them with honey from the rock. (Ps 80: 17)

INTERCESSIONS

O Lord, you feed us on the word of life. Through the intercession of Saint Matthew, we pray:

℟ Jesus, we are hungry; give us this day our daily bread at the table of your word.

O Lord, your word gives wisdom to the simple:
– nourish in us simplicity of heart. ℟

O Lord, your word is sweet to the taste:
– grant us the discernment to prefer its taste to any empty words we may hear this evening. ℟

O Lord, your word is steadfast, abiding for ever:
– strengthen us to walk firmly on the path to everlasting life. ℟

Personal intentions

Our Father…

Let the message of Christ, in all its richness, find a home with you. Amen. (cf. Co 3: 16)

MARIAN ANTIPHON (Text, page 23)

[WEDNESDAY, SEPTEMBER 22]

Prayer for the Morning

Sing praise to God, sing praise!

Glory be to the Father, and to the Son, and to the Holy Spirit, as it was in the beginning, is now and ever shall be, world without end. Amen. Alleluia!

HYMN

Metre: irregular
This hymn can be sung to the tune used for *God's Blessing Sends Us Forth*

O Splendour, Glory bright,
Brought forth as Light from Light!
O Day, all days enlightening!
Angels with one accord
Cry, "Holy, holy Lord!"
To you, our everlasting King.

Come, raise the anthem high!
Let praises fill the sky!
Sing out a new song unto the Lord:
Let all, with heart and voice,
Before the throne rejoice
Of him whom heav'n and earth adore.

PSALM 46

No servant can be the slave of two masters. (Lk 16: 13)

This psalm has consequences. If we say that God is really the ruler of all the earth, and all earthly authorities, we must ask ourselves whom we honour and why, whom we praise and why, whom we obey and why.

All peoples, clap your hands,
cry to God with shouts of joy!

For the Lord, the Most High, we must fear,
great king over all the earth.

He subdues peoples under us
and nations under our feet.
Our inheritance, our glory, is from him,
given to Jacob out of love.

God goes up with shouts of joy;
the Lord goes up with trumpet blast.
Sing praise for God, sing praise,
sing praise to our king, sing praise.

God is king of all the earth.
Sing praise with all your skill.
God is king over the nations;
God reigns on his holy throne.

The princes of the peoples are assembled
with the people of Abraham's God.
The rulers of the earth belong to God,
to God who reigns over all.

Glory be to the Father…

Word of God 1 Corinthians 15: 25-27a, 28

[CHRIST] MUST BE KING until he has put all his enemies under his feet and the last of the enemies to be destroyed is death, for everything is to be put under his feet. —Though when it is said that everything is subjected, this clearly cannot include the One who subjected everything to him. And when everything is subjected to him, then the Son himself will be subject in his turn to the One who subjected all things to him, so that God may be all in all.

For the unsubmissive who refused to take truth for their guide and took depravity instead, there will be anger and fury. (*Rm 2: 8*)

CANTICLE OF ZECHARIAH (Text, back cover B)

You know that if you agree to serve and obey a master you become his slaves. You cannot be slaves of sin that leads to death and at the same time slaves of obedience that leads to righteousness. (Rm 6: 16)

INTERCESSIONS

To the God of heaven and earth, we pray:

℟ Your kingdom come!

God of power and might, all authority comes from you:
– enlighten with your wisdom all those whom you appoint to positions of authority in Church or state. ℟

All obedience is due to you:
– instill in us a spirit of responsible obedience to all those whom you have entrusted with legitimate authority. ℟

All honour is yours by right:
– grant us a spirit of discernment so that we may honour only those who are truly honourable in your sight. ℟

Personal intentions

Our Father…

O Lord our God, you alone are God, and there is no other. Grant us an undivided heart, to love and serve you with all our mind and all our strength, through Jesus Christ our Lord. Amen.

MASS

Wednesday of the Twenty-Fifth Week in Ordinary Time

Christ sends the Twelve out only minimally provisioned. Why? As the Book of Proverbs explains, "Lest, being full, I deny you, saying, 'Who is the Lord?'" In the poverty, trust, and obedience of the Twelve, all the world will recognise that "God is a shield to those who take refuge in him."

(The prayers suggested today are those of the Twenty-Fifth Week in Ordinary Time.)

ENTRANCE ANTIPHON

I am the Saviour of all people, says the Lord. Whatever their troubles, I will answer their cry, and I will always be their Lord.

OPENING PRAYER

Father,
guide us, as you guide creation
according to your law of love.
May we love one another
and come to perfection
in the eternal life prepared for us.
Grant this through our Lord Jesus Christ, your Son,
who lives and reigns with you and the Holy Spirit,
one God, for ever and ever.

● *Give me neither poverty nor riches, grant me only my share of bread to eat.* ●

A reading from
the Book of Proverbs **30: 5-9**

EVERY WORD OF GOD is unalloyed,/ he is the shield of those who take refuge in him./ To his words make no addition,/ lest he reprove you and know you for a fraud. Two things I beg of you,/ do not grudge me them before

I die:/ keep falsehood and lies far from me,/ give me neither poverty nor riches,/ grant me only my share of bread to eat,/ for fear that surrounded by plenty, I should fall away/ and say, "the LORD, Who is the LORD?"/ or else, in destitution, take to stealing/ and profane the name of my God.
This is the word of the Lord.

• PSALM 118 •

℟ (105) Your word is a lamp for my steps, O Lord.

Keep me, Lord, from the way of error
  and teach me your law.
The law from your mouth means more to me
  than silver and gold. ℟

Your word, O Lord, for ever
  stands firm in the heavens.
I turn my feet from evil paths
  to obey your word. ℟

I gain understanding from your precepts
  and so I hate false ways.
Lies I hate and detest
  but your law is my love. ℟

Alleluia, alleluia! The Kingdom of God is close at hand,/ repent and believe the Good News. Alleluia!

● *Jesus sent them out to proclaim the Kingdom of God and to heal.* ●

A reading from
the holy Gospel according to Luke 9: 1-6

JESUS CALLED THE TWELVE together and gave them power and authority over all devils and to cure diseases, and he sent them out to proclaim the kingdom of God and to heal. He said to them, "Take nothing for the journey: neither staff, nor haversack, nor bread, nor money; and let none of you take a spare tunic. Whatever house you enter, stay there; and when you leave, let it be from there. As for those who do not welcome you, when you leave their town shake the dust from your feet as a sign to them." So they set out and went from village to village proclaiming the Good News and healing everywhere. This is the Gospel of the Lord.

PRAYER OVER THE GIFTS

Lord,
may these gifts which we now offer
to show our belief and our love
be pleasing to you.
May they become for us
the Eucharist of Jesus Christ your Son,
who is Lord for ever and ever.

COMMUNION ANTIPHON

You have laid down your precepts to be faithfully kept. May my footsteps be firm in keeping your commands. (Ps 118: 4-5)

PRAYER AFTER COMMUNION

Lord,
help us with your kindness.
Make us strong through the Eucharist.
May we put into action
the saving mystery we celebrate.
We ask this in the name of Jesus the Lord.

MEDITATION OF THE DAY

The New Fundamental Direction of the Twelve

Is it not normal for man to try to assert his independence, his autonomy? Does not accepting poverty mean accepting a conversion, agreeing to change the fundamental direction of one's life? Thereafter, we depend on someone else. The serious factor in refusing one's impoverished state is the refusal to live under the guidance, and in the dependence, of someone else. This is the attitude of the people in the desert: they refuse to live by relying on God, and, what is more, they demand that he account for what has happened to them. This is also the position of the Pharisees toward Christ. And what about ourselves? Do we accept this state of dependence, and more importantly, do we know how to find in it one of the secrets of our existence? Can we recognise in it the true source of peace and joy in love? In examining our religious life and our success in prayer, should we not first of all question ourselves as to whether we accept or refuse this state of dependence on God and on Christ? By accepting and even willing our poverty, we do not rejoice in our state of need, but rejoice in the fact that *it is an opportunity to depend on someone else*. This is one of the meanings of the verb "to believe" in the Bible: "to let oneself be carried along by another." On the other hand, if evangelical poverty were only a lack, only the absence of something we need, should we not justifiably avoid it?

FATHER BERNARD BRO, O.P.

Father Bro is a French Dominican priest, a distinguished theologian, and the author of many books.

Prayer for the Evening

Let us rejoice and sing psalms to our God!

Glory be to the Father, and to the Son, and to the Holy Spirit, as it was in the beginning, is now and ever shall be, world without end. Amen. Alleluia!

HYMN

Metre: LM
This hymn can be sung to the tune used for ***Praise God from Whom All Blessings Flow***

Lord Jesus Christ, abide with us
Now that the sun has run its course;
Let hope not be obscured by night
But may faith's darkness be as light.

Lord Jesus Christ, give us your peace,
And when the trials of earth shall cease,
Grant us the morning light of grace,
The radiant splendour of your face.

Immortal, Holy, Threefold Light,
Yours be the kingdom, pow'r and might;
All glory be eternally
To you, life-giving Trinity.

PSALM 74

2-8, 10-11

Anyone who exalts himself will be humbled, and anyone who humbles himself will be exalted. (Mt 23: 12)

Truly humble people are centres of peace because they fear neither their own failure nor others' success. Let us pray for the wisdom to judge as God judges: to look at our own and others' achievements from God's perspective.

We give thanks to you, O God,
we give thanks and call upon your name.
We recount your wonderful deeds.

"When I reach the appointed time,
then I will judge with justice.
Though the earth and all who dwell in it may rock,
it is I who uphold its pillars.

To the boastful I say: 'Do not boast,'
to the wicked: 'Do not flaunt your strength,

do not flaunt your strength on high.
Do not speak with insolent pride.'"

For neither from the east nor from the west,
nor from desert or mountains comes judgement,
but God himself is the judge.
One he humbles, another he exalts.

As for me, I will rejoice for ever
and sing psalms to Jacob's God.
He shall break the power of the wicked,
while the strength of the just shall be exalted.

Glory be to the Father…

Word of God **Ephesians 4: 1-6**

I, THE PRISONER in the Lord, implore you therefore to lead a life worthy of your vocation. Bear with one another charitably, in complete selflessness, gentleness and patience. Do all you can to preserve the unity of the Spirit by the peace that binds you together. There is one Body, one Spirit, just as you were all called into one and the same hope when you were called. There is one Lord, one faith, one baptism, and one God who is Father of all, over all, through all and within all.

Humble yourselves before the Lord
and he will lift you up. (Jm 4: 10)

CANTICLE OF MARY (Text, back cover A)
If anyone wants to boast, let him boast of the Lord. (2 Co 10: 17)

INTERCESSIONS

Let us pray with confidence to God our strength:

℟ We call upon your name!

Your deeds are wonderful:
– teach us to boast of your love rather than of our accomplishments. ℟

You are the rock upon which the world stands firm:
– grant us faith to depend on you rather than on our own achievements. ℟

You are the true judge of all things:
– open our eyes to see as you see. ℟

You have broken the power of sin and death:
– raise our beloved dead to eternal life. ℟

Personal intentions

Our Father…

May the blessing of almighty God, Father, Son, and Holy Spirit, descend upon us and remain with us always. Amen.

MARIAN ANTIPHON (Text, page 23)

SAINTS
OF TODAY AND YESTERDAY

Be with me, O Lord Jesus,
in all places and at all times.

SAINT IGNATIUS OF SANTHIA
Priest and Religious (1686-1770)

Lorenzo Maurizio Belvisotti, of Santhia, Italy, was ordained a diocesan priest at the age of twenty-four. Six years later, he entered the Capuchin Order, taking the name Ignatius. Following his religious profession, he distinguished himself by his exceptional fidelity to the evangelical counsel of obedience. In 1727, Father Ignatius was sent to the Capuchins' friary of Torino-Monte, having been chosen to serve as the friary's "prefect of the sacristy" and as a confessor for the laity. It was there that he was to spend twenty-eight of the remaining forty-three years of his life, becoming renowned for all the priests, religious, and laity, including the most obstinate sinners, who flocked to his confessional to receive absolution and spiritual direction. His particular gift for counselling wayward souls led to his being called the "father of sinners and the lost". For a time, Father Ignatius also served as a military chaplain, a hospital chaplain, and a master of novices. He developed an eye disorder that nearly blinded him, but his sight subsequently improved sufficiently for him to resume his full round of priestly labours.

Let us remain upon the cross.
Saint Bernard

[THURSDAY, SEPTEMBER 23]

Saint Pio of Pietrelcina

Prayer for the Morning

He was pierced for our offenses:
let us give thanks and praise!

Glory be to the Father, and to the Son, and to the Holy Spirit, as it was in the beginning, is now and ever shall be, world without end. Amen. Alleluia!

HYMN **Metre: LM**

When I survey the wondrous cross
On which the Prince of glory died,
My richest gain I count but loss
And pour contempt on all my pride.

See, from His head, His hands, His feet,
Sorrow and love flow mingled down.
Did e'er such love and sorrow meet
Or thorns compose so rich a crown?

Were the whole realm of nature mine
That were a tribute far too small;
Love so amazing, so divine,
Demands my soul, my life, my all.

CANTICLE OF ISAIAH 52: 13-15; 53: 2-5

While we are still alive, we are consigned to our death every day, for the sake of Jesus, so that in our mortal flesh the life of Jesus, too, may be openly shown. (2 Co 4: 11)

Padre Pio was a man of sorrows. He participated daily in the physical suffering of the wounded Christ, in the humiliation and rejection of the spurned Christ, and in the endless labours of the servant Christ, for the sake of those whom Christ redeemed through the cross. And his reward was to rejoice in the triumph of the cross.

See, my servant will prosper, he shall be lifted up, exalted, rise to great heights.

As the crowds were appalled on seeing him—so disfigured did he look that he seemed no longer human—
so will the crowds be astonished at him, and kings stand speechless before him;
for they shall see something never told and witness something never heard before:
Like a sapling he grew up in front of us, like a root in arid ground.
Without beauty, without majesty (we saw him), no looks to attract our eyes;
a thing despised and rejected by men, a man of sorrows and familiar with suffering,
a man to make people screen their faces; he was despised and we took no account of him.

And yet ours were the sufferings he bore, ours the sorrows he carried.
But we, we thought of him as someone punished, struck by God, and brought low.
Yet he was pierced through for our faults, crushed for our sins.
On him lies a punishment that brings us peace, and through his wounds we are healed.
Glory be to the Father…

Word of God **Galatians 2: 19b-20**

I HAVE BEEN CRUCIFIED with Christ, and I live now not with my own life but with the life of Christ who lives in me.

It makes me happy to suffer for you, as I am suffering now, and in my own body to do what I can to make up all that has still to be undergone by Christ for the sake of his body, the Church. (Co 1: 24)

CANTICLE OF ZECHARIAH **(Text, back cover B)**

I want no more trouble from anybody after this; the marks on my body are those of Jesus.(Ga 6: 17)

INTERCESSIONS

With confidence in the mercy of the Crucified, let us pray through the intercession of Saint Pio:

℟ Lord, have mercy.

For those who give their lives to the mystery of the cross for the sake of others:
– grant them the courage of their vocation. ℟

For those who suffer without understanding the value of their suffering:
– teach them to put their hope in the cross. ℟

For those who reject suffering:
– let the suffering of others enlighten them. ℟

Personal intentions

Our Father…

God of mercy and of love, you called your servant Padre Pio to extend the mystery of the cross visibly into the lives of sinners and sufferers, that they might be converted and believe in the Gospel. Through his intercession, strengthen all believers in willingness to take up the cross daily and follow Jesus Christ your Son, our

Lord, who lives and reigns with you and the Holy Spirit, one God for ever and ever. Amen.

MASS

Thursday of the Twenty-Fifth Week in Ordinary Time

SAINT PIO OF PIETRELCINA *Memorial*

● *"Padre Pio" was born in 1887 in the small Italian village of Pietrelcina. He joined the Capuchin Friars at the age of sixteen and was ordained a priest seven years later. For fifty years at the monastery of San Giovanni Rotundo he was a much sought after spiritual advisor, confessor, and intercessor whose life was devoted to the Eucharist and prayer. Yet despite such notoriety, he would often say, "I only want to be a poor friar who prays."* ●

ENTRANCE ANTIPHON

The Spirit of God is upon me; he has anointed me. He sent me to bring good news to the poor, and to heal the broken-hearted. (Lk 4: 18)

OPENING PRAYER

God our Father,
in Saint Pio of Pietrelcina you gave
a light to your faithful people.
You made him a pastor of the Church
to feed your sheep with his word
and to teach them by his example.
Help us by his prayers to keep the faith he taught
and follow the way of life he showed us.
Grant this through our Lord Jesus Christ, your Son,
who lives and reigns with you and the Holy Spirit,
one God, for ever and ever.

● *There is nothing new under the sun.* ●

A reading from the Book of Ecclesiastes 1: 2-11

VANITY OF VANITIES, the Preacher says. Vanity of vanities. Vanity of vanities. All is vanity! For all his toil, his toil under the sun, what does man gain by it? A generation goes, a generation comes, yet the earth stands firm for ever. The sun rises, the sun sets; then to its place it speeds and there it rises. Southward goes the wind, then turns to the north; it turns and turns again; back then to its circling goes the wind. Into the sea all the rivers go, and yet the sea is never filled, and still to their goal the rivers go. All things are wearisome. No man can say that eyes have not had enough of seeing, ears their fill of hearing. What was will be again; what has been done will be done again; and there is nothing new under the sun. Take anything of which it may be said, "Look now, this is new." Already, long before our time, it existed. Only no memory remains of earlier times, just as in times to come next year itself will not be remembered. This is the word of the Lord.

PSALM 89

℟ (1) O Lord, you have been our refuge from one generation to the next.

You turn men back to dust,
  and say: "Go back, sons of men."
To your eyes a thousand years
  are like yesterday, come and gone,
  no more than a watch in the night. ℟

You sweep men away like a dream,
  like the grass which springs up in the morning.
In the morning it springs up and flowers:
  by evening it withers and fades. ℟

Make us know the shortness of our life
  that we may gain wisdom of heart.
Lord, relent! Is your anger for ever?
  Show pity to your servants. ℟

In the morning, fill us with your love;
  we shall exult and rejoice all our days.
Let the favour of the Lord be upon us:
  give success to the work of our hands. ℟

Alleluia, alleluia! I am the Way, the Truth and the Life, says the Lord;/ no one can come to the Father except through me. Alleluia!

● *I beheaded John, so who is this I hear such reports about?* ●

A reading from
the holy Gospel according to Luke 9: 7-9

HEROD THE TETRARCH had heard about all that was being done by Jesus; and he was puzzled, because some people were saying that John had risen from the dead, others that Elijah had reappeared, still others that one of the ancient prophets had come back to life. But Herod said, "John? I beheaded him. So who is this I hear such reports about?" And he was anxious to see Jesus.
This is the Gospel of the Lord.

PRAYER OVER THE GIFTS
Father of mercy,
we have these gifts to offer in honour of your saints
who bore witness to your mighty power.
May the power of the Eucharist
bring us your salvation.
Grant this through Christ our Lord.

COMMUNION ANTIPHON
I, the Lord, am with you always, until the end of the world. (Mt 28: 20)

PRAYER AFTER COMMUNION

Lord,
may the mysteries we receive
prepare us for the eternal joys
Saint Pio of Pietrelcina won by his faithful ministry.
We ask this in the name of Jesus the Lord.

MEDITATION OF THE DAY

The Grace Herod Lacked

Jesus continues to stay with me and he has not yet left me, for I am finding it increasingly easy to drive away temptation and resign myself to God's will... See, then, Father, how far the tenderness and goodness of Jesus goes, no matter how bad and wicked I am!

Meanwhile, what am I to do to correspond to such great mercy? How am I ever to repay him for such great benefits? If you only knew how many times in the past I have exchanged Jesus for some contemptible thing appertaining to this world! I see something mysterious in myself: I am constantly sorry for the sins I have committed, I resolve continually never to commit them again, yet, I must admit with bitter tears, that in spite of all this I am still very imperfect and it seems to me that I very often offend the Lord. At times I am really in despair because it seems to me almost impossible that Jesus should forgive so many sins; again, more often than not it seems impossible that Jesus should let me go astray. Oh, what on earth is all this? Explain it to me a little.

However, all this happens to me without my perceiving it, for I have by no means the will to offend God even to the slightest extent.

I also suffer greatly, Father, when I see how people ignore Jesus, and what is worse, how they even insult him, especially by those dreadful blasphemies. I should like to die, or at least become deaf rather than hear so many insults offered to God by men.

I have prayed to the Lord as follows: Lord, let me die rather than be present when people are offending you. Please recommend me to the Lord and ask him for this grace for men if it should be for his greater glory.

SAINT PIO OF PIETRELCINA

Saint Pio of Pietrelcina († 1968) was an Italian Capuchin priest who during his lifetime enjoyed a vast reputation for sanctity.

Prayer for the Evening

Too heavy for us our offences! Lord, have mercy!
Glory be to the Father… Alleluia!

HYMN

Metre: 65 65 D
This hymn can be sung to the tune used for *At the Name of Jesus*

Christian! do you see them
On the holy ground,
How the powers of darkness
Rage your steps around?
Christian! up and smite them,
Counting gain but loss;
In the strength that fills you
From the holy cross.

Christian! do you hear them,
How they speak you fair?

"Always fast and vigil?
Always watch and prayer?"
Christian! answer boldly:
"While I breathe I pray!"
Peace shall follow battle,
Night shall end in day.

"Well I know your trouble,
O my servant true;
You are very weary –
I was weary too;
But that toil shall make you
Some day all my own –
And the end of sorrow
Shall be near my throne."

PSALM 64 2-5

Now you must repent and turn to God, so that your sins may be wiped out. (Ac 3: 19)

At great cost to himself, Padre Pio devoted himself especially to the personal and sacramental work of penance, that all sinners might know and receive the mercy that flows upon us from the cross of Christ.

To you our praise is due
in Sion, O God.
To you we pay our vows,
you who hear our prayer.

To you all flesh will come
with its burden of sin.
Too heavy for us, our offences,
but you wipe them away.

Blessed is he whom you choose and call
to dwell in your courts.
We are filled with the blessings of your house,
of your holy temple.

Glory be to the Father…

Word of God Luke 24: 46-48

AND [JESUS] SAID to them, "So you see how it is written that the Christ would suffer and on the third day rise from the dead, and that, in his name, repentance for the forgiveness of sins would be preached to all the nations, beginning from Jerusalem. You are witnesses to this."

Come now, let us talk this over,/ says the LORD:/ Though your sins are like scarlet,/ they shall be white as snow;/ Though they are red as crimson,/ they shall be like wool. (Is 1: 18)

CANTICLE OF MARY (Text, back cover A)

We must realise that our former selves have been crucified with [Christ] to destroy this sinful body and to free us from the slavery of sin. (Rm 6: 6)

INTERCESSIONS

Through the intercession of Padre Pio, let us pray:

℟ Forgive us, O Lord, that we may be healed!

For all believers in whom the Gospel witness burns only dimly: ℟

For all who fail to recognise and benefit from the power of the sacrament of penance: ℟

For all who persist in their sins: ℟

Personal intentions

Our Father…

May rich recompense be made to you by the LORD, the God of Israel, to whom you have come, to find shelter beneath his wings. Amen. (cf. Rt 2: 12)

MARIAN ANTIPHON (Text, page 23)

SAINTS
OF TODAY AND YESTERDAY

You know, O Lord, what is best.

BLESSEDS ANTHONY AND JOHN
Martyrs († 1529)

Anthony was born in Tizatlan, Mexico, around 1516 when the Gospel had not yet reached his native land. The son of a wealthy Mexican government official, Anthony was baptised into the Catholic faith at the Franciscan mission of Tlaxcala by one of the priests who had arrived following the 1521 Spanish Conquest. He proved to be an exceptionally devout convert. With Anthony at his baptism was another youth named John, a fellow convert to the Catholic faith who is thought to have been a servant of Anthony's family. Anthony and John both volunteered to accompany the Dominican priest Bernardino de Minaya in setting out on a dangerous missionary journey to the Mexican region of Oaxaca. Both Anthony and John suffered martyrdom for their faith, most probably in 1529. They, together with another youth, (Blessed) Christopher, are venerated as the earliest lay martyrs of the Americas.

O my Jesus, who with a single word from the cross to your heavenly Father have converted so many obstinate sinners "who returned striking their breasts," speak from the tabernacle a second time that word which will be sufficient to change sinful men, as they are, into so many devoted and faithful followers of you.

Saint Joseph Cafasso

[FRIDAY, SEPTEMBER 24]
Our Lady of Walsingham

Prayer for the Morning

In honour of Mary, the Mother of God,
let us give praise and thanks to the Lord!

Glory be to the Father… Alleluia!

HYMN **Metre: 88 88 88 88**

Traditional melody Henri Friedrich Hemy
Words by John Lingard, based on the *Salve Regina*

Hail Queen of heav'n, the ocean star,
Guide of the wand'rer here below:
Thrown on life's surge, we claim thy care,
Save us from peril and from woe.
Mother of Christ, Star of the Sea,
Pray for the wanderer, pray for me.

O gentle, chaste, and spotless Maid,
We sinners make our prayers through thee;
Remind thy Son that he has paid
The price of our iniquity.
Virgin most pure, Star of the Sea,
Pray for the sinner, pray for me.

Sojourners in this vale of tears,
To thee, blest advocate, we cry;
Pity our sorrows, calm our fears,
And soothe with hope our misery.
Refuge in grief, Star of the Sea,
Pray for the mourner, pray for me.
And while to him who reigns above,
In Godhead One, in Persons Three,
The source of life, of grace, of love,
Homage we pay on bended knee;

Do thou, bright Queen, Star of the Sea,
Pray for thy children, pray for me.

PSALM 51 10-11

I am like a vine putting out graceful shoots,/ my blossoms bear the fruit of glory and wealth. (Si 24: 17)

One tradition holds that the tree of life in the garden of Eden was the olive tree. In the Mediterranean world of the Bible, its fruit provided food, and oil for light, heat, and healing. Mary bore the One who is the light of the world and the healing of the nations.

I am like a growing olive tree
in the house of God.
I trust in the goodness of God
for ever and ever.

I will thank you for evermore;
for this is your doing.
I will proclaim that your name is good,
in the presence of your friends.

Glory be to the Father…

Word of God Sirach 24: 12-14

I HAVE TAKEN ROOT in a privileged people,/ in the LORD's property, in his inheritance./ I have grown tall as a cedar on Lebanon,/ as a cypress on Mount Hermon;/ I have grown tall as a palm in Engedi,/ as the rose bushes of Jericho,/ as a fine olive in the plain,/ as a plane tree I have grown tall.

Every tree can be told by its own fruit.
(Lk 6: 44)

CANTICLE OF ZECHARIAH (Text, back cover B)

Of all women you are the most blessed, and blessed is the fruit of your womb (Lk 1: 42)

INTERCESSIONS

Brought to life by the fruit of Mary's womb, let us pray:

℟ Give life, O Lord!

The Virgin Mary received your Word in faith and brought forth fruit in love:
– through her intercession, may your Church bear fruit that will last. ℟

The Virgin Mary gave birth to your Son, our Saviour:
– through her intercession, bring your Church to full maturity in your kingdom. ℟

The Virgin Mary is honoured as the Mother of God:
– through her intercession, gather children from every land into your family through the proclamation of the word and the celebration of the sacraments. ℟

Personal intentions

Our Father…

O God, you give life to the world through the life, death, and resurrection of your Son, our Lord Jesus Christ. Through the intercession of his mother, grant us the light and healing he brings, who lives and reigns with you and the Holy Spirit, one God for ever and ever. Amen.

MASS

Friday of the Twenty-Fifth Week in Ordinary Time

OUR LADY OF WALSINGHAM *Memorial*

● *In 1061, Lady Richeldis de Faverches was taken in spirit from Norfolk to Nazareth and asked by Our*

Lady to build a replica of the Holy House of the Annunciation. The Shrine of Our Lady of Walsingham was a place of pilgrimage until it was destroyed at the Reformation. In the 19th century the Slipper Chapel nearby was restored and pilgrimage to Walsingham began once more. In 1934, the English Bishops named the Slipper Chapel the Roman Catholic National Shrine of Our Lady. ●

ENTRANCE ANTIPHON

Hail, holy Mother! The child to whom you gave birth is the King of heaven and earth for ever. (Sedulius)

OPENING PRAYER

Lord God,
give to your people the joy
of continual health in mind and body.
With the prayers of the Virgin Mary to help us,
guide us through the sorrows of this life
to eternal happiness in the life to come.
Grant this through our Lord Jesus Christ, your Son,
who lives and reigns with you and the Holy Spirit,
one God, for ever and ever.

● *There is a time for every occupation under heaven.* ●

A reading from the Book of Ecclesiastes

3: 1-11

THERE IS a season for everything, a time for every occupation under heaven:/ A time for giving birth, a time for dying;/ a time for planting, a time for uprooting what has been planted./ A time for killing, a time for healing;/ a time for knocking down, a time for building./ A time for tears, a time for laughter;/ a time for mourning, a time for dancing./ A time for throwing stones away, a time for gathering them up;/ a time for embracing, a time to refrain from embracing./ A time for searching, a time for losing;/ a time for keeping, a time for throwing away./ A time for tearing, a time for sewing;/ a time for keeping silent, a time for speaking./ A time for loving, a time for hating;/ a time for war, a time for peace.

What does a man gain for the efforts that he makes? I contemplate the task that God gives mankind to labour at. All that he does is apt for its time; but though he has permitted man to consider time in its wholeness, man cannot comprehend the work of God from beginning to end.
This is the word of the Lord.

PSALM 143

℟ (1) **Blessed be the Lord, my rock.**

Blessed be the LORD, my rock,
He is my love, my fortress;
he is my stronghold, my saviour,
my shield, my place of refuge. ℟

LORD, what is man, that you care for him;
mortal man, that you take keep him in mind;
man, who is merely a breath;
whose life fades like a passing shadow. ℟

Alleluia, alleluia! The Son of Man came to serve/ and to give his life as a ransom for many. Alleluia!

● *You are the Christ of God. The Son of Man is destined to suffer grievously.* ●

A reading from
the holy Gospel according to Luke 9: 18-22

ONE DAY WHEN JESUS was praying alone in the presence of his disciples he put this question to them, "Who do the crowds say I am?" And they answered, "John the Baptist; others Elijah; and others say one of the ancient prophets come back to life." "But you," he said, "who do you say I am?" It was Peter who spoke up. "The Christ of God," he said. But he gave them strict orders not to tell anyone anything about this.

"The Son of Man", he said, "is destined to suffer grievously, to be rejected by the elders and chief priests and scribes and to be put to death, and to be raised up on the third day."
This is the Gospel of the Lord.

PRAYER OVER THE GIFTS

Father,
the birth of Christ your Son
deepened the virgin mother's love for you,
and increased her holiness.
May the humanity of Christ
give us courage in our weakness;
may it free us from our sins,
and make our offering acceptable.
We ask this through Christ our Lord.

COMMUNION ANTIPHON

Blessed is the womb of the Virgin Mary; she carried the Son of the eternal Father. (See Lk 11: 27)

PRAYER AFTER COMMUNION

Lord,
we rejoice in your sacraments and ask your mercy
as we honour the memory of the Virgin Mary.
May her faith and love
inspire us to serve you more faithfully
in the work of salvation.
Grant this in the name of Jesus the Lord.

MEDITATION OF THE DAY

"Who do people say that I am?"

I ask, then, do you know the feeling of expecting a friend, expecting him to come, and he delays?... This is a state of mind, when our Lord and Saviour is its Object, not intelligible at first sight to the world, not easy to nature, yet of so ordinary fulfillment in the Church in all ages, as to become the sign of the Presence of him who is unseen, and to be a sort of note of the divinity of our religion. You know there are subtle instincts in the inferior animals, by which they apprehend the presence of things which man cannot discern, as atmospheric changes, or convulsions of the earth, or their natural enemies, whom yet they do not actually see; and we consider the uneasiness or the terror which they exhibit to be a proof that there is something near them which is the object of the feeling, and is the evidence of its own reality. Well, in some such way the continuous watching and waiting for Christ, which prophets, apostles, and the Church built upon them, have manifested, age after age, is a demonstration that the Object of it is not a dream or a fancy, but really exists; in other words, that he lives still, that he has ever lived, who was once upon earth, who died, who disappeared, who said he would come again.

For centuries before he came on earth, prophet after prophet was upon his high tower, looking out for him, through the thick night, and watching for the faintest glimmer of the dawn. "I will stand upon my watch," says one of them, "fix my feet upon the tower, and I will watch to see what will be said to me. For, as yet, the vision is far off, and it shall appear at the end, and shall not lie; if it make any delay, wait for it, for it shall surely come, and it shall not be slack." Another prophet says, "O God, my God, to Thee do I watch at break of day. For Thee my soul hath thirsted in a desert land, where there is no way nor water."... And another, "O that Thou wouldst rend the heavens, and come down! – the mountains would melt away at Thy presence, they would melt, as at the burning of fire; the waters would burn with fire. From the beginning of the world the eye hath not seen, O God, besides Thee, what things Thou hast prepared for them that wait on Thee."

BLESSED JOHN HENRY NEWMAN

Blessed John Henry Newman († 1890) established the Oratory in Birmingham, England, and was a preacher of great eloquence.

Prayer for the Evening

By his wounds, we were healed:
let us give thanks and praise!

Glory be to the Father, and to the Son, and to the Holy Spirit, as it was in the beginning, is now and ever shall be, world without end. Amen. Alleluia!

HYMN

Metre: 87 87 D
This hymn can be sung to the tune used for *There's a Wideness in God's Mercy*

Lord, whose love in humble service
Bore the weight of human need,
Who did on the Cross forsaken,
Show us mercy's perfect deed;
We, your servants, bring the worship
Not of voice alone but heart:
Consecrating to your purpose
Ev'ry gift which you impart.

Still your children wander homeless;
Still the hungry cry for bread;
Still the captives long for freedom;
Still in grief we mourn our dead.
As, O Lord, your deep compassion
Healed the sick and freed the soul,
Use the love your Spirit kindles
Still to save and make us whole.

As we worship, grant us vision,
Till your love's revealing light,
Till the height and depth and greatness
Dawns upon our human sight:
Making known the needs and burdens
Your compassion bids us bear,
Stirring us to faithful service,
Your abundant life to share.

PSALM 40 **2-6, 8-14**

Power came out of Jesus that cured them all. (cf. Lk 6: 19)

Human need of every kind cries out to God for healing. The sharpest cry is the plea of the human heart betrayed and wounded by the sin of self and others. The Lord hears every call for help and heals by taking upon himself the suffering of all who are impoverished and weakened by failure, sin, and death.

Happy the man who considers the poor and the weak.
The Lord will save him in the day of evil,
will guard him, give him life, make him happy in the land
and will not give him up to the will of his foes.
The Lord will help him on his bed of pain,
he will bring him back from sickness to health.

As for me, I said: "Lord, have mercy on me,
heal my soul for I have sinned against you."

My foes are speaking evil against me.
"How long before he dies and his name be forgotten?"

My enemies whisper together against me.
They all weigh up the evil which is on me:
"Some deadly thing has fastened upon him,
he will not rise again from where he lies."
Thus even my friend, in whom I trusted,
who ate my bread, has turned against me.

But you, O Lord, have mercy on me.
Let me rise once more and I will repay them.
By this I shall know that you are my friend,
if my foes do not shout in triumph over me.
If you uphold me I shall be unharmed
and set in your presence for evermore.

Blessed be the Lord, the God of Israel
from age to age. Amen. Amen.

Glory be to the Father…

Word of God Isaiah 53: 4-5

OURS WERE THE SUFFERINGS he bore,/ ours the sorrows he carried./ But we, we thought of him as someone punished,/ struck by God and brought low./ Yet he was pierced through for our faults,/ crushed for our sins./ On him lies a punishment that beings us peace,/ and through his wounds we are healed.

Lord, have mercy on me,
heal my soul for I have sinned against you.

CANTICLE OF MARY (Text, back cover A)
Lord, you hear the prayer of the poor. (cf. Ps 9a: 17)

INTERCESSIONS

In the name of all who seek to heal the sufferings of the world, we pray:

℟ Hear us, O Lord.

You lifted upon your own shoulders the burdens of the poor and the weak:
– strengthen those who follow in your footsteps in caring for those in need. ℟

You bore the pain of the disbelief of your relatives and neighbours:
– strengthen those who encounter ridicule in their efforts to live the Gospel. ℟

You shunned no leper and turned away from no sinner:
– strengthen those who seek to grow in love for all who suffer. ℟

You died for all who live under the weight of mortality:
– raise to life all our beloved dead. ℟

Personal intentions

Our Father…

For the kingdom, the power, and the glory are yours, now and for ever! Amen.

MARIAN ANTIPHON (Text, page 23)

SAINTS
OF TODAY AND YESTERDAY

Now indeed, I tread a path that is obscured by darkness. Yet with you, O divine Leader of mankind, I know that I am safe.

SAINTS ANDOCHIUS, THYRSUS, AND FELIX
Martyrs (3rd century)

Andochius, a priest of Smyrna (what is now Izmir, Turkey), was sent as a missionary to Gaul (France) with a fellow priest, Saint Benignus, the deacon Thyrsus, and the subdeacon Andeolus. They preached the Gospel near Autun, where they received hospitality from a Christian named Felix. Andochius, Thyrsus, and Felix were ultimately apprehended by the pagans and suffered martyrdom in Saulieu. The specific era in which they died cannot be established with any certainty, but they would have been victims of one of the persecutions under the Roman emperors. Traditionally Saint Benignus has been commemorated separately from the other three martyrs, having suffered for the faith on a different occasion.

SAINT RUSTICUS
Bishop (5th century)

Rusticus served as a priest of Clermont-Ferrand, France. In 423 he was consecrated bishop of this see. He is commemorated as a saint on September 24 in the 2004 edition of the *Roman Martyrology.*

My Jesus, fling open that book of life in which are set down the deeds of every saint. I want to perform them all for you!
Saint Thérèse of Lisieux

[SATURDAY, SEPTEMBER 25]

Prayer for the Morning

Merciful is the Lord: come, let us sing praise!

Glory be to the Father, and to the Son, and to the Holy Spirit, as it was in the beginning, is now and ever shall be, world without end. Amen. Alleluia!

HYMN Metre: 76 76 D

This hymn can be sung to the tune used for *O Sacred Head Surrounded*

Our Father, we have wandered
And hidden from your face;
In foolishness have squandered
Your legacy of grace.
But now, in exile dwelling,
We rise with fear and shame,
As distant but compelling,
We hear you call our name.

And now at length discerning
The evil that we do,
Behold us, Lord, returning
With hope and trust to you.
In haste you come to meet us
And home rejoicing bring,
In gladness there to greet us
With calf and robe and ring.

O Lord of all the living,
Both banished and restored,
Compassionate, forgiving
And ever caring Lord,

Grant now that our transgressing,
Our faithlessness may cease,
Stretch out your hand in blessing,
In pardon and in peace.

PSALM 37 2-11, 22-23

I know the plans I have in mind for you – it is the LORD who speaks – plans for peace, not disaster, reserving a future full of hope for you. (Jr 29: 11)

The penitential psalms very often speak of sin as sickness brought on by the attack of enemies. Their vivid descriptions of the sinner's suffering remind us again and again that the misery of sin is not what God wants for his beloved children.

O Lord, do not rebuke me in your anger;
do not punish me, Lord, in your rage.
Your arrows have sunk deep in me;
your hand has come down upon me.

Through your anger all my body is sick:
through my sin, there is no health in my limbs.
My guilt towers higher than my head;
it is a weight too heavy to bear.

My wounds are foul and festering,
the result of my own folly.
I am bowed and brought to my knees.
I go mourning all the day long.

All my frame burns with fever;
all my body is sick.
Spent and utterly crushed,
I cry aloud in anguish of heart.

O Lord, you know all my longing:
my groans are not hidden from you.
My heart throbs, my strength is spent;
the very light has gone from my eyes.

O Lord, do not forsake me!
My God, do not stay afar off!
Make haste and come to my help,
O Lord, my God, my saviour!

Glory be to the Father…

Word of God **Isaiah 57: 18-19**

I HAVE SEEN THE WAY/ he went. "But I will heal him, and console him,/ I will comfort him to the full,/ both him and his afflicted fellows,/ bringing praise to their lips.

"Peace, peace to far and near,/ I will indeed heal him," says the LORD.

I will heal their disloyalty,/ I will love them with all my heart. (*Ho 14: 5*)

CANTICLE OF ZECHARIAH **(Text, back cover B)**
I will restore you to health/ and heal your wounds – it is the LORD who speaks. (Jr 30: 17)

INTERCESSIONS

Let us pray to the Divine Physician:

℟ Have mercy on us, Lord, for we have sinned.

Hold back the punishment we fear:
– grant us the healing for which we long. ℟

Lift from us the burden of our guilt:
– grant us the freedom we have sold for illusions of pleasure or power. ℟

Strengthen our longing for goodness:
– remove our foolish preferences for sinful rewards. ℟

Personal intentions

Our Father…

O God, our Healer and our Good, you sent your Son to cure the world's sickness by taking upon himself the burden of its guilt. Heal the diseased vision which causes us to mistake evil for good; heal the sickened mind which causes us to mistake selfishness for love; heal the unhealthy habits which we have made our own, that we may stand before you, whole in body, soul, and spirit, to sing your praise for ever with all the saints, through Jesus Christ our Lord. Amen.

MASS

Saturday of the Twenty-Fifth Week in Ordinary Time

Jesus warns, "The Son of Man is to be handed over into the power of men." In effect, the Lord says, "Remember your creator… before evil days come… before sun and light… grow dark." How do we do this? By following "the promptings of your heart and the desires of your eyes" which lead to the cross of Jesus Christ for which our heart was made.

ENTRANCE ANTIPHON
I am the Saviour of all people, says the Lord. Whatever their troubles, I will answer their cry, and I will always be their Lord.

OPENING PRAYER
Father,
guide us, as you guide creation
according to your law of love.
May we love one another
and come to perfection
in the eternal life prepared for us.
Grant this through our Lord Jesus Christ, your Son,
who lives and reigns with you and the Holy Spirit,
one God, for ever and ever.

● *Remember your creator in the days of your youth, before the dust returns to the earth, and the breath to God.* ●

A reading from the Book of Ecclesiastes 11: 9-12: 8

REJOICE, in your youth, you who are young;/ let your heart give you joy in your young days./ Follow the promptings of your heart/ and the desires of your eyes./ But this you must know: for all these things God will bring you to judgement./ Cast worry from your heart,/ shield your flesh from pain.

Yet youth, the age of dark hair, is vanity. And remember your creator in the days of your youth, before evil days come and the years approach when you say, "These give me no pleasure," before sun and light and moon and stars grow dark, and the clouds return after the rain;/ the day when those who keep the house tremble/ and strong men are bowed;/ when the women grind no longer at the mill,/ because day is darkening at the windows/ and the street doors are shut;/ when the sound of the mill is faint,/ when the voice of the bird is silenced,/ and song notes are stilled,/ when to go uphill is an ordeal/ and a walk is something to dread./ Yet the almond tree is in flower,/ the grasshopper is heavy with food/ and the caper bush bears its fruit,/ while man goes to his everlasting home. And the mourners are already walking to and fro in the street/ before the silver cord has snapped,/ or the golden lamp been broken,/ or the pitcher shattered at the spring,/ or the pulley cracked at the well,/ or before the dust returns to the earth as it once came from it, and the breath to God who gave it.

Vanity of vanities, the Preacher says. All is vanity.

This is the word of the Lord.

PSALM 89

℟ (1) O Lord, you have been our refuge from one generation to the next.

You turn men back to dust,
and say, "Go back, sons of men."
To your eyes a thousand years
are like yesterday, come and gone,
no more than a watch in the night. ℟

You sweep men away like a dream,
like the grass which springs up in the morning.
In the morning it springs up and flowers:
by evening it withers and fades. ℟

Make us know the shortness of our life
that we may gain wisdom of heart.
LORD, relent! Is your anger for ever?
Show pity to your servants. ℟

In the morning, fill us with your love;
we shall exult and rejoice all our days.
Let the favour of the Lord be upon us:
give success to the work of our hands. ℟

Alleluia, alleluia! Our Saviour Christ Jesus abolished death/ and he has proclaimed life through the Good News. Alleluia!

● *The Son of Man is going to be handed over. They were afraid to ask him about what he had said.* ●

**A reading from
the holy Gospel according to Luke** 9: 43b-45

AT A TIME WHEN everyone was full of admiration for all he did, Jesus said to his disciples, "For your part, you must

have these words constantly in your mind: The Son of Man is going to be handed over into the power of men." But they did not understand him when he said this; it was hidden from them so that they should not see the meaning of it, and they were afraid to ask him about what he had just said.
This is the Gospel of the Lord.

PRAYER OVER THE GIFTS

Lord,
may these gifts which we now offer
to show our belief and our love
be pleasing to you.
May they become for us
the Eucharist of Jesus Christ your Son
who is Lord for ever and ever.
We ask this through Christ our Lord.

COMMUNION ANTIPHON

I am the Good Shepherd, says the Lord; I know my sheep, and mine know me. (See Jn 10: 14)

PRAYER AFTER COMMUNION

Lord,
help us with your kindness.
Make us strong through the Eucharist.
May we put into action
the saving mystery we celebrate.
Grant this in the name of Jesus the Lord.

MEDITATION OF THE DAY

One with the One to Be Handed Over

Our supernatural life is our natural life with Christ given to it, inseparable from Christ, as the divinity and humanity of Christ are inseparable in him, and as our souls and bodies in this life are inseparable from one another in us. Since Christ has given himself to us, our lives have the redemptive quality of his, and our relationships with one another are a communion in him. They are a meeting and one-ing of Christ with Christ, an impact of unimaginable love, the never ceasing generation and increase of eternal love on earth, the fulfillment of Christ's words, "I came that they should have life and have it more abundantly." We live our Christ-life, offer our Christ to God, and give Christ to one another by the means that Christ used on earth: by natural means. We give him with our hands and eyes and ears, with the words we speak, the journeys we make, by our human friendships and human loves. It is even truer to say that to our eyes Christ has given his eyes, to our ears he has given his ears, to our words he has given his words, to our hands he has given his hands, to our pain he has given his pain, to our hearts he has given his heart. We see then through his eyes, listen with his ears, speak with his words, work with his hands, suffer with his suffering, rejoice with his joy, love with his heart. It stands to reason that if we surrender our will to God's will, we will make our lives the echo of our Lady's prayer, "Be it done to me according to Thy word" – that is to say, may Christ live in me the life he wants to live in me, where, with whom, and how he wants to live it. Christ in us attracts to us those whom we can truly love; he radiates from those in whom he abides. But he is not only the beauty of life but its strength; it is he who gives the restraint and the tenderness that are the security of passion. It is his strength in us which makes us able to accept responsibilities and to bear one another's burdens.

CARYLL HOUSELANDER

Caryll Houselander († 1954) was a British mystic, poet, and spiritual teacher.

Prayer for the Evening

Vigil of the Twenty-Sixth Sunday in Ordinary Time

God is the giver of all good gifts:
come, give him thanks and praise!

Glory be to the Father, and to the Son, and to the Holy Spirit, as it was in the beginning, is now and ever shall be, world without end. Amen. Alleluia!

HYMN **Metre: 88 88 88**

This hymn can be sung to the tune used for ***Eternal Father, Strong to Save***

The rich man meant no hurt or harm;
He wore his purple, rich and warm,
And dined in comfort with no heed
For Lazarus, who died in need,
Of hunger and of bleeding sores
Before the rich man's very doors.

Still wounded Lazarus awaits,
A world in need before our gates.
And will we bar the door and feast
On hoarded wealth when these, the least
Cry out in pain where deafened ears
Refuse to hear or heed their tears?

Let us arise, the hour is late,
And open wide our bolted gate
To let the poor and suffering in,
Lest we discover that our sin
Lay not in any wrong we did
But in the good from which we hid.

For we must learn what Christ declared:
All gifts are given to be shared.
Where suff'rers are, he also is;

Whatever wounds we heal are his;
Whatever love we have denied
We have refused the Crucified.

PSALM 48 6-10, 13-15

I tell you solemnly, in so far as you neglected to do this to one of the least of these, you neglected to do it to me. (Mt 25: 45)

Treasure of every kind, material or not, is a gift from God, given to be shared and not hoarded. Trust in God rather than one's own stockpile of personal resources is the source of our salvation. Wickedness is not always overt: the neglect of simple kindness, great or small, kills as surely as open violence.

Why should I fear in evil days
the malice of the foes who surround me,
men who trust in their wealth,
and boast of the vastness of their riches?

For no man can buy his own ransom,
or pay a price to God for his life.
The ransom of his soul is beyond him.
He cannot buy life without end,
nor avoid coming to the grave.

In his riches, man lacks wisdom:
he is like the beasts that are destroyed.

This is the lot of those who trust in themselves,
who have others at their beck and call.
Like sheep they are driven to the grave,
where death shall be their shepherd
and the just shall become their rulers.

Glory be to the Father…

Word of God **Jeremiah 5: 27b-29**

THEY HAVE GROWN RICH and powerful,/ fat and sleek./ Yes, in wickedness they go to any lengths,/ they have no respect for rights,/ for orphans' rights, to support them;/ they do not uphold the cause of the poor./ And must I not punish them for such things – it is the LORD who speaks –/or from such a nation exact my vengeance?

He who trusts in riches will have his fall,/
the virtuous will flourish like the leaves. (Pr 11: 28)

CANTICLE OF MARY **(Text, back cover A)**

Is there a poor man among you, one of your brothers, in any town of yours in the land that the LORD your God is giving you? Do not harden your heart or close your hand against that poor brother of yours. (Dt 15: 7)

INTERCESSIONS

Absorption in one's own interests causes the heart to grow hard and die. Let us pray for the gift of life for all our sisters and brothers:

℟ Lord of life, grant life to all.

For those who are rich in this world's goods:
– that they may find blessing in generosity to the poor and hungry. ℟

For those who are rich in the gifts of the mind:
– that they may find blessing in putting their abilities to work for the common good. ℟

For those who are rich in the gifts of the heart:
– that they may find blessing by loving those who are unlovable and unloved. ℟

Personal intentions

Our Father…

May Christ live in our hearts through faith, planted in love and built on love. Amen. (*cf. Ep 3: 17*)

MARIAN ANTIPHON **(Text, page 23)**

SAINTS
OF TODAY AND YESTERDAY

O Mary, my Mother, obtain for me an ardent love for the Most Holy Sacrament.

BLESSED JOSEPH STANEK
Priest, Religious, and Martyr (1916-1944)

A native of Poland, Joseph Stanek entered the Pallottine congregation in 1935 at the age of eighteen. In the autumn of 1939, the Nazis invaded Poland, subjecting this largely Catholic country to the aggression of a regime that in pursuance of its evil agenda sought to destroy the Catholic Church. It was during the Nazi occupation that Joseph was ordained to the priesthood at the age of twenty-four, courageously risking his life to receive the sacrament of holy orders at a time when priests were in grave danger from the Nazis. Less than three and a half years later, Father Stanek was arrested by the Nazis, who hung him in Warsaw, Poland on September 23, 1944, at the age of twenty-seven. In 1992, the cause for beatifying Father Stanek and one hundred and seven other martyrs of Poland who had suffered for their faith during World War II was introduced in response to their popular reputation for holiness and the many favours attributed to their intercession. They were beatified in June of 1999.

The purifying of the soul by the punishment of purgatory is nothing else than the expiation of the guilt that hinders it from obtaining glory.

Saint Thomas Aquinas

Suggested Prayer of the Faithful

(Each local community should compose its own Universal Prayer, but may find inspiration in the texts proposed here.)

The Father has sent us his Son so that we might know the way of righteousness and follow it with all our heart. Calling on the mercy of the Father, we turn to him now with our intercessions:

That God will bring about in the Church many new vocations to the priesthood and religious life, and that the Lord will bless and guide the work of all vocation directors.

For those in public office: that they will secure justice for the oppressed and safeguard the freedom of all.

For the reverence and protection of human life, from natural birth to natural death.

For the homeless and the destitute in our society: that they may be loved and provided for according to Christ's own heart.

For the sick and the suffering: that God who gives life to all things will share his life with those who are most afflicted.

For the grace this week to pursue righteousness, devotion, faith, love, patience, and gentleness.

Loving Father, you dwell in unapproachable light. Grant us the grace to compete well for the faith and to lay hold of eternal life. We ask this through Christ our Lord. Amen.

[SUNDAY, SEPTEMBER 26]

Twenty-Sixth Sunday in Ordinary Time

Prayer for the Morning

Come, let us give thanks to God for all his gifts to us!

Glory be to the Father, and to the Son, and to the Holy Spirit, as it was in the beginning, is now and ever shall be, world without end. Amen. Alleluia!

HYMN — Metre: CM

This hymn can be sung to the tune used for *Lord, Who Throughout These Forty Days*

We sinned each day we passed you by
And did not bind your wound,
To this one's pain and that one's cry
Remaining unattuned.

So doing to the very least,
We did, O Lord, to you;
For, like the Levite and the priest,
We had so much to do.

We left you lying there for dead,
Abandoned and unhealed;
In your unheeded cry for bread
Is selfishness revealed!

PSALM 9b — 1-6, 14, 17-18

If a man who was rich enough in this world's goods saw that one of his brothers was in need, but closed his heart to him, how could the love of God be living in him? (1 Jn 3: 17)

The poor are all those who stand in need of our love, our time, our interest, our concern. Our wealth is not necessarily our money. It is whatever good God has done for us and given to us.

Lord, why do you stand afar off
and hide yourself in times of distress?
The poor man is devoured by the pride of the wicked:
he is caught in the schemes that others have made.

For the wicked man boasts of his heart's desires;
the covetous blasphemes and spurns the Lord.
In his pride the wicked says: "He will not punish.
There is no God." Such are his thoughts.

His path is ever untroubled;
your judgement is far from his mind.
His enemies he regards with contempt.
He thinks: "Never shall I falter:
misfortune shall never be my lot."

But you have seen the trouble and sorrow,
you note it, you take it in hand.
The helpless trusts himself to you;
for you are the helper of the orphan.

Lord, you hear the prayer of the poor;
you strengthen their hearts; you turn your ear
to protect the rights of the orphan and oppressed
so that mortal man may strike terror no more.

Glory be to the Father…

Word of God — 1 Timothy 6: 17-19

WARN THOSE WHO ARE RICH in this world's goods that they are not to look down on other people; and not to set their hopes on money, which is untrustworthy, but on God who, out of his riches, gives us all that we need for our happiness. Tell them that they are to do good, and be rich in good works, to be generous and willing to share – this is the way they can save up a good capital sum for the future if they want to make sure of the only life that is real.

Woe to those ensconced so snugly in Sion/ and to those who feel so safe on the mountain of Samaria. (Am 6: 1)

CANTICLE OF ZECHARIAH (Text, back cover B)

In the day of wrath riches will be of no advantage,/ but virtuous conduct delivers from death. (Pr 11: 4)

INTERCESSIONS

Many are the needs of those around us; few are our resources; great is the generosity of God, and so we pray:

℟ Lord, you hear the prayer of the poor!

For those who go to bed hungry:
– that they may be fed by those who have more food than they need. ℟

For those who suffer the diseases of poverty:
– that they may find help from those who suffer the diseases of affluence. ℟

For those who are neglected:
– that they may find care from those who are loved. ℟

For those who have died:
– that they may be raised to eternal life. ℟

Personal intentions

Our Father…

O God, you loved the world so much that you gave your only-begotten Son for our salvation. Grant that we who have received such a gift from you may withhold from those in need no gift that lies within our power to give, through Christ our Lord. Amen.

MASS

Twenty-Sixth Sunday in Ordinary Time

Perhaps the most scandalous thing about the parable of the rich man is that the sore-ridden beggar "lying at his door" was not some anonymous, faceless stranger, for the first one to speak the name of the "poor man" – "Lazarus" – was the rich man! *"Woe to those esconced so snugly in Sion," for their complacency not only deprives the poor of what they need – it goes so far as to deny their very humanity, their personal dignity. To steer clear of this temptation, we pursue righteousness, devotion, faith, love, patience, and gentleness. The King of kings and Lord of lords dwells in unapproachable light – a light that he shares with us so that we will approach the poor who dwell with us.*

ENTRANCE ANTIPHON

O Lord, you had just cause to judge men as you did: because we sinned against you and disobeyed your will. But now show us your greatness of heart, and treat us with your unbounded kindness. (Dn 3: 31, 29, 30, 43, 42)

GLORIA —— page 450

OPENING PRAYER

Father,
you show your almighty power
in your mercy and forgiveness.
Continue to fill us with your gifts of love.
Help us to hurry toward the eternal life you promise
and come to share in the joys of your kingdom.
Grant this through our Lord Jesus Christ, your Son,
who lives and reigns with you and the Holy Spirit,
one God, for ever and ever.

ALTERNATIVE OPENING PRAYER

Father of our Lord Jesus Christ,
in your unbounded mercy
you have revealed the beauty of your power
through your constant forgiveness of our sins.

May the power of this love be in our hearts
to bring your pardon and your kingdom to all we meet.
We ask this through Christ our Lord.

● *Those who sprawl and those who bawl will be exiled.* ●

A reading from
the Book of the Prophet Amos 6: 1a, 4-7

THE ALMIGHTY LORD SAYS THIS: / Woe to those ensconced so snugly in Sion/ and to those who feel so safe on the mountain of Samaria./ Lying on ivory beds/ and sprawling on their divans,/ they dine on lambs from the flock,/ and stall-fattened veal;/ they bawl to the sound of the harp,/ they invent new instruments of music like David,/ They drink wine by the bowlful,/ and use the finest oil for anointing themselves,/ but about the ruin of Joseph they do not care at all./ That is why they will be the first to be exiled;/ the sprawlers' revelry is over.
This is the word of the Lord.

• PSALM 145 •

℟ (1b) My soul, give praise to the Lord.

Or: Alleluia.

It is the LORD who keeps faith for ever,
who is just to those who are oppressed.
It is he who gives bread to the hungry,
The LORD, who sets prisoners free, ℟

It is the LORD who gives sight to the blind,
who raises up those who are bowed down,
The LORD, who protects the stranger
and upholds the widow and orphan. ℟

It is the LORD who loves the just
 but thwarts the path of the wicked.
The LORD will reign for ever;
 Sion's God, from age to age. ℟

● *Do all that you have been told until the Appearing of the Lord Jesus Christ.* ●

A reading from
the first Letter of Saint Paul to Timothy 6: 11-16

AS A MAN DEDICATED TO GOD, you must aim to be saintly and religious, filled with faith and love, patient and gentle. Fight the good fight of the faith and win for yourself the eternal life to which you were called when you made your profession and spoke up for the truth in front of many witnesses. Now, before God the source of all life and before Christ, who spoke up as a witness for the truth in front of Pontius Pilate, I put to you the duty of doing all that you have been told, with no faults or failures, until the Appearing of our Lord Jesus Christ, who at the due time will be revealed by God, the blessed and only Ruler of all, the King of kings and the Lord of lords, who alone is immortal, whose home is in inaccessible light, whom no man has seen and no man is able to see: to him be honour and everlasting power. Amen.
This is the word of the Lord.

Alleluia, alleluia! The sheep that belong to me listen to my voice, says the Lord,/ I know them and they follow me. Alleluia!

● *Good things came your way, just as bad things came the way of Lazarus. Now he is being comforted here while you are in agony.* ●

A reading from
the holy Gospel according to Luke 16: 19-31

JESUS SAID TO THE PHARISEES: "There was a rich man who used to dress in purple and fine linen and feast magnificently every day. And at his gate there lay a poor man called Lazarus, covered with sores, who longed to fill himself with the scraps that fell from the rich man's table. Dogs even came and licked his sores. Now the poor man died and was carried away by the angels to the bosom of Abraham. The rich man also died and was buried. In his torment in Hades he looked up and saw Abraham a long way off with Lazarus in his bosom. So he cried out, 'Father Abraham, pity me and send Lazarus to dip the tip of his finger in water and cool my tongue, for I am in agony in these flames.' 'My son,' Abraham replied, 'remember that during your life good things came your way, just as bad things came the way of Lazarus. Now he is being comforted here while you are in agony. But that is not all: between us and you a great gulf has been fixed, to stop anyone, if he wanted to, crossing from our side to yours, and to stop any crossing from your side to ours.' The rich man replied, 'Father, I beg you then to send Lazarus to my father's house, since I have five brothers, to give them warning so that they do not come to this place of torment too.' 'They have Moses and the prophets,' said Abraham, 'let them listen to them.' 'Ah no, father Abraham,' said the rich man, 'but if someone comes to them from the dead, they will repent.' Then Abraham said to him, 'If they will not listen either to Moses or to the prophets, they will not be convinced even if someone should rise from the dead.'"

This is the Gospel of the Lord.

CREDO ——— page 452

PRAYER OVER THE GIFTS

God of mercy,
accept our offering
and make it a source of blessing for us.
We ask this in the name of Jesus the Lord.

PREFACE OF SUNDAYS IN ORDINARY TIME ——— page 455

COMMUNION ANTIPHON

O Lord, remember the words you spoke to me, your servant, which made me live in hope and consoled me when I was downcast. (Ps 118: 49-50)

Or:

This is how we know what love is: Christ gave up his life for us; and we too must give up our lives for our brothers. (1 Jn 3: 16)

PRAYER AFTER COMMUNION

Lord,
may this Eucharist
in which we proclaim the death of Christ
bring us salvation
and make us one with him in glory,
for he is Lord for ever and ever.

DAY BY DAY

Lazarus – The Unknown Friend

Sometimes those of us who have more power, more money, more time, or more knowledge bend down to those who have less power, less knowledge, or less wealth; there is a movement from the "superior" to the "inferior." When people are generous they are in control. You can imagine someone in the street falling down and your going to help that person to get up. Then something happens. As you listen to that person you become friends. Perhaps you discover that he or she is living in squalor and has little money. You are not just being generous, you are entering into a relationship which will change your life. You are no longer in control. You have become vulnerable; you have come to love that person. You have listened to her story. You have been touched by that incredible, beautiful person who has lived something incredibly difficult. You are no longer in control, you are no longer just the generous one; you have become vulnerable. You have become a friend.

There is a very moving text in the Gospel of Luke. Jesus says when you give a meal don't invite the members of your family, your friends, or rich neighbours. When you give a really good meal, a banquet, invite the poor, the disabled, and the blind and you will be blessed (Lk 14). In biblical language to give a meal, or to be at a meal, is to become a friend. It is to enter into a covenant relationship. So Jesus is asking us to come up from behind the walls of our group and open our hearts to those who have been marginalised because of their poverty, because of their handicaps, and become their friend. In the heart of Christ there is a yearning to bring people together to meet as friends. To make that move from generosity to communion of hearts will imply a new way of living. It will imply a transformation, because we will have lost power.

JEAN VANIER

Jean Vanier is the founder of l'Arche, an international network of communities for the mentally disabled.

Prayer for the Evening

God is our great desire: come, let us seek his face.

Glory be to the Father, and to the Son, and to the Holy Spirit, as it was in the beginning, is now and ever shall be, world without end. Amen. Alleluia!

HYMN **Metre: SM**

Blest are the pure in heart,
For they shall see our God;
The secret of the Lord is theirs,
Their soul is Christ's abode.

The Lord who left the heav'ns
Our life and peace to bring,
To dwell in lowliness with men,
Their pattern and their king.

Still to the lowly soul
He does himself impart,
And for his dwelling and his throne
Chooses the pure in heart.

We seek your presence, Lord;
This grace to us impart:
Make us a temple fit for you,
A pure and lowly heart.

PSALM 23 **1-6**

Avoid all that. You must aim to be saintly and religious, filled with faith and love, patient and gentle. (1 Tm 6: 11)

Taking Paul's exhortation to heart, let us avoid the pursuit of the kind of selfish hoarding against which the Gospel warns, and let us instead put our energy into pursuing these worthier goals.

The Lord's is the earth and its fullness,
the world and all its peoples.
It is he who set it on the seas;
on the waters he made it firm.

Who shall climb the mountain of the Lord?
Who shall stand in his holy place?
The man with clean hands and pure heart,
who desires not worthless things,
who has not sworn so as to deceive his neighbour.

He shall receive blessings from the Lord
and reward from the God who saves him.
Such are the men who seek him,
seek the face of the God of Jacob.

Glory be to the Father…

Word of God 2 Timothy 2: 21-22

NOW, TO AVOID THESE FAULTS that I am speaking about is the way for anyone to become a vessel for special occasions, fit for the Master himself to use, and kept ready for any good work. Instead of giving in to your impulses like a young man, fasten your attention on holiness, faith, love and peace, in union with all those who call on the Lord with pure minds.

What the Spirit brings is: love, joy, peace, patience, kindness, goodness, trustfulness.
(Ga 5: 22)

CANTICLE OF MARY (Text, back cover A)
Fight the good fight of the faith and win for yourself the eternal life to which you were called. (1 Tm 6: 12)

INTERCESSIONS

To live in and for Christ is a goal worth the devotion of our lives. Let us pray:

℟ Make us holy in your sight, O Lord.

Free us from all worthless pursuits:
– that we may seek your kingdom first. ℟

Cleanse us of all destructive desires:
– that we may seek the true good of all. ℟

Purify our hearts of useless clutter and distractions:
– that we may always seek your face. ℟

Personal intentions

Our Father…

May the Lord rescue us from all evil attempts on us, and bring us safely to his heavenly kingdom. Amen. (cf. 2 Tm 4: 18)

MARIAN ANTIPHON (Text, page 23)

[MONDAY, SEPTEMBER 27]

Saint Vincent de Paul

Prayer for the Morning

The Lord hears the cry of the poor:
let us go into his presence and pray.

Glory be to the Father, and to the Son, and to the Holy Spirit, as it was in the beginning, is now and ever shall be, world without end. Amen. Alleluia!

HYMN

Metre: LM
This hymn can be sung to the tune used for
O Jesus, Joy of Loving Hearts

With glowing light sent from above,
O Vincent, how you guide our way!
Your virtues and example pure
Show us the path to heaven's day.

Amidst the graces of your life
Your charity sheds brightest fire:
How many of the poor it fed,
Filled many hearts with Christ's desire.

Urged on by zeal and charity,
You preached in town and countryside,
Proclaiming all God's mysteries
To poor and rich, both far and wide.

PSALM 111 1, 4-6, 9

He who looks down on his neighbour sins,/ blessed is he who takes pity on the poor. (Pr 14: 21)

Saint Vincent was a man of many talents, but he is remembered especially as the great apostle to the poor.

Happy the man who fears the Lord,
who takes delight in all his commands.
He is a light in the darkness for the upright:
he is generous, merciful and just.

The good man takes pity and lends,
he conducts his affairs with honour.
The just man will never waver:
he will be remembered for ever.

Open-handed, he gives to the poor;
his justice stands firm for ever.
His head will be raised in glory.

Glory be to the Father…

Word of God Matthew 6: 19-21

DO NOT STORE UP treasures for yourselves on earth, where moths and woodworms destroy them and thieves can break in and steal. But store up treasures for yourselves in heaven, where neither moth nor woodworms destroy them and thieves cannot break in and steal. For where your treasure is, there will your heart be also.

The man who is kind to the poor lends to the LORD, he will repay him for what he has done.
(Pr 19: 17)

CANTICLE OF ZECHARIAH (Text, back cover B)
Jesus said, "If you wish to be perfect, go and sell what you own and give the money to the poor, and you will have treasure in heaven; then come, follow me." (Mt 19: 21)

INTERCESSIONS

Through the intercession of Saint Vincent de Paul, let us pray:

℟ Lord, hear the cry of the poor!

For those who follow in Saint Vincent's footsteps in caring for the poor:
– may God repay their good deeds. ℟

For those who use their goods and gifts wisely in service of their neighbours:
– may God store up for them treasure in heaven. ℟

For those who are destitute, hungry, and homeless:
– may God send compassionate and creative men and women to assist them. ℟

Personal intentions

Our Father…

God of mercy, you sent your only-begotten Son to preach the Gospel to the poor. Continue to inspire your people with a love for all those in need; bless the work of those who serve those in want; and grant relief to those who suffer the lack of food, shelter, and clothing. We ask this in the name of Christ the Lord. Amen.

MASS

Monday of the Twenty-Sixth Week in Ordinary Time

SAINT VINCENT DE PAUL *Memorial*

● *Saint Vincent de Paul was born in Gascony in 1581. After completing his studies, he was ordained a priest and went to Paris where he served in a parish. He founded the Congregation of the Mission to supervise the formation of priests and to give support to the poor. With the help of Saint Louise de Marillac, he also founded the Congregation of the Daughters of Charity. He died in Paris in 1660.* ●

ENTRANCE ANTIPHON

The Spirit of God is upon me; he has anointed me. He sent me to bring good news to the poor, and to heal the broken-hearted. (Lk 4: 18)

OPENING PRAYER

God our Father,
you gave Vincent de Paul
the courage and holiness of an apostle
for the well-being of the poor
and the formation of the clergy.
Help us to be zealous in continuing his work.
Grant this through our Lord Jesus Christ, your Son,
who lives and reigns with you and the Holy Spirit,
one God, for ever and ever.

● *The Lord gave, the Lord has taken back. Blessed be the name of the Lord!* ●

A reading from the Book of Job 1: 6-22

ONE DAY, the Sons of God came to attend on the LORD, and among them was Satan. So the LORD said to Satan, "Where have you been?" "Round the earth," he answered, "roaming about." So the LORD asked him, "Did you notice my servant Job? There is no one like him on the earth: a sound and honest man who fears God and shuns evil." "Yes," Satan said "but Job is not God-fearing for nothing, is he? Have you not put a wall round him and his house and all his domain? You have blessed all he undertakes, and his flocks throng the countryside. But stretch out your hand and lay a finger on his possessions: I warrant you, he will curse you to your face." "Very well," the LORD said to Satan, "all he has is in your power. But keep your hands off his person." So Satan left the presence of the LORD.

On the day when Job's sons and daughters were at their meal and drinking wine at their eldest brother's house, a messenger came to Job. "Your oxen," he said, "were at the plough, with the donkeys grazing at their side, when the Sabaeans swept down on them and carried them off. Your servants they put to the sword: I alone escaped to tell you." He had not finished speaking when another messenger arrived. "The fire of God," he said, "has fallen from the heavens and burnt up all your sheep, and your shepherds too: I alone escaped to tell you." He had not finished speaking when another messenger arrived. "The Chaldaeans," he said, "three bands of them, have raided your camels and made off with them. Your servants they put to the sword: I alone escaped to tell you." He had not finished speaking when another messenger arrived. "Your sons and daughters" he said, "were at their meal and drinking wine at their eldest brother's house, when suddenly from the wilderness a gale sprang up, and it battered all four corners of the house which fell in on the young people. They are dead: I alone escaped to tell you." Job rose and tore his gown and shaved his head. Then falling to the ground he worshipped and said:

"Naked I came from my mother's womb,/ naked shall I shall return./ The LORD gave, the LORD has taken back./ Blessed be the name of the LORD!"

In all this misfortune Job committed no sin nor offered any insult to God.
This is the word of the Lord.

• PSALM 16 •

℟ (6) Turn your ear to me, O Lord; hear my words.

LORD, hear a cause that is just,
pay heed to my cry;
Turn your ear to my prayer;
no deceit is on my lips. ℟

From you may my judgement come forth.
Your eyes discern the truth.
You search my heart, you visit me by night.
You test me and you find in me no wrong. ℟

I am here and I call, you will hear me, O God.
Turn your ear to me; hear my words.
Display your great love, you whose right hand saves
your friends from those who rebel against them. ℟

Alleluia, alleluia! The Son of Man came to serve/ and to give his life as a ransom for many. Alleluia!

• *The least among you, that is the one who is great.* •

A reading from
the holy Gospel according to Luke **9: 46-50**

AN ARGUMENT started between the disciples about which of them was the greatest. Jesus knew what thoughts were going through their minds, and he took a little child and set him by his side and then said to them, "Anyone who welcomes this little child in my name welcomes me; and anyone who welcomes me welcomes the one who sent me. For the least among you all, that is the one who is great."

John spoke up. "Master," he said, "we saw a man casting out devils in your name, and because he is not with us we tried to stop him." But Jesus said to him, "You

must not stop him: anyone who is not against you is for you."
This is the Gospel of the Lord.

PRAYER OVER THE GIFTS

Lord,
you helped Saint Vincent
to imitate the love he celebrated in these mysteries.
By the power of this sacrifice
may we also become an acceptable gift to you.
We ask this in the name of Jesus the Lord.

COMMUNION ANTIPHON

Give praise to the Lord for his kindness, for his wonderful deeds toward men. He has filled the hungry with good things, he has satisfied the thirsty. (Ps 106: 8-9)

PRAYER AFTER COMMUNION

Lord,
hear the prayers
of those you have renewed with your sacraments
from heaven.
May the example and prayers of Saint Vincent
help us to imitate your Son
in preaching the good news to the poor.
We ask this in the name of Jesus the Lord.

MEDITATION OF THE DAY

Greatness in Being Least

Our soul can never be at peace in these worldly things, because they are all less than we are. They have been made for us, not we for them. And we have been made for God, so that we may experience his supreme eternal good. Only God, then, can satisfy us. In him we are at peace, and in him we find rest, because there is nothing we can desire or want that we do not find in God. Once we have found it, we cannot fail to find in God the goodness that knows how to gift us and the wisdom that knows how to do it. We have proof of this, for not only has he gifted us when we've asked, but he gifted us even before we existed. Without our ever asking, he created us in his own image and likeness. And he created us anew to grace in the blood of his Son. So our soul is at peace in him and in no one or nothing else. It is he who is supreme wealth, supreme wisdom, supreme goodness, and supreme beauty. He is such an unimaginable good that no one but he himself can measure or fully appreciate how good and great and delightful he is – so much so that he knows how to satisfy and fulfill the holy desires of those who are willing to strip themselves of the world and clothe themselves in him – and he can do it and wants to do it.

SAINT CATHERINE OF SIENA

Saint Catherine of Siena († 1380), Doctor of the Church, was a Dominican, stigmatist, and papal counsellor.

Prayer for the Evening

God does not forget his people:
let us give him thanks and praise!

Glory be to the Father, and to the Son, and to the Holy Spirit, as it was in the beginning, is now and ever shall be, world without end. Amen. Alleluia!

HYMN — Metre: LM

This hymn can be sung to the tune used for ***Again We Keep This Solemn Fast***

Thou, Lord of life, our saving health,
Who mak'st thy suff'ring ones our care,
Our gifts are still our truest wealth,
To serve thee our sincerest prayer.

As on the river's rising tide
Flow strength and coolness from the sea,
So through the ways our hands provide
May quick'ning life flow in from thee,

To heal the wound, to still the pain,
And strength to failing pulses bring,
Till the lame feet shall leap again,
And the parched lips with gladness sing.

PSALM 9 5, 8-13

It was those who are poor according to the world that God chose, to be rich in faith and to be the heirs to the kingdom which he promised to those who love him. (Jm 2: 5)

God does not forget the cry of the poor. Christ sends disciples like Saint Vincent and all his followers to defend the widow and orphan, the poor and oppressed, and to raise them up to the dignity which is rightfully theirs as children of God.

You upheld the justice of my cause;
you sat enthroned, judging with justice.

But the Lord sits enthroned for ever.
He has set up his throne for judgement;
he will judge the world with justice,
he will judge the peoples with his truth.

For the oppressed let the Lord be a stronghold,
a stronghold in times of distress.
Those who know your name will trust you:
you will never forsake those who seek you.

Sing psalms to the Lord who dwells in Sion.
Proclaim his mighty works among the peoples;
for the Avenger of blood has remembered them,
has not forgotten the cry of the poor.

Glory be to the Father…

Word of God

Matthew 25: 34-36

COME, you whom my Father has blessed, take for your heritage the kingdom prepared for you since the foundation of the world. For I was hungry and you gave me food; I was thirsty and you gave me drink; I was a stranger and you made me welcome; naked and you clothed me, sick and you visited me, in prison and you came to see me.

When men were dying,
I it was who had their blessing. (Jb 29: 13)

CANTICLE OF MARY (Text, back cover A)

I tell you solemnly, in so far as you did this to one of the least of these brothers of mine, you did it to me. (Mt 25: 40)

INTERCESSIONS

All Christians are called to the work of prayer for those in need. Let us pray:

℟ Arise, Lord, lift up your hand!

For the helpless and those who defend them: ℟

For the hungry and those who give or prepare food for them: ℟

For the lonely and those who visit them: ℟

For the oppressed and those who work for their liberation: ℟

Personal intentions

Our Father…

May the Lord deliver us from all evil and bring us to life everlasting! Amen.

MARIAN ANTIPHON (Text, page 23)

SAINTS
OF TODAY AND YESTERDAY

I hope for your salvation, O Lord.

BLESSED JEAN-BAPTISTE LABORIER DU VIVIER
Deacon and Martyr (1734-1794)

Jean-Baptiste Laborier du Vivier served as a deacon at the cathedral of Macon, France. On November 29, 1791, the Jacobin regime of the French Revolution ordered all French priests to take the oath of the "Civil Constitution of the Clergy," an edict of the revolutionary regime demanding that bishops be appointed by the votes of the local clergy rather than by the authority of the papacy. In August of 1792 the Jacobins threatened to imprison or deport to French Guiana all priests refusing to take this oath. Jean-Baptiste, although a deacon, was also pressed to take the oath, but refused. He was arrested and brought to Rochefort, where he was put aboard a docked fleet of prison ships with over eight hundred priests and religious refusing the oath. Falling ill from the squalid conditions on the ships, he died on September 26 or 27, 1794, at the age of sixty.

Only God has brought in with the grace of the sacrament, that men are so supplied and made humble in heart, that they will willingly go show themselves their own sins to the priest, whom God has there appointed in his stead… and humbly submit themselves to such pain and penance as their confessor shall assign them.

Saint Thomas More

[TUESDAY, SEPTEMBER 28
Saint Wenceslaus; Saint Lawrence Ruiz and his companions]

Prayer for the Morning

God gives life to all that lives:
come, let us return thanks and praise!

Glory be to the Father, and to the Son, and to the Holy Spirit, as it was in the beginning, is now and ever shall be, world without end. Amen. Alleluia!

Hymn **Metre: 88 88 88**

This hymn can be sung to the tune used for ***Eternal Father, Strong to Save***

Untended and unloved, the earth
Would ravel into tangled void,
But God who drew its filaments
From waste is ceaselessly employed
In spinning frames of time and space
Around our fragile dwelling place.

As days and seasons weave their web
Of warmth and cold, of wet and dry,
The cattle forage for their feed,
And overhead the sparrows fly
Where God keeps count of every one
Whose span is measured by the sun.

The wheel of time entwines the strands
Of death and life we think to be
Our loss and gain, and makes of them
One single thread: eternity.
The lilies of the field know best:
Where God provides, let spindles rest.

PSALM 103 1, 14-18, 33-34, 35b

So do not worry; do not say, "What are we to eat? What are we to drink? How are we to be clothed?" (Mt 6: 31)

God did not create the world only to abandon it to its own devices. He cares day by day for all that he has made, though we do not always recognise his hand at work.

Bless the Lord, my soul!
Lord God, how great you are!

You make the grass grow for the cattle
and the plants to serve man's needs,
that he may bring forth bread from the earth
and wine to cheer man's heart;
oil, to make his face shine
and bread to strengthen man's heart.

The trees of the Lord drink their fill,
the cedars he planted on Lebanon;
there the birds build their nests:
on the tree-top the stork has her home.
The goats find a home on the mountains
and rabbits hide in the rocks.

I will sing to the Lord all my life,
make music to my God while I live.
May my thoughts be pleasing to him.
I find my joy in the Lord.
Bless the Lord, my soul.

Glory be to the Father…

Word of God Matthew 6: 26-30

LOOK AT THE BIRDS in the sky. They do not sow or reap or gather into barns; yet your heavenly Father feeds them. Are you not worth much more than they are? Can any of you, for all his worrying, add one single cubit to his span of life? And why worry about clothing? Think of the flowers growing in the fields; they never have to work or spin; yet I assure you that not even Solomon in all his regalia was robed like one of these. Now if that is how God clothes the grass in the field which is there today and thrown into the furnace tomorrow, will he not much more look after you, you men of little faith?

Surely life means more than food, and the body more than clothing! (Mt 6: 25)

CANTICLE OF ZECHARIAH **(Text, back cover B)**

Your heavenly Father knows that you need all these things. (cf. Mt 6: 32)

INTERCESSIONS

With trust in the love our heavenly Father has for us, we pray:

℟ You are our life, O Lord!

You care for all the works of your hands:
– teach us to help and not to hinder your loving providence. ℟

You feed and clothe all your children:
– forgive us the greediness that seeks to deprive others for our own benefit. ℟

You provide for all the earth:
– grant us the wisdom to see and to serve your purposes. ℟

Personal intentions

Our Father…

Loving Father, you desire to feed, clothe, and shelter all your children. Forgive the sin which seeks to feed, to dress, and to live at the expense of those in need; grant the generosity which seeks to care for all that you have given, through Christ our Lord. Amen.

MASS

Tuesday of the Twenty-Sixth Week in Ordinary Time

SAINT WENCESLAUS *Optional memorial*

● *Saint Wenceslaus was born in Bohemia around the year 907. Brought up as a Christian by his grandmother, he began his reign around the year 925. Having experienced many difficulties in ruling over his subjects and in leading them to the faith, he was betrayed by his brother Boleslaus and killed by assassins in 935. He was immediately recognised as a martyr and is venerated as the patron saint of Bohemia.* ●

ENTRANCE ANTIPHON

This holy man fought to the death for the law of his God, never cowed by the threats of the wicked; his house was built on solid rock.

OPENING PRAYER

Lord,
you taught your martyr Wenceslaus
to prefer the kingdom of heaven
to all that the earth has to offer.
May his prayers free us from our self-seeking
and help us to serve you with all our hearts.
We ask this through our Lord Jesus Christ, your Son,
who lives and reigns with you and the Holy Spirit,
one God, for ever and ever.

● *Why give light to a man of grief?* ●

A reading from the Book of Job **3: 1-3, 11-17, 20-23**

JOB BROKE THE SILENCE and cursed the day of his birth. This is what he said:

May the day perish when I was born,/ and the night that told of a boy conceived.

Why did I not die new-born,/ not perish as I left the womb?/ Why were there two knees to receive me,/ two breasts for me to suck?/

Had there not been, I should now be lying in peace,/ wrapped in a restful slumber,/ with the kings and high viziers of earth/ who build themselves vast vaults,/ or with princes who have gold and to spare/ and houses crammed with silver.

Or put away like a still-born child that never came to be,/ like unborn babes that never see the light./ Down there, bad men bustle no more,/ there the weary rest.

Why give light to a man of grief?/ Why give life to those bitter of heart,/ who long for a death that never comes,/ and hunt for it more than for a buried treasure?/ They would be glad to see the grave-mound/ and shout with joy if they reached the tomb.

Why make this gift of light to a man who does not see his way,/ whom God baulks on every side?
This is the word of the Lord.

PSALM 87

℟ (3) **Let my prayer come into your presence, O Lord.**

LORD my God, I call for help by day;
  I cry at night before you.
Let my prayer come into your presence.
  O turn your ear to my cry. ℟

For my soul is filled with evils;
my life is on the brink of the grave.
I am reckoned as one in the tomb:
I have reached the end of my strength. ℟

Like one alone among the dead;
like the slain lying in their graves;
like those you remember no more,
cut off, as they are, from your hand. ℟

You have laid me in the depths of the tomb,
in places that are dark, in the depths.
Your anger weighs down upon me:
I am drowned beneath your waves. ℟

Alleluia, alleluia! The Son of Man came to serve/ and to give his life as a ransom for many. Alleluia!

● *Jesus resolutely took the road for Jerusalem.* ●

A reading from the holy Gospel according to Luke 9: 51-56

AS THE TIME DREW NEAR for him to be taken up to heaven, Jesus resolutely took the road for Jerusalem and sent messengers ahead of him. These set out, and they went into a Samaritan village to make preparations for him, but the people would not receive him because he was making for Jerusalem. Seeing this, the disciples James and John said, 'Lord, do you want us to call down fire from heaven to burn them up?' But he turned and rebuked them, and they went off to another village.
This is the Gospel of the Lord.

PRAYER OVER THE GIFTS

Lord,
bless our offerings and make them holy.

May these gifts fill our hearts
with the love which gave Saint Wenceslaus victory
over all his suffering.
We ask this through Christ our Lord.

COMMUNION ANTIPHON
If anyone wishes to come after me, he must renounce himself, take up his cross, and follow me, says the Lord. (Mt 16: 24)

PRAYER AFTER COMMUNION
Lord,
may the mysteries we receive
give us the spiritual courage which made your martyr Wenceslaus
faithful in your service and victorious in his suffering.
Grant this in the name of Jesus the Lord.

MEDITATION OF THE DAY

How to Join Jesus on his Journey

The future will be what we make it; let us reflect on this thought so that it may motivate us to act. Especially, let us realize that all collective reform must first be individual reform. Let us work at transforming ourselves and our lives. Let us influence those around us, not by useless preaching, but by the irresistible power of our spirituality and the example of our lives.

Let us give ourselves generously and try to strengthen our faith and expand our understanding, confident that all will come to us to be rekindled and to enlighten their hearts and minds.

The world is unable to recognize spiritual reality; it does not know how to penetrate the outer covering that veils our inmost self. Any unconquerable strength, purity, and truth in us is seen in our depths only by him who lives in us and judges us with more justice and love than men and women. What a reason to be faithful and courageous in daily life!

Nothing goes unnoticed by our eternal Guest; the least of our actions has a profound effect on others.

Let us love. Let our lives be a perpetual song of love for God, first of all, and for all human beings who suffer, love, and mourn. Let deep joy live in us. Let us be like the lark, enemy of the night, who always announces the dawn and awakens in each creature the love of light and life. Let us awaken others to the spiritual life.

Why do we put off doing the good until tomorrow? Why do we wait to be wealthy before giving? Is not the gift of ourselves better than money, and is there any time when we could not offer a tear or a smile to someone who is suffering? Cannot a word from us strengthen someone in distress? Cannot an act of pure love coming from our depths brighten a sad life?

ELISABETH LESEUR

Elisabeth Leseur († 1914) was a French married laywoman whose cause for canonisation is underway.

Prayer for the Evening

God speaks of peace:
come, let us give thanks and praise!

Glory be to the Father, and to the Son, and to the Holy Spirit, as it was in the beginning, is now and ever shall be, world without end. Amen. Alleluia!

HYMN Metre: LM

Remember, Lord, thy works of old,
The wonders that our fathers told;
Remember not our sin's dark stain;
Give peace, O God, give peace again!

Whom shall we trust but thee, O Lord?
Where rest but on thy faithful Word?
None ever called on thee in vain,
Give peace, O God, give peace again!

Where saints and angels dwell above
All hearts are knit in holy love;
O bind us in that heavenly chain;
Give peace, O God, give peace again!

PSALM 84 2-4, 7-14

The Lord of heaven favour you, and grant you his grace and peace. (cf. Tb 7: 11)

In the Word made flesh in the incarnation, God's mercy and human faithfulness become one Saviour, Christ, who is our peace. In him are all people knit together into one Body.

O Lord, you once favoured your land
and revived the fortunes of Jacob,
you forgave the guilt of your people
and covered all their sins.
You averted all your rage,
you calmed the heat of your anger.

Will you not restore again our life
that your people may rejoice in you?
Let us see, O Lord, your mercy
and give us your saving help.

I will hear what the Lord God has to say,
a voice that speaks of peace,
peace for his people and his friends
and those who turn to him in their hearts.
His help is near for those who fear him
and his glory will dwell in our land.

Mercy and faithfulness have met;
justice and peace have embraced.
Faithfulness shall spring from the earth
and justice look down from heaven.

The Lord will make us prosper
and our earth shall yield its fruit.
Justice shall march before him
and peace shall follow his steps.

Glory be to the Father…

Word of God

Isaiah 45: 8

SEND VICTORY LIKE A DEW, you heavens,/ and let the clouds rain it down./ Let the earth open for salvation to spring up./ Let deliverance, too, bud forth/ which I, the LORD, shall create.

God lowered the heavens and came down.
(Ps 17: 10)

CANTICLE OF MARY

(Text, back cover A)

For I mean to spread peace everywhere; the vine will give its fruit, the earth its increase, and heaven its dew. (Zc 8: 12)

INTERCESSIONS

Let us pray to the God of our salvation:

℟ Give peace, O Lord.

You forgave the guilt of your people:
– make all one in the love of Christ. ℟

You spoke the final Word of salvation in the incarnation:
– make all holy by the dying and rising of Christ. ℟

You revealed your faithfulness through the longed-for Messiah:
– make us servants of your justice and peace for all who wait for you. ℟

Personal intentions

Our Father…

To you all, who are God's beloved, may God our Father and the Lord Jesus Christ send grace and peace. Amen. *(cf. Rm 1: 7)*

MARIAN ANTIPHON **(Text, page 23)**

SAINTS
OF TODAY AND YESTERDAY

O Saviour, who have shed the last drop of your blood for me, I throw myself down at your feet and pray for pardon.

BLESSEDS MICHAEL ICHINOSE SUKIZAYEMON, JOHN MUTSUNOO CHOZABURO, AND PETER SAWAGUCHI KUHYOYE
Martyrs († 1630)

In 1614 Japan's pagan shogun ruler Iyeyasu issued an edict ordering all foreign missionaries to depart. The priests who thereafter remained in Japan or entered the country risked their lives to do so. Michael Ichinose Sukizayemon, a native Japanese member of the Augustinian Hermits' Third Order, assisted the Augustinian priests in their dangerous labours. On September 28, 1630, Michael was beheaded in Nagasaki for having given lodging to the missionaries. Five other Third Order Augustinians died with him, including John Mutsunoo Chozaburo, a lay catechist who had assisted the Mexican-born Augustinian priest and future martyr (Blessed) Bartholomew Gutierrez. Another of the martyrs, Peter Sawaguchi Kuhyoye, who had taken the name Peter of the Mother of God, was like Michael condemned to death for having sheltered the missionaries.

Bring up your children well for God, and God will settle their future a hundred thousand times better than you can do it.
Blessed Charles de Foucauld

[WEDNESDAY, SEPTEMBER 29
Saint Michael, Saint Gabriel, and Saint Raphael]

Prayer for the Morning

Let us praise God above all for ever!

Glory be to the Father, and to the Son, and to the Holy Spirit, as it was in the beginning, is now and ever shall be, world without end. Amen. Alleluia!

HYMN — Metre: LM

This hymn can be sung to the tune used for *Praise God from Whom All Blessings Flow*

O Lord, the angels' sheer delight!
Their life reflects your splendour bright;
As we today their praise declare,
May we their joy forever share.

Saint Michael, be our refuge here,
Preserve us from all useless fear;
Through you may God his peace bestow
On all the nations here below.

Saint Gabriel, be with us this day,
Reveal God's will to us, we pray;
As Mary once did answer you,
May our response be firm and true.

Saint Raphael, heal our sinful heart,
May God his grace to us impart,
And may you guide us on the way
That we may never go astray. Amen.

PSALM 102 — 19-22

You walk on the wings of the wind,/ you make the winds your messengers/ and flashing fire your servants. (cf. Ps 103: 3-4)

The great archangels – Michael, Gabriel, and Raphael – lead the choirs of those awesome servants of God whom we picture as "wings of the wind" and "flashes of fire" and to whom we give the name "angel", meaning "messenger".

The Lord has set his sway in heaven
and his kingdom is ruling over all.
Give thanks to the Lord, all his angels,
mighty in power, fulfilling his word,
who heed the voice of his word.

Give thanks to the Lord, all his hosts,
his servants who do his will.
Give thanks to the Lord, all his works,
in every place where he rules.
My soul, give thanks to the Lord!

Glory be to the Father…

Word of God

Isaiah 6: 1-3

I SAW THE LORD seated on a high throne; his train filled the sanctuary; above him stood seraphs, each one with six wings: two to cover its face, two to cover its feet and two for flying.

And they cried out one to another in this way, "Holy, holy, holy is the LORD Sabaoth. His glory fills the whole earth."

Holy, holy, holy is the LORD Sabaoth
(Is 6: 3)

CANTICLE OF ZECHARIAH **(Text, back cover B)**
Heavens, rejoice with him,/ let the sons of God pay him homage! (Dt 32: 43)

INTERCESSIONS

To God who is enthroned upon the seraphim, we pray:

℟ We give you thanks and praise!

Through the power of Michael, leader of the heavenly armies in the war against evil:
– protect your people, Lord! ℟

Through the word of Gabriel, message-bearer of the Gospel:
– save your people, Lord! ℟

Through the intervention of Raphael, companion and healer:
– comfort your people, Lord! ℟

Personal intentions

Our Father…

O God, in your great wisdom you have given to your angels and to your people each their proper tasks. Grant us their protection, who serve ever in your presence, through Jesus Christ, your Son, our Lord, who lives and reigns with you and the Holy Spirit, one God for ever and ever. Amen.

MASS

Feast of Saints Michael, Gabriel, and Raphael

It is on the anniversary of the dedication of a basilica in honour of Saint Michael in the northeastern part of Rome, during the fifth century, that we celebrate the feast of the Holy Angels. "Their splendour shows us your greatness, which surpasses in goodness the whole of creation" (Preface).

Scripture mentions but briefly the archangels Michael and Gabriel, and speaks of Raphael only in the Book of Tobit. In the

New Testament, Gabriel is the messenger who announces the birth of John the Baptist and that of Jesus, while Michael appears at the head of the heavenly hosts, the conqueror of Satan in the great battle of the endtime (First Reading from Revelation). From the paradise of Genesis to that of Revelation, however, the angels fill the entire span of the history of salvation with their invisible presence. They are the Lord's "angels" or messengers (Entrance Antiphon), revealing his designs and carrying out his commands. Above all, they sing his praises (Communion Antiphon), an immense host of adorers seen by Daniel and John around the throne of the living God: "A thousand thousand waited on him, ten thousand times ten thousand stood before him (First Reading from Daniel).

Earth's liturgy joins us to that of the angels in heaven. Not only do we "make their hymn of praise our own" (Preface), proclaiming that the Lord is holy, but in offering the sacrifice we ask God "that your angel may take this sacrifice to your altar in heaven" (Eucharistic Prayer I).

ENTRANCE ANTIPHON

Bless the Lord, all you his angels, mighty in power, you obey his word and heed the sound of his voice. (Ps 102: 20)

GLORIA —— page 450

OPENING PRAYER

God our Father,
in a wonderful way you guide the work of angels and men.
May those who serve you constantly in heaven
keep our lives safe from all harm on earth.
Grant this through our Lord Jesus Christ, your Son,
who lives and reigns with you and the Holy Spirit,
one God, for ever and ever.

● *A thousand thousand waited on him.* ●

A reading from
the Book of the Prophet Daniel **7: 9-10, 13-14**

AS I WATCHED:/ Thrones were set in place/ and one of great age took his seat./ His robe was white as snow,/ the hair of his head as pure as wool./ His throne was a blaze of flames,/ its wheels were a burning fire./ A stream of fire poured out/ issuing from his presence./ A thousand thousand waited on him,/ ten thousand times ten thousand stood before him.

A court was held/ and the books were opened./ I gazed into the visions of the night.

And I saw, coming on the clouds of heaven,/ one like a son of man./He came to the one of great age/ and was led into his presence./ On him was conferred sovereignty, glory, and kingship,/ and men of all peoples, nations and languages became his servants./ His sovereignty is an eternal sovereignty/ which shall never pass away,/ nor will his empire ever be destroyed.

This is the word of the Lord.

Or:

● *Michael and his angels attacked the dragon.* ●

A reading from
the Book of Revelation **12: 7-12ab**

NOW WAR BROKE OUT in heaven, when Michael with his angels attacked the dragon. The dragon fought back with his angels, but they were defeated and driven out of heaven. The great dragon, the primeval serpent, known as the devil or Satan, who had deceived all the world, was hurled down to the earth and his angels were hurled down with him. Then

I heard a voice shout from heaven, "Victory and power and empire for ever have been won by our God, and all authority for his Christ, now that the persecutor, who accused our brothers day and night before our God, has been brought down. They have triumphed over him by the blood of the Lamb and by the witness of their martyrdom, because even in the face of death they would not cling to life. Let the heavens rejoice and all who live there."
This is the word of the Lord.

• PSALM 137 •

℟ (1) In the presence of the angels I will bless you, O Lord.

I thank you, LORD, with all my heart:
you have heard the words of my mouth;
in the presence of the angels I will bless you.
I will adore before your holy temple. ℟

I thank you for your faithfulness and love,
which excel all we ever knew of you.
On the day I called, you answered;
you increased the strength of my soul. ℟

All earth's kings shall thank you
when they hear the words of your mouth.
They shall sing of the LORD's ways:
"How great is the glory of the LORD." ℟

Alleluia, alleluia! Give thanks to the LORD, all his hosts,/ his servants who do his will. Alleluia!

● *You will see the angels of God ascending and descending above the Son of Man.* ●

A reading from
the holy Gospel according to John 1: 47-51

WHEN JESUS SAW NATHANAEL coming he said of him, "There is an Israelite who deserves the name, incapable of deceit." "How do you know me?" said Nathanael. "Before Philip came to call you," said Jesus "I saw you under the fig tree." Nathanael answered, "Rabbi, you are the Son of God, you are the King of Israel." Jesus replied, "You believe that just because I said: I saw you under the fig tree. You will see greater things than that." And then he added, "I tell you most solemnly, you will see heaven laid open and, above the Son of Man, the angels of God ascending and descending."
This is the Gospel of the Lord.

PRAYER OVER THE GIFTS

Lord,
by the ministry of your angels
let our sacrifice of praise come before you.
May it be pleasing to you and helpful to our own salvation.
We ask this through Christ our Lord.

PREFACE OF THE ANGELS

Father, all-powerful and ever-living God,
we do well always and everywhere to give you thanks.

In praising your faithful angels and archangels,
we also praise your glory,
for in honouring them, we honour you, their creator.
Their splendour shows us your greatness,
which surpasses in goodness the whole of creation.
Through Christ our Lord
the great army of angels rejoices in your glory.
In adoration and joy
we make their hymn of praise our own: **Holy…**

COMMUNION ANTIPHON
In the sight of the angels I will sing your praise, my God. (Ps 137: 1)

PRAYER AFTER COMMUNION
Lord,
hear the prayers of those you renew with the bread of life.
Made strong by the courage it gives,
and under the watchful care of the angels,
may we advance along the way of salvation.
We ask this in the name of Jesus the Lord.

MEDITATION OF THE DAY

Honouring the Archangels

The angels show forth God's greatness and perfection. "Each symbolises individually some attribute or other of that infinite Being. In some we see his power, in others his love, in others his strength. Each is a reproduction of some beauty of the divine Original; each adores him and glorifies him in the perfection it portrays." It is God, then, whom we honour in the angels. They are like mirrors reflecting the perfections of their infinite Creator. Raised to the supernatural order, they share in the life of God; and victorious in trial, they enjoy the beatific vision: "Their angels in heaven always see the face of my Father who is in heaven."

If we consider their relations with Jesus Christ, it may not appear absolutely certain that they hold their grace from him; but this much does appear with certainty, that in heaven they unite themselves with him, the Mediator of all religion, in order to adore, praise, and glorify the majesty of the Most High. It is their bliss to add in this wise a greater worth to their worship: "Through whom the angels praise, the dominations adore and the powers hold in awe your majesty." Hence, when we unite ourselves to Jesus Christ to adore God we join at the same time with the angels and saints in a heavenly harmony which renders the praise of the Godhead still more perfect. We can well make our own the words of Father Olier: "May all the angelic host, the mighty powers that move the spheres of heaven, forever pour forth in Jesus Christ whatever be wanting to our song of praise. May they forever thank you, Lord, for all those gifts both of nature and of grace which from the goodness of your hand we all receive."

FATHER ADOLPHE TANQUEREY, S.S.

Father Adolphe Tanquerey († 1932) was a Sulpician priest and theologian who was born in France. His work The Spiritual Life: A Treatise on Ascetic and Mystical Theology *is considered a classic.*

Prayer for the Evening

In the presence of the angels
let us praise our God!

Glory be to the Father, and to the Son, and to the Holy Spirit, as it was in the beginning, is now and ever shall be, world without end. Amen. Alleluia!

HYMN Metre: LM

This hymn can be sung to the tune used for *All Creatures of Our God and King*

Ye watchers and ye holy ones,
Bright seraphs, cherubim, and thrones,
Raise the glad strain, Alleluia!
Cry out, dominions, princedoms, powers,
Virtues, archangels, angels' choirs,
Alleluia, Alleluia, Alleluia, Alleluia, Alleluia!

O friends, in gladness let us sing
Supernal anthems echoing,
Alleluia, Alleluia

To God the Father, God the Son,
And God the Spirit, Three in One.
Alleluia, Alleluia, Alleluia, Alleluia, Alleluia!

PSALM 137 1-5

The angel who was talking to me then said to me, "Make this proclamation: the LORD Sabaoth says this: I feel most jealous love for Jerusalem and Sion." (Zc 1: 14)

In whatever form they appear, the great angels of God bear the message of God's faithfulness and love for his people and proclaim the glory of his saving power.

I thank you, Lord, with all my heart,
you have heard the words of my mouth.
In the presence of the angels I will bless you.
I will adore before your holy temple.

I thank you for your faithfulness and love
which excel all we ever knew of you.
On the day I called, you answered;
you increased the strength of my soul.

All earth's kings shall thank you
when they hear the words of your mouth.
They shall sing of the Lord's ways:
"How great is the glory of the Lord!"

Glory be to the Father…

Word of God Isaiah 63: 9

IT WAS NEITHER MESSENGER nor angel/ but his Presence that saved them./ In his love and pity/ he redeemed them himself,/ he lifted them up, carried them,/ throughout the days of old.

Blessed be God for ever!

CANTICLE OF MARY (Text, back cover A)

Suddenly with the angel there was a great throng of the heavenly host, praising God and singing: "Glory to God in the highest heaven,/ and peace to men who enjoy his favour." (Lk 2: 13-14)

INTERCESSIONS

To the One who reigns above the angels yet stoops down to hear the prayers of earth, let us pray:

℟ With the angels, we sing your praise!

You are all-holy and all-loving: ℟

You send your messengers to bear the tidings of salvation: ℟

You will to gather your people into your glory with all the angels: ℟

Personal intentions

Our Father…

May mercy, peace, and love be ours in abundance. Amen. *(cf. Jude 2)*

MARIAN ANTIPHON (Text, page 23)

[THURSDAY, SEPTEMBER 30]

Saint Jerome

Prayer for the Morning

The word of the Lord endures for ever:
let us give thanks and praise!

Glory be to the Father, and to the Son, and to the Holy Spirit, as it was in the beginning, is now and ever shall be, world without end. Amen. Alleluia!

HYMN **Metre: 77 77**

This hymn can be sung to the tune used for *Saviour of the Nations, Come*

Word of life, most pure and strong,
Lo! for thee the nations long,
Spread, till from its dreary night
All the world awakes to light.

Up! the ripening fields you see,
Mighty shall the harvest be;
But the reapers still are few,
Great the work they have to do.

Lord of harvest, let there be
Joy and strength to work for thee,
Till the nations, far and near,
See thy light, and learn thy fear.

PSALM 118 **105-112**

Now I know you are a man of God and the word of the LORD in your mouth is truth itself. (cf. 1 K 17: 24)

Saint Jerome lived intensely by the light of God's word through study, prayer, and the painstaking work of translating it into the vernacular, which was Latin at the time, and writing commentaries on it.

Your word is a lamp for my steps
and a light for my path.
I have sworn and have made up my mind
to obey your decrees.

Lord, I am deeply afflicted:
by your word give me life.
Accept, Lord, the homage of my lips
and teach me your decrees.

Though I carry my life in my hands,
I remember your law.
Though the wicked try to ensnare me
I do not stray from your precepts.

Your will is my heritage for ever,
the joy of my heart.
I set myself to carry out your statutes
in fullness, for ever.

Glory be to the Father…

Word of God 2 Timothy 3: 14-17

YOU MUST KEEP to what you have been taught and know to be true; remember who your teachers were, and how, ever since you were a child, you have known the holy scriptures – from these you can learn the wisdom that leads to salvation through faith in Christ Jesus. All scripture is inspired by God and can profitably be used for teaching, for refuting error, for guiding people's lives and teaching them to be holy. This is how the man who is dedicated to God becomes fully equipped and ready for any good work.

Now I will make my words/ a fire in your mouth.
(Jr 5: 14b)

CANTICLE OF ZECHARIAH (Text, back cover B)
Jesus replied: "If anyone loves me he will keep my word, and my Father will love him, and we shall come to him and make our home with him." (cf. Jn 14: 23)

INTERCESSIONS

God speaks his word to all peoples. In gratitude, let us pray:

℟ Speak, Lord, your servants are listening!

For all students and teachers of your word:
– fill them with the spirit of wisdom and understanding. ℟

For all translators of your word:
– grant them patience and perseverance at their difficult task. ℟

For all who pray your word:
– fill us with love for you and for the gift of the Scriptures. ℟

Personal intentions

Our Father…

O God, you illumined Saint Jerome with love for your word and for the task of proclaiming it to others. Shine on your people's path that we may walk always in the light of your word toward your heavenly kingdom, through Jesus Christ, your Son, our Lord, who lives and reigns with you and the Holy Spirit, one God for ever and ever. Amen.

MASS

Thursday of the Twenty-Sixth Week in Ordinary Time

SAINT JEROME *Memorial*

● *Saint Jerome was born in Stridon, Dalmatia, around the year 340. He studied the classical authors in Rome, and was baptised there. He embraced a life of asceticism and went to the East where he was ordained a priest. Returning to Rome, he became a secretary to Pope Damasus. In Rome he began to translate the holy Scriptures into Latin and to promote the monastic life. Eventually he settled in Bethlehem where he served the needs of the Church. He wrote many works, especially commentaries on holy Scripture. He died in Bethlehem in 420.* ●

ENTRANCE ANTIPHON

The book of the law must be ever on your lips; reflect on it night and day. Observe and do all that it commands: then you will direct your life with understanding. (Jos 1: 8)

OPENING PRAYER

**Father,
you gave Saint Jerome delight
in his study of holy Scripture.
May your people find in your word
the food of salvation and the fountain of life.
We ask this through our Lord Jesus Christ, your Son,
who lives and reigns with you and the Holy Spirit,
one God, for ever and ever.**

● *I know that my Avenger lives.* ●

A reading from the Book of Job **19: 21-27**

JOB SAID:/ Pity me, pity me, you, my friends,/ for the hand

of God has struck me!/ Why do you hound me down like God,/ will you never have enough of my flesh?

Ah, would that my words were written down,/ inscribed in some monument/ with iron chisel and engraving tool,/ cut into the rock forever./ This I know: that my Avenger lives,/ and he, the Last, will take his stand on earth./ After my awakening, he will set me close to him,/ and from my flesh I shall look on God./ He whom I shall see will take my part:/ these eyes will gaze on him and find him not aloof.

This is the word of the Lord.

PSALM 26

℟ (13) I am sure I shall see the Lord's goodness in the land of the living.

O LORD, hear my voice when I call;
have mercy and answer.
Of you my heart has spoken: "Seek his face." ℟

It is your face, O LORD, that I seek;
hide not your face.
Dismiss not your servant in anger;
you have been my help. ℟

I am sure I shall see the LORD's goodness
in the land of the living.
Hope in him, hold firm and take heart.
Hope in the LORD. ℟

Alleluia, alleluia! The Kingdom of God is at hand,/ repent and believe the Good News. Alleluia!

● *Your peace will rest on him.* ●

A reading from
the holy Gospel according to Luke 10: 1-12

THE LORD APPOINTED seventy-two others and sent them out ahead of him, in pairs, to all the towns and places he himself was to visit. He said to them, "The harvest is rich but the labourers are few, so ask the Lord of the harvest to send labourers to his harvest. Start off now, but remember, I am sending you out like lambs among wolves. Carry no purse, no haversack, no sandals. Salute no one on the road. Whatever house you go into, let your first words be, 'Peace to this house!' And if a man of peace lives there, your peace will go and rest on him; if not, it will come back to you. Stay in the same house, taking what food and drink they have to offer, for the labourer deserves his wages; do not move from house to house. Whenever you go into a town where they make you welcome, eat what is set before you. Cure those in it who are sick, and say, 'The kingdom of God is very near to you.' But whenever you enter a town and they do not make you welcome, go out into its streets and say, 'We wipe off the very dust of your town that clings to our feet, and leave it with you. Yet be sure of this: the kingdom of God is very near.' I tell you, on that day it will not go as hard with Sodom as with that town."
This is the Gospel of the Lord.

PRAYER OVER THE GIFTS

Lord,
help us to follow the example of Saint Jerome.
In reflecting on your word
may we better prepare ourselves
to offer you this sacrifice of salvation.
We ask this in the name of Jesus the Lord.

COMMUNION ANTIPHON

When I discovered your teaching, I devoured it. Your words brought me joy and gladness; you have called me your own, O Lord my God. (Jr 15: 16)

PRAYER AFTER COMMUNION

Lord,
let this holy Eucharist we receive
on the feast of Saint Jerome
stir up the hearts of all who believe in you.
By studying your sacred teachings,
may we understand the Gospel we follow
and come to eternal life.
Grant this through Christ our Lord.

MEDITATION OF THE DAY

Ascending the Highways with the Seventy-Two

"Happy the man whose strength you are!" Truly, do we long for your tabernacles, and your courts, and your house, but to attain our hearts' desire is not within our power; it does not depend upon our strength, but upon your help. "Their hearts are set upon the pilgrimage." Who have set their hearts upon pilgrimage? The blessed who find their strength in the Lord; they are the ones who determine to ascend step by step. Day by day, the saint reaches out for the better things before him, unmindful of what is past. That is, in fact, why in the Psalter there are fifteen gradual canticles, and the first song of ascent begins with the words: "In my distress I call to the Lord, and he answered me"; the second with: "I lift up my eyes toward the mountains; whence shall help come to me?"; the third: "I rejoiced because they said to me." The saint is always moving forward, advancing steadily and ascending to heights ever more sublime; that is the meaning of "their hearts are set upon the pilgrimage." Happy the man who makes progress daily, who does not weigh what he did yesterday, but makes his resolution for today and keeps it. The holy man sets his heart on ascending; the sinner, on descending. Just as the saintly man progresses day by day, the sinner regresses day by day. Happy the man who wholeheartedly ascends the highway.

SAINT JEROME

Saint Jerome († 420) was a hermit, papal secretary, and Scripture scholar.

Prayer for the Evening

God's word is our glory:
let us give him thanks and praise!

Glory be to the Father, and to the Son, and to the Holy Spirit, as it was in the beginning, is now and ever shall be, world without end. Amen. Alleluia!

HYMN **Metre: 76 76 D**

This hymn can be sung to the tune used for *The Church's One Foundation*

O Word of God incarnate,
O Wisdom from on high,
O Truth, unchanged, unchanging,
O Light of our dark sky,
We praise you for the radiance
That from the hallowed page,
A lantern to our footsteps,
Shines on from age to age.

PSALM 17 29-33

The city did not need the sun or the moon for light, since it was lit by the radiant glory of God and the Lamb was a lighted torch for it. (Rv 21: 23)

Saint Jerome saw and loved Christ in the word of God. He said, "Whoever is ignorant of the Scriptures is ignorant of Christ."

You, O Lord, are my lamp,
my God who lightens my darkness.
With you I can break through any barrier,
with my God I can scale any wall.

As for God, his ways are perfect;
the word of the Lord, purest gold.
He indeed is the shield
of all who make him their refuge.

For who is God but the Lord?
Who is a rock but our God?
The God who girds me with strength
and makes the path safe before me.

Glory be to the Father…

Word of God John 1: 1, 14

IN THE BEGINNING was the Word,/ and the Word was with God,/ and the Word was God.

The Word was made flesh,/ he lived among us,/ and we saw his glory,/ the glory that is his as the only Son of the Father,/ full of grace and truth.

God's word has made its home in you.
(1 Jn 2: 14)

CANTICLE OF MARY **(Text, back cover A)**

Remember your leaders, who preached the word of God to you, and as you reflect on the outcome of their lives, imitate their faith. (He 13: 7)

INTERCESSIONS

To the living Word of God we pray:

℟ Lead us; guide us.

Your word is the light of the Church:
– let us read and meditate that we may see the way. ℟

Your word is bread for the hungry:
– let us seek its nourishment that we may find strength to walk in your way. ℟

Your word is refreshment and peace:
– let us rest in it that we may one day rest for ever in you. ℟

Personal intentions

Our Father…

May the grace of the Lord Jesus Christ be with our spirit. Amen. (cf. Phm 25)

MARIAN ANTIPHON **(Text, page 23)**

SAINTS
OF TODAY AND YESTERDAY

Let us test and examine our ways,
and return to the Lord!

SAINT MICHAEL DE AOZARAZA
Priest, Religious, and Martyr (1598-1637)

Michael de Aozaraza, of Ozate, Spain, entered the Dominican Order and became a priest. He served for a time as a professor of philosophy at the Dominicans' friary in Madrid before leaving for the missions in the Philippines. In 1636, after having laboured for a year on the northern Philippine island of Luzon, he went to Japan, where the harshly persecuted Catholic population lacked priests. Over two decades earlier, all foreign missionaries had been ordered to depart. Priests who entered Japan thereafter did so in peril of their lives. Soon after his arrival, Father Michael was captured by the regime of the pagan ruler Tokugawa Yemitsu. He was condemned to a horrific death by "gallows and hole", in which the victim was hung upside down and gradually suffocated within a sealed hole in the ground. He and several other martyrs had begun to undergo this agonising form of execution on September 29, 1637, when the magistrate charged with carrying out their death sentence, eager to leave, decided to have them quickly beheaded.

Let the dwelling-place of our hearts be cleansed from sin, and filled with virtue; closed to the devil, and open to Christ.
Saint Augustine

If you liked praying with MAGNIFICAT *before and after the Papal visit, we urge you to become part of the growing* MAGNIFICAT *family. The UK edition is now available!*

If you would like to receive regularly each month a resource that would help you to develop your prayer life…

MAGNIFICAT is the answer.

If you would like to have a companion to accompany you each day in the growth of your spiritual life…

MAGNIFICAT is the answer.

If you would like to benefit from a worship aid that helps you participate in the Holy Mass with greater fervour…

MAGNIFICAT is the answer.

If you would like to enter fully into the Church's liturgical rhythms and spiritual legacy…

MAGNIFICAT is the answer.

An annual subscription to MAGNIFICAT *promises thirteen issues – one per month with a special issue for Holy Week – filled with spiritual insight, exquisite art, and invaluable inspiration. You will discover the most beautiful prayers, readings, and hymns of the Church in this lavishly printed, easy-to-read, pocket-sized worship aid.*

ORDER FORM

To: Magnificat Papal Visit Offer
15 Lamb's Passage
Off Bunhill Row
London EC1Y 8TQ

☐ I would like to take advantage of the special introductory offer subscription price of £29 (€39 Ireland) for a 12-month subscription to MAGNIFICAT.

☐ I enclose cheque for £29 or €39

Name ....

Address ....

....

....

Postcode ....

Telephone ....

Order at
www.magnificat.com/pope

The Order of Mass

Greeting

■ In the name of the Father, and of the Son, and of the Holy Spirit.
■ **Amen.**

A

■ The grace of our Lord Jesus Christ and the love of God and the fellowship of the Holy Spirit be with you all.
■ **And also with you.**

B

■ The grace and peace of God our Father and the Lord Jesus Christ be with you.
■ **Blessed be God, the Father of our Lord Jesus Christ.**

Or:

■ **And also with you.**

C

■ The Lord be with you.
■ **And also with you.**

Penitential rite

A

■ As we prepare to celebrate the mystery of Christ's love,
let us acknowledge our failures
and ask the Lord for pardon and strength.

B

■ Coming together as God's family,
with confidence let us ask the Father's forgiveness,
for he is full of gentleness and compassion.

C

■ My brothers and sisters,
to prepare ourselves to celebrate the sacred mysteries,
let us call to mind our sins.

A

■ **I confess to almighty God,**
and to you, my brothers and sisters,
that I have sinned through my own fault
(The people strike their breast:)
in my thoughts and in my words,
in what I have done,
and in what I have failed to do;
and I ask blessed Mary, ever virgin,
all the angels and saints,
and you, my brothers and sisters,
to pray for me to the Lord our God.

B

■ Lord, we have sinned against you:
Lord, have mercy.
■ **Lord, have mercy.**
■ Lord, show us your mercy and love.
■ **And grant us your salvation.**

C

(The priest [or other suitable minister] makes the following or other invocations:)

■ You were sent to heal the contrite:
Lord, have mercy.
■ **Lord, have mercy.**
■ You came to call sinners:
Christ, have mercy.
■ **Christ, have mercy.**
■ You plead for us at the right hand of the Father:
Lord, have mercy.
■ **Lord, have mercy.**

■ May almighty God have mercy on us,
forgive us our sins,
and bring us to everlasting life.
■ **Amen.**

Kyrie

(The Kyrie is omitted if it has already been used in one of the forms of the act of penance.)

■ Lord, have mercy.	Kyrie, eleison.
■ Lord, have mercy.	Kyrie, eleison.
■ Christ, have mercy.	Christe, eleison.
■ Christ, have mercy.	Christe, eleison.
■ Lord, have mercy.	Kyrie, eleison.
■ Lord, have mercy.	Kyrie, eleison.

Gloria

Glory to God in the highest,
and peace to his people on earth.

Lord God, heavenly King,
almighty God and Father,
we worship you, we give you thanks,
we praise you for your glory.

Lord Jesus Christ, only Son of the Father,
Lord God, Lamb of God,
you take away the sin of the world:
have mercy on us;
you are seated at the right hand of the Father:
receive our prayer.

For you alone are the Holy One,
you alone are the Lord,
you alone are the Most High,
Jesus Christ,
with the Holy Spirit,
in the glory of God the Father. Amen.

Gloria in excelsis Deo
et in terra pax hominibus bonae voluntatis.
Laudamus te, benedicimus te, adoramus te,
glorificamus te, gratias agimus tibi
propter magnam gloriam tuam,
Domine Deus, Rex caelestis,

Deus Pater omnipotens.
Domine Fili unigenite, Iesu Christe,
Domine Deus, Agnus Dei, Filius Patris,
qui tollis peccata mundi, miserere nobis;
qui tollis peccata mundi,
suscipe deprecationem nostram;
qui sedes ad dexteram Patris, miserere nobis.
Quoniam tu solus Sanctus,
tu solus Dominus,
tu solus Altissimus, Iesu Christe,
cum Sancto Spiritu:
in gloria Dei Patris. Amen.

Opening prayer

LITURGY OF THE WORD

First reading

Responsorial psalm

Second reading

Alleluia or Gospel acclamation

Gospel

The priest [or the deacon] bows before the altar and says inaudibly:
Almighty God, cleanse my heart and my lips that I may worthily proclaim your Gospel.

- The Lord be with you.
- **And also with you.**

- A reading from the holy Gospel according to…
- **Glory to you, Lord.**

At the end of the Gospel:

- This is the Gospel of the Lord.
- **Praise to you, Lord Jesus Christ.**

Then the priest [or the deacon] kisses the book, saying inaudibly:
May the words of the Gospel wipe away our sins.

Homily

Profession of faith

The Nicene Creed

We believe in one God,
the Father, the Almighty,
maker of heaven and earth,
of all that is seen and unseen.

We believe in one Lord, Jesus Christ,
the only Son of God,
eternally begotten of the Father,
God from God, Light from Light,
true God from true God,
begotten, not made, of one Being with the Father.
Through him all things were made.
For us men and for our salvation
he came down from heaven:

All bow during these two lines:

by the power of the Holy Spirit he became incarnate
from the Virgin Mary, and was made man.

For our sake he was crucified under Pontius Pilate;
he suffered death and was buried.
On the third day he rose again
in accordance with the Scriptures;
he ascended into heaven
and is seated at the right hand of the Father.

He will come again in glory to judge the living and the dead,
and his kingdom will have no end.

We believe in the Holy Spirit, the Lord, the giver of life,
who proceeds from the Father and the Son.
With the Father and the Son he is worshipped and glorified.
He has spoken through the Prophets.
We believe in one holy catholic and apostolic Church.
We acknowledge one baptism for the forgiveness of sins.
We look for the resurrection of the dead,
and the life of the world to come. Amen.

Credo in unum Deum,
Patrem omnipotentem, factorem caeli et terrae,
visibilium omnium et invisibilium.
Et in unum Dominum Iesum Christum,
Filium Dei unigenitum,
et ex Patre natum ante omnia saecula.
Deum de Deo,
lumen de lumine,
Deum verum de Deo vero,
genitum, non factum, consubstantialem Patri:
per quem omnia facta sunt.
Qui propter nos homines et propter nostram salutem
descendit de caelis.
Et incarnatus est de Spiritu Sancto ex Maria Virgine,
et homo factus est.
Crucifixus etiam pro nobis sub Pontio Pilato,
passus et sepultus est,
et resurrexit tertia die, secundum Scripturas,
et ascendit in caelum, sedet ad dexteram Patris.
Et iterum venturus est cum gloria,
iudicare vivos et mortuos,
cuius regni non erit finis.
Et in Spiritum Sanctum,
Dominum et vivificantem:
qui ex Patre Filioque procedit;
qui cum Patre et Filio,
simul adoratur et conglorificatur:
qui locutus est per prophetas.
Et unam, sanctam, catholicam et apostolicam Ecclesiam.
Confiteor unum baptisma in remissionem peccatorum.
Et exspecto resurrectionem mortuorum,
et vitam venturi saeculi. Amen.

The Apostles' Creed

I believe in God, the Father almighty,
creator of heaven and earth.

I believe in Jesus Christ, his only Son, our Lord.
He was conceived by the power of the Holy Spirit
and born of the Virgin Mary.
He suffered under Pontius Pilate,
was crucified, died, and was buried.
He descended to the dead.
On the third day he rose again.
He ascended into heaven,
and is seated at the right hand of the Father.
He will come again to judge the living and the dead.
I believe in the Holy Spirit,
the holy catholic Church,
the communion of saints,
the forgiveness of sins,
the resurrection of the body,
and the life everlasting. Amen.

Prayer of the faithful

LITURGY OF THE EUCHARIST

Preparation of the altar and the gifts

■ Blessed are you, Lord, God of all creation.
Through your goodness we have this bread to offer,
which earth has given and human hands have made.
It will become for us the bread of life.
■ **Blessed be God for ever.**

By the mystery of this water and wine may we come
to share in the divinity of Christ, who humbled himself
to share in our humanity.

■ Blessed are you, Lord, God of all creation.
Through your goodness we have this wine to offer,
fruit of the vine and work of human hands.
It will become our spiritual drink.
■ **Blessed be God for ever.**

Lord God, we ask you to receive us and be pleased with the sacrifice we offer you with humble and contrite hearts.

Lord, wash away my iniquity; cleanse me from my sin.

■ Pray, brethren, that our sacrifice
may be acceptable to God, the almighty Father.

■ **May the Lord accept the sacrifice at your hands**
for the praise and glory of his name,
for our good, and the good of all his Church.

Prayer over the gifts

Eucharistic prayer

■ The Lord be with you.
■ **And also with you.**
■ Lift up your hearts.
■ **We lift them up to the Lord.**
■ Let us give thanks to the Lord our God.
■ **It is right to give him thanks and praise.**

Preface of Sundays in Ordinary Time V

Father, all-powerful and ever-living God,
we do well always and everywhere to give you thanks.

All things are of your making,
all times and seasons obey your laws,
but you chose to create man in your own image,
setting him over the whole world in all its wonder.
You made man the steward of creation,
to praise you day by day for the marvels of your wisdom and power,
through Jesus Christ our Lord.

We praise you, Lord, with all the angels
in their song of joy: Holy…

Preface of Weekdays V

Father, all-powerful and ever-living God,
we do well always and everywhere to give you thanks
through Jesus Christ our Lord.

With love we celebrate his death.
With living faith we proclaim his resurrection.
With unwavering hope we await his return in glory.

Now, with the saints and all the angels
we praise you for ever:

Holy, holy, holy Lord, God of power and might,
heaven and earth are full of your glory.
Hosanna in the highest.
Blessed is he who comes in the name of the Lord.
Hosanna in the highest.

■ **Sanctus, Sanctus, Sanctus**
Dominus Deus Sabaoth.
Pleni sunt caeli et terra gloria tua.
Hosanna in excelsis.
Benedictus qui venit in nomine Domini.
Hosanna in excelsis.

Eucharistic prayer I (Roman canon)

(I: below; II: p. 460; III: p. 463; IV: p. 465)

(In the first eucharistic prayer the words in brackets may be omitted.)

We come to you, Father,
with praise and thanksgiving,
through Jesus Christ your Son.
Through him we ask you to accept and bless
these gifts we offer you in sacrifice.
We offer them for your holy catholic Church,
watch over it, Lord, and guide it;
grant it peace and unity throughout the world.
We offer them for … our Pope,
for … our bishop,
and for all who hold and teach the catholic faith
that comes to us from the apostles.

Remember, Lord, your people,
especially those for whom we now pray, … and …
Remember all of us gathered here before you.
You know how firmly we believe in you
and dedicate ourselves to you.
We offer you this sacrifice of praise
for ourselves and those who are dear to us.

We pray to you, our living and true God,
for our well-being and redemption.

In union with the whole Church
we honour Mary,
the ever-virgin mother of Jesus Christ our Lord and God.
We honour Joseph, her husband,
the apostles and martyrs
Peter and Paul, Andrew,
[James, John, Thomas,
James, Philip,
Bartholomew, Matthew, Simon and Jude;
we honor Linus, Cletus, Clement, Sixtus,
Cornelius, Cyprian, Lawrence, Chrysogonus,
John and Paul, Cosmas and Damian]
and all the saints.
May their merits and prayers
gain us your constant help and protection.
[Through Christ our Lord. Amen.]

Father, accept this offering
from your whole family.
Grant us your peace in this life,
save us from final damnation,
and count us among those you have chosen.
[Through Christ our Lord. Amen.]

Bless and approve our offering;
make it acceptable to you,
an offering in spirit and in truth.
Let it become for us
the body and blood of Jesus Christ,
your only Son, our Lord.
[Through Christ our Lord. Amen.]

The day before he suffered,
he took bread in his sacred hands
and looking up to heaven,
to you, his almighty Father,
he gave you thanks and praise.

He broke the bread,
gave it to his disciples, and said:
Take this, all of you, and eat it:
this is my body which will be given up for you.

When supper was ended,
he took the cup.
Again he gave you thanks and praise,
gave the cup to his disciples, and said:
Take this, all of you, and drink from it:
this is the cup of my blood,
the blood of the new and everlasting covenant.
It will be shed for you and for all
so that sins may be forgiven.
Do this in memory of me.

■ Let us proclaim the mystery of faith:

A

■ **Christ has died,**
Christ is risen,
Christ will come again.

B

■ **Dying you destroyed our death,**
rising you restored our life.
Lord Jesus, come in glory.

C

■ **When we eat this bread and drink this cup,**
we proclaim your death, Lord Jesus,
until you come in glory.

D

■ **Lord, by your cross and resurrection**
you have set us free.
You are the Saviour of the world.

Father, we celebrate the memory of Christ, your Son.
We, your people and your ministers,
recall his passion,
his resurrection from the dead,
and his ascension into glory;

and from the many gifts you have given us
we offer to you, God of glory and majesty,
this holy and perfect sacrifice:
the bread of life
and the cup of eternal salvation.

Look with favour on these offerings
and accept them as once you accepted
the gifts of your servant Abel,
the sacrifice of Abraham, our father in faith,
and the bread and wine offered by your priest Melchisedech.

Almighty God,
we pray that your angel may take this sacrifice
to your altar in heaven.
Then, as we receive from this altar
the sacred body and blood of your Son,
let us be filled with every grace and blessing.
[Through Christ our Lord. Amen.]

Remember, Lord, those who have died
and have gone before us marked with the sign of faith,
especially those for whom we now pray, … and …

May these, and all who sleep in Christ,
find in your presence
light, happiness, and peace.
[Through Christ our Lord. Amen.]

For ourselves, too, we ask
some share in the fellowship of your apostles and martyrs,
with John the Baptist, Stephen, Matthias, Barnabas,
    [Ignatius, Alexander, Marcellinus, Peter,
    Felicity, Perpetua, Agatha, Lucy,
    Agnes, Cecilia, Anastasia]
and all the saints.
Though we are sinners,
we trust in your mercy and love.
Do not consider what we truly deserve,

but grant us your forgiveness.
Through Christ our Lord.

Through him you give us all these gifts.
You fill them with life and goodness,
you bless them and make them holy.

Through him,
with him,
in him,
in the unity of the Holy Spirit,
all glory and honour is yours,
almighty Father,
for ever and ever.

■ **Amen.** (Our Father: page 469)

Eucharistic prayer II

Father, it is our duty and our salvation,
always and everywhere
to give you thanks
through your beloved Son, Jesus Christ.

He is the Word through whom you made the universe,
the Saviour you sent to redeem us.
By the power of the Holy Spirit
he took flesh and was born of the Virgin Mary.

For our sake he opened his arms on the cross;
he put an end to death
and revealed the resurrection.
In this he fulfilled your will
and won for you a holy people.

And so we join the angels and the saints
in proclaiming your glory
as we say: Holy…

Lord, you are holy indeed,
the fountain of all holiness.
Let your Spirit come upon these gifts to make them holy,

so that they may become for us
the body and blood of our Lord, Jesus Christ.

Before he was given up to death,
a death he freely accepted,
he took bread and gave you thanks.
He broke the bread,
gave it to his disciples, and said:
Take this, all of you, and eat it:
this is my body which will be given up for you.

When supper was ended, he took the cup.
Again he gave you thanks and praise,
gave the cup to his disciples, and said:
Take this, all of you, and drink from it:
this is the cup of my blood,
the blood of the new and everlasting covenant.
It will be shed for you and for all
so that sins may be forgiven.
Do this in memory of me.

■ Let us proclaim the mystery of faith:

A

■ **Christ has died,**
Christ is risen,
Christ will come again.

B

■ **Dying you destroyed our death,**
rising you restored our life.
Lord Jesus, come in glory.

C

■ **When we eat this bread and drink this cup,**
we proclaim your death, Lord Jesus,
until you come in glory.

D

■ **Lord, by your cross and resurrection**
you have set us free.
You are the Saviour of the world.

In memory of his death and resurrection,
we offer you, Father, this life-giving bread,
this saving cup.
We thank you for counting us worthy
to stand in your presence and serve you.
May all of us who share in the body and blood of Christ
be brought together in unity by the Holy Spirit.

Lord, remember your Church throughout the world;
make us grow in love,
together with ... our Pope,
... our bishop, and all the clergy.

Remember our brothers and sisters
who have gone to their rest
in the hope of rising again;
bring them and all the departed
into the light of your presence.
Have mercy on us all;
make us worthy to share eternal life
with Mary, the virgin Mother of God,
with the apostles, and with all the saints
who have done your will throughout the ages.
May we praise you in union with them,
and give you glory
through your Son, Jesus Christ.

Through him,
with him,
in him,
in the unity of the Holy Spirit,
all glory and honour is yours,
almighty Father,
for ever and ever.

■ **Amen.** **(Our Father: page 469)**

Eucharistic prayer III

Father, you are holy indeed,
and all creation rightly gives you praise.
All life, all holiness comes from you
through your Son, Jesus Christ our Lord,
by the working of the Holy Spirit.
From age to age you gather a people to yourself,
so that from east to west
a perfect offering may be made
to the glory of your name.

And so, Father, we bring you these gifts.
We ask you to make them holy by the power of your Spirit,
that they may become the body and blood
of your Son, our Lord Jesus Christ,
at whose command we celebrate this Eucharist.

On the night he was betrayed,
he took bread and gave you thanks and praise.
He broke the bread, gave it to his disciples, and said:
Take this, all of you, and eat it:
this is my body which will be given up for you.

When supper was ended, he took the cup.
Again he gave you thanks and praise,
gave the cup to his disciples, and said:
Take this, all of you, and drink from it:
this is the cup of my blood,
the blood of the new and everlasting covenant.
It will be shed for you and for all
so that sins may be forgiven.
Do this in memory of me.

■ Let us proclaim the mystery of faith:

A

■ **Christ has died,**
Christ is risen,
Christ will come again.

B

- **Dying you destroyed our death,**
  rising you restored our life.
  Lord Jesus, come in glory.

C

- **When we eat this bread and drink this cup,**
  we proclaim your death, Lord Jesus,
  until you come in glory.

D

- **Lord, by your cross and resurrection**
  you have set us free.
  You are the Saviour of the world.

Father, calling to mind the death your Son endured for
our salvation,
his glorious resurrection and ascension into heaven,
and ready to greet him when he comes again,
we offer you in thanksgiving this holy and living sacrifice.

Look with favour on your Church's offering,
and see the Victim whose death has reconciled us to yourself.
Grant that we, who are nourished by his body and blood,
may be filled with his Holy Spirit,
and become one body, one spirit in Christ.

May he make us an everlasting gift to you
and enable us to share in the inheritance of your saints,
with Mary, the virgin Mother of God;
with the apostles, the martyrs,
(Saint ... the saint of the day or the patron saint)
and all your saints,
on whose constant intercession we rely for help.

Lord, may this sacrifice,
which has made our peace with you,
advance the peace and salvation of all the world.
Strengthen in faith and love your pilgrim Church on earth;
your servant, Pope ..., our bishop ...,
and all the bishops,

with the clergy and the entire people your Son
has gained for you.
Father, hear the prayers of the family you have gathered
here before you.
In mercy and love unite all your children wherever
they may be.

Welcome into your kingdom our departed brothers and sisters,
and all who have left this world in your friendship.
We hope to enjoy for ever the vision of your glory,
through Christ our Lord, from whom all good things come.

Through him,
with him,
in him,
in the unity of the Holy Spirit,
all glory and honour is yours,
almighty Father,
for ever and ever.
■ **Amen.** **(Our Father: page 469)**

Eucharistic prayer IV

Father in heaven,
it is right that we should give you thanks and glory:
you are the one God, living and true.
Through all eternity you live in unapproachable light.
Source of life and goodness, you have created all things,
to fill your creatures with every blessing
and lead all men to the joyful vision of your light.
Countless hosts of angels stand before you to do your will;
they look upon your splendour
and praise you, night and day.
United with them,
and in the name of every creature under heaven,
we too praise your glory as we say: **Holy...**

Father, we acknowledge your greatness:
all your actions show your wisdom and love.

You formed man in your own likeness
and set him over the whole world
to serve you, his creator,
and to rule over all creatures.
Even when he disobeyed you and lost your friendship
you did not abandon him to the power of death,
but helped all men to seek and find you.
Again and again you offered a covenant to man,
and through the prophets taught him to hope for salvation.
Father, you so loved the world
that in the fullness of time you sent your only Son to be
our Saviour.
He was conceived through the power of the Holy Spirit,
and born of the Virgin Mary,
a man like us in all things but sin.
To the poor he proclaimed the good news of salvation,
to prisoners, freedom,
and to those in sorrow, joy.
In fulfillment of your will
he gave himself up to death;
but by rising from the dead,
he destroyed death and restored life.
And that we might live no longer for ourselves but for him,
he sent the Holy Spirit from you, Father,
as his first gift to those who believe,
to complete his work on earth
and bring us the fullness of grace.

Father, may this Holy Spirit sanctify these offerings.
Let them become the body and blood of Jesus Christ our Lord
as we celebrate the great mystery
which he left us as an everlasting covenant.

He always loved those who were his own in the world.
When the time came for him to be glorified by you, his
heavenly Father,
he showed the depth of his love.

While they were at supper,
he took bread, said the blessing, broke the bread,
and gave it to his disciples, saying:
Take this, all of you, and eat it:
this is my body which will be given up for you.

In the same way, he took the cup, filled with wine.
He gave you thanks, and giving the cup to his disciples, said:
Take this, all of you, and drink from it:
this is the cup of my blood,
the blood of the new and everlasting covenant.
It will be shed for you and for all
so that sins may be forgiven.
Do this in memory of me.

■ Let us proclaim the mystery of faith:

A

■ **Christ has died,**
Christ is risen,
Christ will come again.

B

■ **Dying you destroyed our death,**
rising you restored our life.
Lord Jesus, come in glory.

C

■ **When we eat this bread and drink this cup,**
we proclaim your death, Lord Jesus,
until you come in glory.

D

■ **Lord, by your cross and resurrection**
you have set us free.
You are the Saviour of the world.

Father, we now celebrate this memorial of our redemption.
We recall Christ's death, his descent among the dead,
his resurrection, and his ascension to your right hand;
and, looking forward to his coming in glory,

we offer you his body and blood,
the acceptable sacrifice
which brings salvation to the whole world.

Lord, look upon this sacrifice which you have given to
your Church;
and by your Holy Spirit, gather all who share this one bread
and one cup
into the one body of Christ, a living sacrifice of praise.

Lord, remember those for whom we offer this sacrifice,
especially … our Pope,
… our bishop, and bishops and clergy everywhere.
Remember those who take part in this offering,
those here present and all your people,
and all who seek you with a sincere heart.
Remember those who have died in the peace of Christ
and all the dead whose faith is known to you alone.
Father, in your mercy grant also to us, your children,
to enter into our heavenly inheritance
in the company of the Virgin Mary, the Mother of God,
and your apostles and saints.
Then, in your kingdom, freed from the corruption of sin
and death,
we shall sing your glory with every creature through
Christ our Lord,
through whom you give us everything that is good.

Through him,
with him,
in him,
in the unity of the Holy Spirit,
all glory and honour is yours,
almighty Father,
for ever and ever.

■ Amen.

COMMUNION RITE

Lord's prayer

A

■ Let us pray with confidence to the Father
in the words our Saviour gave us.

B

■ Jesus taught us to call God our Father,
and so we have the courage to say:

C

■ Let us ask our Father to forgive our sins
and to bring us to forgive those who sin against us.

D

■ Let us pray for the coming of the kingdom
as Jesus taught us.

**Our Father, who art in heaven,
hallowed be thy name;
thy kingdom come;
thy will be done on earth
as it is in heaven.
Give us this day our daily bread;
and forgive us our trespasses
as we forgive those who trespass against us;
and lead us not into temptation,
but deliver us from evil.**

**Pater noster, qui es in caelis:
sanctificetur nomen tuum;
adveniat regnum tuum;
fiat voluntas tua,
sicut in caelo, et in terra.
Panem nostrum quotidianum
da nobis hodie;
et dimitte nobis debita nostra,
sicut et nos dimittimus
debitoribus nostris;
et ne nos inducas in tentationem;
sed libera nos a malo.**

■ Deliver us, Lord, from every evil,
and grant us peace in our day.
In your mercy keep us free from sin
and protect us from all anxiety
as we wait in joyful hope
for the coming of our Saviour,
Jesus Christ.

■ **For the kingdom, the power, and the glory are yours,**
now and for ever.

Sign of peace

■ Lord Jesus Christ, you said to your apostles:
I leave you peace, my peace I give you.
Look not on our sins, but on the faith of your Church,
and grant us the peace and unity of your kingdom
where you live for ever and ever.

■ **Amen.**

■ The peace of the Lord be with you always.

■ **And also with you.**

(Then the deacon [or the priest] may add:)

Let us offer each other the sign of peace.

Breaking of the bread

■ **Lamb of God, you take away the sins of the world:**
have mercy on us.
Lamb of God, you take away the sins of the world:
have mercy on us.
Lamb of God, you take away the sins of the world:
grant us peace.

■ **Agnus Dei, qui tollis peccata mundi:**
miserere nobis.
Agnus Dei, qui tollis peccata mundi:
miserere nobis.
Agnus Dei, qui tollis peccata mundi:
dona nobis pacem.

(Meanwhile, he takes the host and breaks it over the paten. He places a small piece in the chalice, saying inaudibly:)

May this mingling of the body and blood of our Lord Jesus Christ bring eternal life to us who receive it.

Private preparation of the priest

(Then the priest joins his hands and says inaudibly:)

Lord Jesus Christ, Son of the living God, by the will of the Father and the work of the Holy Spirit your death brought life to the world. By your holy body and blood free me from all my sins and from every evil. Keep me faithful to your teaching, and never let me be parted from you.

Or:

Lord Jesus Christ, with faith in your love and mercy I eat your body and drink your blood. Let it not bring me condemnation, but health in mind and body.

Communion

(The priest genuflects. Taking the host, he raises it slightly over the paten and, facing the people, says aloud:)

■ This is the Lamb of God
who takes away the sins of the world.
Happy are those who are called to his supper.

■ **Lord, I am not worthy to receive you,**
but only say the word and I shall be healed.

(Facing the altar, the priest says inaudibly:)

May the body of Christ bring me to everlasting life.

(He reverently consumes the body of Christ. Then he takes the chalice and says inaudibly:)

May the blood of Christ bring me to everlasting life.

(He reverently drinks the blood of Christ.)

Communion song

Period of silence or song of praise

Prayer after communion

CONCLUDING RITE

Brief announcements

Greeting

- The Lord be with you.
- **And also with you.**

Blessing

- May almighty God bless you,
  the Father, and the Son, and the Holy Spirit.
- **Amen.**

Dismissal

(The deacon [or the priest], with hands joined, sings or says:)

A

- Go in the peace of Christ.

B

- The Mass is ended, go in peace.

C

- Go in peace to love and serve the Lord.

A, B, C

- **Thanks be to God.**

MAGNIFICAT

MAGNIFICAT

ACKNOWLEDGMENTS

Music engraved by The Art of Music, Dunblane – theartofmusic.com.

For Calamus: Decani Music, Oak House, 70 High Street, Brandon, Suffolk, IP27 0AU.

Editor: Fr Allen Morris (who offers grateful thanks to all who have contributed their thoughts and skills to the writing and the proof-reading of the articles.).

COVER IMAGE

Most Christians are familiar with the stories of the second evangelisation of "mainland" Britain during the 6th and 7th centuries, with the mission of Columba, of Aidan and Cuthbert in Scotland and North of England, and with that of Augustine in the South of England. But there was a first and earlier evangelisation in England and Wales – not so well known and which faded during the Dark Ages, but which bore rich fruit, amongst whom must be counted St David of Wales and Saint Patrick, apostle to Ireland.

That first evangelisation began during the time of the Roman occupation. Scarcely anything is known of the organisation of the Church here during that time, and perhaps it came to these shores only because it had first been embraced by Roman traders and settlers. But it took root quickly and firmly. We know of the fervour of the faith of these early communities through the accounts of the martyrdoms of Saints Alban, Julius and Aaron during the Diocletian persecution. And we know something of the way they practised faith through the traces of their homes and places of worship recovered by archaeologists. It is still possible to visit the remains of the chapel in the Roman Villa at Lullingstone, Kent, and in the British Museum to see the Christian paintings which decorated its walls.

More perfectly preserved is a mosaic floor now in the British Museum but which comes from a Roman villa at Hinton St Mary, Dorset. This mosaic from the 4th century contains what is one of the very earliest known representations of Christ not only in Britain, but anywhere. The image is featured on the cover of this book and it shows Christ as a clean-shaven young man. The bust is placed before the Greek letters chi and rho, the first two letters of Christ's name: a sign adopted in AD

312 by Constantine, the first Christian Emperor. The Chi Rho was a common symbol for Christianity from this time, and also features in the decoration of the chapel at Lullingstone. Also in this image, flanking the head of Jesus are two pomegranates, symbols of eternal life, and of the resurrection.

The image of Christ is incorporated into a larger mosaic made of two panels. The first and smaller panel includes hunting scenes and a central roundel which shows the hero Bellerophon mounted on his winged horse Pegasus, slaying the three-headed monster, Chimaera. A pagan scene is depicted, but perhaps it is intended for a Christian audience as a scene which illustrates the triumph of good over evil. The second, larger, panel contains the image of Christ, but also images of the four winds, or are they the four apostles? Probably both.

Pagan imagery was commonly used in Christian art, and for a variety of reasons. It was relatively anonymous, accessible to the initiate, but "hidden" from persecutors of the Church. It indicated an ascendency of Christianity over the pagan cults, and the fulfilment of all which these promised – so a Christian looking at an image of Apollo saw not Apollo the Sun God but Jesus the Son of God, and not Hermes carrying a ram ready for slaughter and sacrifice, but Jesus, the Good Shepherd, carrying the lost lamb home for which he himself was the sacrifice who saves and wins us life, and freedom for those who will receive his love.

The mosaic of Hinton St Mary stands at the end of that practice, for with the prominent Christian symbolism accompanying the image of Christ, there is no mistaking who is portrayed. And this explicitly Christian mosaic stands at the beginning of the great mosaic tradition which would come to its fullest expression in the mosaics of the Christian basilicas of Rome, Constantinople and Ravenna.

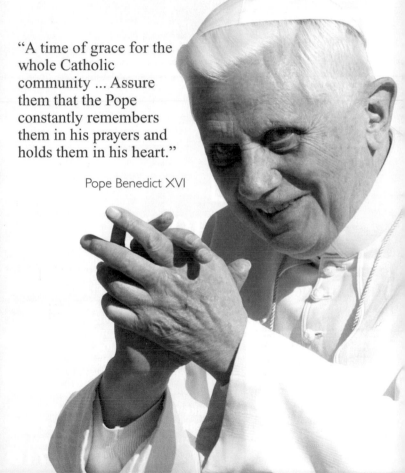

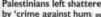

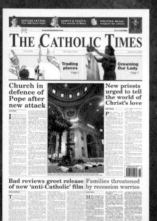

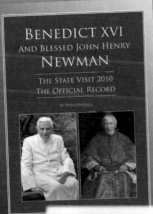

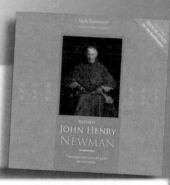

CAFOD
great
livesimply
10

The Blessed Virgin Mary

Illustration: Wilton Diptych (1395-1399), National Gallery, London, England, U.K.
Text: Allen Morris

The religious reformations of the 16th and 17th Centuries led to the wholesale destruction of virtually all Christian paintings and sculpture in England, Wales and Scotland. Fragments remain and one or two pieces. It is all the more remarkable then that one of the pieces remaining is the exceptional painting known as the Wilton Diptych. Probably commissioned for King Richard II or perhaps for his Queen (and now in the National Gallery, London) it shows on one panel Our Lady and the Christ Child surrounded by the glory of angels, and on the other, King Richard kneeling in homage, accompanied by Sts Edmund Martyr, Edward the Confessor and John the Baptist, his patrons. It is a powerful symbol of the close association between Crown and Church, of Faith and State.

Our principal focus is on the image of Mary and the Christ Child and the reminder this provides of Mary, Handmaid of the Lord, the one who gives of herself so that Christ can take flesh and be born into our world for its salvation.

A solemn declaration made by Archbishop Arundel in 1399, with the support of King Richard, insisted: '*The contemplation of the great mystery of the Incarnation has brought all Christian nations to venerate her from whom came the beginnings of redemption. But we, as the humble servants of her inheritance, and liege-men of her especial dower - as we are approved by common parlance ought to excel all others in the favour of our praises and devotions to her.*'

Richard in fact had placed his kingdom under the protection of Mary in 1381, having recovered it from its 'loss' during the Peasants Revolt. From this event, almost certainly, is derived the idea of England as Mary's Dowry.

The Monarch's veneration of Mary is depicted in the painting, and the warmth of response which we see made by Jesus, Mary and heavenly host assure of God's continued blessing to Monarch and nation, and urge veneration and piety on those who gaze on this exquisite piece.

Devotion to Mary, and wonder at her role in Salvation History is also at the heart of one of the best known Middle English verses, 'I sing of a maiden' dating from perhaps the 1400s, a little after the Wilton diptych.

I syng of a mayden	*I sing of a maiden*
bat is makeles,	*That is matchless,*
kyng of alle kynges	*King of all kings*
to here sone che ches.	*For her son she chose.*
He came also style	*He came as still*
ber his moder was	*Where his mother was*
as dew in aprylle,	*As dew in April*
bat fallyt on be gras.	*That falls on the grass.*
He cam also style	*He came as still*
to his moderes bowr	*To his mother's bower*
as dew in aprille,	*As dew in April*
bat fallyt on be flour.	*That falls on the flower.*
He cam also style	*He came as still*
ber his moder lay	*Where his mother lay*
as dew in Aprille,	*As dew in April*
bat fallyt on be spray;	*That falls on the spray.*
Moder & mayden	*Mother and maiden*
was neuer non but che –	*There was never, ever one but she;*
wel may swych a lady	*Well may such a lady*
Godes moder be	*God's mother be.*

In the simplest language the poem celebrates the incarnation and evokes its wonder through the most accessible imagery. The sheer gratuity of God's self-gift overwhelms us: the only appropriate response is thanksgiving and worship.

HOW TO PRAY EVERY DAY

MAGNIFICAT *provides a rich programme of daily prayer conveniently adapted for busy family and professional lives – a complete Missal for each day of the month, together with psalms, hymns, canticles, readings, intercessions and meditations for Morning and Evening Prayer.*

HOW TO PARTICIPATE MORE DEEPLY IN THE MASS

MAGNIFICAT *is designed to enhance personal participation in the Divine Liturgy of the Church.* MAGNIFICAT *will help you follow and learn about the Mass, both on Sundays and throughout the week.* MAGNIFICAT *contains everything you need for the prayerful celebration of the daily Eucharist, including readings for the Masses celebrated throughout the month, the responses spoken by the congregation, and the prayers spoken by the priest.*

HOW TO GROW IN YOUR SPIRITUAL LIFE

In addition, MAGNIFICAT *is an exceptional source of spiritual reading to nurture a deeper Christian spirituality. Each day offers a carefully selected meditation drawn from the very best writings from the Fathers of the Church as well as from recent spiritual teachers. The great heroes of the faith come alive in* MAGNIFICAT'S *lives of the Saints. Each issue begins with a number of short essays by the country's finest Catholic authors, treating spirituality, liturgy, scripture and the concerns of the New Evangelisation.* MAGNIFICAT *also features full-colour reproductions of great works of sacred art, complete with explanatory notes. Truth, goodness and beauty – the foundations of the new Culture of Life are in your hands.*

MAGNIFICAT®

Become part of the growing MAGNIFICAT *family*

ORDER FORM

To: Magnificat Papal Visit Offer

15 Lamb's Passage

Off Bunhill Row

London EC1Y 8TQ

☐ I would like to take advantage of the special introductory offer subscription price of £29 (€39 Ireland) for a 12-month subscription to MAGNIFICAT.

☐ I enclose cheque for £29 or €39

Name ....

Address...

....

....

Postcode...

Telephone ....

Order at

www.magnificat.com/pope